DEVELOPING DECISION-MAKING SKILLS FOR BUSINESS

DEVELOPING
DECISION-
MAKING
SKILLS FOR
BUSINESS

Julian L. Simon

M.E. Sharpe
Armonk, New York
London, England

H   Copyright © 2000 by M. E. Sharpe, Inc.

Library of Congress Cataloging-in-Publication Data

Simon, Julian Lincoln, 1932–
    Developing decision-making skills for business / Julian L. Simon.
        p. cm.
    Includes bibliographical references and index.
    ISBN 0-7656-0676-3 (alk. paper)
        1. Decision-making. 2. Corporate culture. 3. Psychology, Industrial. I. Title.

HD30.23 .S556 2001
158.7—dc21   00-030118

Contents

Preface

Some Personal Reflections on Writing This Book

No one could write with authority about all the topics in a book that ranges as widely as this one does. Even to attempt to do so requires chutzpah. Yet I believe the attempt is worth making even if the book is not wholly successful in knitting together these disparate subjects into a common framework and a single volume. In such a venture, new ideas inevitably arise about the kinship (and lack of it) among various kinds of thinking, and about the similarities and differences among them. As Eudora Welty put it about writing fiction: "In writing, as in life, the connections of all sorts of relationships and kinds lie in wait of discovery, and give out their signals to the Geiger counter of the charged imagination, once it is drawn into the right field." This axiom has made it worthwhile for me, and I hope for you, too. And if someone with a peculiar background like mine doesn't try, who will?

The Author's Qualifications to Write a Book Like This One

Such as they are, these are my qualifications: First and foremost, the book is mainly about "how to," in both the broad and the narrow senses—such as how to choose the problems a scientific laboratory should study, and how to decide whether to rent or buy a large computer. Many of my early books also have been about "how to"—how to do research in social science, a very broad topic; how to make business decisions, also rather broad; the very specific *How to Start and Operate a Mail-order Business*; how university libraries can identify and reduce the cost of storing books that are not used frequently, a very technical how-to-do-it; how to do (and teach students to do) all probability and statistics problems by the Monte Carlo "resampling" method; and how to manage advertising. Many of my technical articles also have been "how to"—how to handle airline oversales with a volunteer auction plan (in use since 1978 on all U.S. airlines), how to value a country's population size, and so on. My viewpoint is practical even when the subject of discussion is very unbusinesslike. This fits with the pragmatic thought of William James, many traces of which can be seen in various chapters.

During my younger years, I worked at a variety of down-to-earth jobs such as menial labor in a brewery and a beer can factory; service occupations such as caddying, driving a taxi, selling encyclopedias, stocking at Sears, and clerking in a drugstore; white-collar work such as technical-manual writer; bookkeeper, advertising copywriter, and market researcher; self-employed painter of house numbers, and starting my own mail-order business; lawyering as defense counsel in low-level Navy trials; serving as a deck officer aboard a destroyer and as a gunfire liaison officer with the Marines; business consultant; free-lance columnist. There is something to be learned in each of these jobs, and each of them casts light on the others.

It may also be of benefit that my intellectual sympathies embrace a wide range of writers. Although I admire David Hume and Adam Smith for their realistic view of human nature and for the analysis of society that follows from that view, and though I have a corresponding negative view of Karl Marx's thought about human nature and society, I admire Marx's muckraker writing about the ills of English industrial life in the nineteenth century. The prose of Genesis, Shakespeare's rhyming sonnets, and Whitman's free verse all inspire awe and joy in me; Blake's poems cast me into despair. I am a Jew by loyalty and I am attached to Judaism, but I honor Jesus, the Buddha, and the Zen masters as teachers and heroes. This catholicity of interest and sympathy, together with my belief that there are ridiculous and funny aspects to almost everything, should help a person write a book like this one.

More generally, I must confess the most serious of academic sins—I am an eclectic. (I first heard this sin denounced in an undergraduate course in experimental psychology. The moral immediately struck me with force, but I knew that I was cut out to sin the sin anyway.) I usually find useful truth in apparently opposed views of a subject, and the disparity between different views of the same subject often produces new ideas in me. (One of the pleasures of writing this book has been the exploration of these interpenetrations.) I believe that single-mindedness and intellectual imperialism usually damage scholarship, though they are invaluable in promoting ideas. This fits together with my sense of the universe as an open system made up of open subsystems, even though I recognize that closed-system analysis can often be a useful approximation for analysis.

Interchange Among the Social and Decision Sciences

For decades there has been talk that the social sciences were in the process of convergence. Yet they seem to have drifted ever farther apart. In the 1990s there have been some encouraging signs, especially in the field of decision-making where psychologists, economists, philosophers, and mathematicians are arguing with each other, and also in the field of organizational behavior where sociologists and economists are finding common ground. The book benefits from these contacts among the social sciences, and I hope that it contributes to this movement of interchange, too, even if the convergence is only for a few brief years.

When one looks beneath the surface of many political and intellectual controversies, one often finds that the participants are divided not only by differences in their preferences and beliefs about the "facts," but also by differences in their modes of thinking. Often the two sides in a dispute have entirely different world views—that is, different ways of thinking about the way that nature and human nature operate. If one can identify these differences, one can sometimes reduce the distance between the contending parties, or at least reduce the intensity of conflict by making clear the underlying nature of the dispute. Perhaps this book can contribute by helping build such intellectual bridges.

The History of the Book

It is now nearly three decades that I have been planning this work. You will find quotations from newspaper articles dating back to 1970; on the clippings I scribbled "Thinking," my file name for this book during all these years. During that long period of preparation, I have had the opportunity—and sometimes the necessity—of learning about subjects and ideas that on the surface have no connection to one another. Yet many or even most of those subjects turn out to hinge upon thinking processes, one way or another.

My desire to write this book was greatly intensified by experiences over three decades in my main special field, the economics of population. Unsound modes of thinking account for many of the false beliefs that are commonly held about population growth, natural resources, and the environment. A key example is people's focus only on short-run and local effects rather than upon the long-run and diffuse effects of additional people being born. Another example is the differences in underlying values between those people who would reduce immigration to the United States and those people who would increase it.

Please Enjoy It

I hope that you will enjoy this book even a little bit as much as I have enjoyed collecting and developing and then writing about the ideas in it. I am grateful that it has been my lot in life to have had this opportunity.

Note

Julian Simon died on February 8, 1998. With the help of my son Daniel, who is a professor of business at Texas A&M, I have edited this manuscript, and am delighted that M.E. Sharpe has agreed to publish it. Julian considered this a very important book in his rather large arsenal of publications.

Rita Simon

Overview of Business Psychology

The Book's Purpose

This book teaches ways to improve your mind so that you can live better. The skills it teaches range from making business decisions to choosing life goals and getting to sleep quickly.

Life Is Complicated

The sensible place to begin thinking about any task or problem is to ask what it is that you would like to accomplish. But figuring out what you want from life is probably the most difficult problem in thinking that you will ever address. Everything affects everything else. The preferences you now hold must influence the choices you make now. But the choices you now make affect not only what happens to you in the immediate future, but also the preferences and desires you will hold in the future, hence affecting the choices you make then. And events that one cannot now foresee and probably cannot control are likely to cause twists and turns in most lives. These uncertainties are only a portion of the difficulties. Nevertheless, we must press on and try to make some reasonable plans, and that requires that we not try to deal with everything at once, but instead try to mark off matters that we can reasonably think about separate from other matters. And that is how we shall proceed, starting with our preferences.

The Outline of the Book

Part I of the book tackles the problem of assessing our wants and capacities and then using that knowledge to select goals. Chapter 1 deals with desires, chapter 2 deals with capacities, and chapter 3 discusses setting the goals.

Part II discusses "cost-benefit analysis"—the comparative evaluation of a list of available alternatives. Though the method of cost-benefit thinking was developed for economic situations, it often can usefully be extended to other types of choices—into science and psychotherapy, for example. The reason we discuss it at length is that business-type analysis is wonderfully simpler than any other analysis because it assumes only a single, known goal. But in some choices—such as your choice of loyalties, or what to do with your life, or whether it is worth the effort needed to make yourself happier—cost-benefit thinking may cause more damage than benefit.

Chapter 4 presents the framework for making cost-benefit evaluations, and illustrates its use when the outcomes are rather certain and where all the important consequences occur within a single period. That is, these first types of situations are unencumbered with the two most important sources of difficulty in evaluation—uncertainty and delayed effects. But the power of the intellectual framework is shown by its easy handling of such complexities as the pricing of several products whose sales affect each other.

Chapter 5 presents the concept of *time discounting,* which enables us to appropriately weigh incomes and outgoes in various future periods, and then add the set of them into a single overall sum. That sum is called the *present value* of the stream of future revenues and expenditures. This idea is at the core of decisions about investments and other actions taken in the present that will have ramifications long into the future. It is the single most important and powerful idea in all of managerial decision-making.

The negative elements connected with an alternative—call them "expenditures" when they are monetary, and "costs" otherwise—are easy to deal with conceptually. But they are difficult to handle psychologically and organizationally, which often causes firms and individuals to reach disastrously wrong decisions. Chapter 6 describes devices to avoid these cost pitfalls.

Uncertainty is a key difficulty in decision-making. Chapter 7 presents intellectual machinery for dealing with uncertainty in a systematic fashion when valuing and comparing alternatives.

People sometimes enjoy uncertainty, and some even are willing to pay for it in gambling. More commonly, though, uncertainty is a negative consequence that people will purchase insurance to avoid. Chapter 8 explains how to allow for risk when you prefer avoiding uncertainty.

The cost-benefit analyses presented in chapters 4 to 8 presupposes that you have a single criterion of success on which to compare the various alternatives. In ordinary business situations, money profit—or, more accurately, the present value criterion—serves as the goal and hence the measure of success. But in many of life's situations, you have more than one goal in mind. Chapter 9 provides some devices to integrate multiple goals for organizations and individuals.

Part II also assumes that you *know* your goals. But often when we make tough decisions in our personal and professional lives, we find that we are *not* sure of our goals. The two main inputs into choosing goals are (1) our *desires*, the satisfaction of which constitutes benefits for us, and (2) our human and physical *resources*, which enable us to work toward satisfying our desires.

Part III analyzes the processes of creating ideas, developing alternatives, and obtaining sound knowledge of the world around you. Chapter 10 offers techniques for developing ideas by recourse to experience and imagination, and also techniques for eliminating inferior ideas from further consideration. A key issue is whether radical ideas with far-reaching consequences will be considered further, or whether the scope will be limited to less far-reaching adjustments where no attempt is made to do an overall analysis. This sort of "myopic" adjustment process is known (inaccurately) as "muddling through"—inelegant, but often the most effective way of doing things.

Knowledge can usefully be categorized as (1) *tacit*—such as knowing how to ride a bicycle, (2) *applied*—such as knowing how to fix a bicycle, and (3) *abstract*—such as understanding why the rider and bicycle don't fall down. This book is mainly about abstract and applied knowledge. The first place to turn for such knowledge is where it may already exist—libraries and experts. Chapter 11 tells you how to mine those resources.

Casual observation adequately provides most of the information we need for our work and personal lives. But when casual observation is insufficient, and when experts and libraries do not yield the answers you need, you must turn to scientifically disciplined research for reliable knowledge. Chapter 12 presents the basic principles of scientific research. Violations of these same principles are much the same as the errors we make in drawing everyday conclusions, as will be discussed in chapter 18. And many of the same scientific principles are the converse of the logical fallacies that have been discussed by philosophers since the ancient Greeks. This is a nice example of how the same principles of thinking appear in several different contexts.

Chapter 13 takes up the special scientific problem of estimating the probabilities of uncertain events.

Part IV discusses the mental operations that we may (or may not) apply to the new knowledge that we obtain.

Unbiased and error-free thinking is impossible in principle, and perfect rationality is not even a good standard of comparison. Chapter 14 discusses a variety of pitfalls that may ensnare our thinking and especially our judgments. And chapter 15 focuses on some of the most frequent and most troublesome of these pitfalls. Both chapters 14 and 15, as well as chapters 16 and 17, offer some guides around the pitfalls so as to arrive more closely at mental clarity and self-discipline. Chapter 18 focuses on dealings with people and managing social interactions.

The entire business of creating ideas, obtaining relevant information, evaluating the alternatives, and drawing conclusions—the subjects of parts III and IV—is a back-and-forth process rather than a neat series of steps, even though it is necessary to neaten up the process when presenting it here on the printed page.

The Book in a Nutshell

The single most important practical idea in this book: When in doubt about whether some scheme will work, or whether you will like something, or whether someone will be interested in your offer, or whether your new product will sell, or whether almost anything . . . try it. Experiment. Don't just turn the matter around in your mind. Simulate the situation with a small model. Take a small bite. Call the person whose interest you wonder about. Put some paint on and see whether it matches. Take some of your new product into a local store, hang up a sign, and see if anyone buys. . . . Yes, theorize—but don't *just* theorize. Theorize, and then try it out.

And then try it another way. If the conclusions from the two experiments coincide, you can be much more confident than with the results of only one investigation in hand. And if the results do not coincide, you should be wary of proceeding on the basis of one investigation alone, and study the situation more fully.

DEVELOPING
DECISION-
MAKING
SKILLS FOR
BUSINESS

PART I

WANTS, ABILITIES, AND GOALS

You must know your goals, and you must be able to specify your criteria of success in life, in order to make use of the machinery for evaluative analysis that helps you make decisions among various possible courses of conduct—the analytic system described in part II. But as we struggle with the toughest decisions in our personal and professional lives, we often find that we are unsure of our goals. Therefore, the next three chapters in part I tackle the difficult problem of selecting our goals and our criteria of success.

There are two main inputs for the process of selecting goals: (1) Our wants, the satisfaction of which pleases us and makes us feel good—call this satisfaction "benefits." The most important and fundamental of these wants, apart from the needs of sheer subsistence, are the general desires that we call our *values*. (2) Our human and physical resources, which enable us to work toward satisfying our desires. We usually refer to the usage of these resources as "costs," though using our talents may be a benefit as well as a cost; this interpenetration of work and play is one of the many interesting complications that pop up as we choose goals. These topics of benefit and cost are discussed in chapters 1 and 2, respectively. Chapter 3 discusses how to combine our values and our capacities in choosing our goals.

Chapter 1

Tastes, Preferences, Wants, and Values

Brief Outline

- What Do You Want?
- What Are We Talking About Here?
- The Basics of Understanding Desires
- Some Useful Tactics for Sorting Out Desires
- Tastes Are Tricky
- You May Wish to Increase Your Desires Rather Than Satisfy Them
- Analyzing the Aims of Organizations
- Summary

What Do You Want?

What you do want? Ask yourself what matters to you. Your family? Your car? The human species? Chocolate rather than vanilla? Lots of money? The environment? Religion? Quietness?

Our wants constitute one of the two elements of the life goals we set for ourselves. (Our capacities constitute the other element.) Satisfying one or more of our desires is the benefit part of cost-benefit analysis of alternatives. Therefore, in this chapter we turn to the task of clarifying our institutional and personal values, as well as our more ordinary needs and desires.

This is a very tough job, however. Our wants are slippery when we try to grasp and understand them. One reason that wants are elusive is that they change, and sometimes we change them by the very process of thinking about them. So we have hard work to do in this chapter.

What Are We Talking About Here?

Your desires are the sensible starting point for your efforts to think better and live well. But one's desires are a very complex matter, perhaps the most complex matter in your life. It is simple enough to say "I want the French onion" when a waiter asks you to choose a soup. But especially when you are young, or at any other time when you face major choices, the question "What do I want?" can be unbearably difficult. It is such a difficult question that we often can hardly bear to ask it. Facing up to this question in a very explicit manner often is the crucial first step to resolving one's confusion and making sound decisions.

Even Definitions and Distinctions Are Difficult to Come By

Even specifying and defining the subject of this chapter is a messy business. The word "want" can often be ambiguous, and sometimes it is just a single part of the overall issue you are grappling with. The economist and the psychologist can both agree that we should define "desire"—the rather vague word I've used so far—by the fact that you are willing to give up something else you desire in order to obtain the object of your desire and, even more so, by your actually behaving in such manner. Both the psychologist and the economist emphasize that talk is cheap with respect to wants; when someone acts in accordance with the talk, it is time to take the matter more seriously.

That is, a "good"—the object of a desire—is defined as something you are willing to pay for in effort, money, or the like. This can encompass the most noble of desires—which we may call values—as well as the most trivial of desires. Our desires include not only values but also tastes, preferences, and wants, with all those categories overlapping each other.

Values Compared to Other Wants

The difference between what are called "values" and our other desires is chiefly a difference in their importance to ourselves and to others, though people may also attach moral valences to their values. By *values* I mean the desires that are intertwined with our most basic beliefs, such as the belief that humanity should progress, or that children should grow up in decent homes rather than on the street. In contrast, *tastes*—say your taste for chocolate ice cream and your distaste for snake meat, or even your dislike of live snakes and your visceral reaction to the sight of blood—are not the products of deep thought but instead seem to stem from some combination of instinct and experience. This is not to say that these tastes are unimportant. Indeed, you might run away from an accident where there is blood even though you have a strong value to provide help in a disaster. Nevertheless you are not likely to say that avoiding the sight of blood is *important* to you.

We must also distinguish between values and *goals*, which will be discussed in part I, chapter 3. I recognize that I *value* having my children be healthy more highly than almost any other value. Then I think about *ways to achieve* this value, which is then a *goal*. That is, goals imply initiating actions whereas values imply setting priorities. The goals follow from the values, and from our capacity to achieve goals.

The Basics of Understanding Desires

The Conflicts Among Desires

Each of us has many desires that may conflict with each other. Rare indeed is the person who is so integrated that there is no pulling and tugging among her/his desires. We constantly want to eat the cake and stay thin, too. Indeed, such conflict is inevitable because we must satisfy our desires within limited lifetime budgets of time, strength, and material resources. Furthermore, if there were no conflict among desires, each desire would be unchecked and we would go careening without limit in one direction after another.

Conflict may arise because satisfying one desire means not satisfying the other, as the desire to smoke is incompatible with the desire to be fit. Or conflict may arise because the desires are inconsistent with each other, as the value for equal treatment of all people is inconsistent with the desire that your own ethnic group be given preference.

Conflicts Among Desires Appear Everywhere

Mutually inconsistent desires appear in all contexts. Abraham Lincoln agonized because he wanted peace and he also wanted to prevent the southern U.S. states from seceding, and then afterward he also wanted to free the slaves. Our desires differ in their immediacy. We want to eat and drink beyond moderation tonight, and we also want not to get fat or to be hungover tomorrow. This example, and even more so the example of drug and alcohol addiction, illustrates the perennial conflict between short-run versus long-run desires. Struggling with the conflicts helps you better understand your values, however. And responding to several values at once requires the sorts of techniques discussed in part II, chapter 9, on dealing with multiple goals.

Often we deal with conflicts in desires by not examining them closely, or by closing our eyes to the conflicts while we act. And, indeed, this may be the only practical way of getting on with your life. Demanding perfect clarity of yourself would lead you into an infinite regress with ever finer analysis of your desires but with ever worse paralysis of action. I once heard Herbert Simon (no relation, but a Nobel Prize-winning economist and psychologist), who knows as much about decision-making as any living person, refer to the ultimate decision-making tool—and then took a coin out of his pocket and flipped it.

Biological and Learned Wants

Our desires also differ in their different relationships to our biological needs. The need to void one's bladder is more "primitive" and more urgent than the desire to arrange the greeting cards on the mantelpiece. We can think of our "higher" desires as being caused more by learning and less by instinct than our "lower" desires. And the higher desires come more into play as our skills and wealth enable us to satisfy our lower wants. Though the higher wants are built on the lower desires, they eventually develop existences of their own. In the words of Gordon Allport, the higher desires become "functionally autonomous" of the lower desires. Abraham Maslow formalized this idea into a *hierarchy* of wants, with the biological needs at the bottom and what he called the "self-actualization" desires for creative activity at the top. The place in the hierarchy corresponds to the distance from the purest biological needs of food, shelter, and so on, rather than to the importance of the needs.

Whether a given desire should best be considered learned or congenital is a murky matter, though genetic and social scientists are making rapid progress in this field. For example, for the first time, studies in the 1990s seemed to find solid evidence that a propensity for homosexual attraction derives from the genetic constitutions of at least some people, and that people differ greatly in their desires to eat large quantities of food. The strength of one's curiosity—the desire to understand one's world—may well derive from biological factors, too, though surely modified by experience. Research seems to trace ever more of our desires and behavior to congenital biology, as many great earlier scholars of human nature, such as David Hume, believed. The interactions between genetics and learning are so tangled, however, that it is exceedingly difficult to understand the roles of each.

There is further discussion in part II, chapter 9, of how to resolve the difficult matter of conflicting desires.

A Single Controlling Goal?

Despite the pyramidal, control-like image of a hierarchy, there is seldom a single goal atop the pyramid that rules the others uncontested. Trying to determine which is the emperor goal usually is a fruitless pursuit that can cause confusion and distress. The question "Who am I?" usually makes sense only if you translate it into "What do I want?" Looking for a single dominant want seems to follow from searching for the unique essence of "I." I recommend that you do neither.

There are exceptions. Some people do discover a "life mission" for themselves—to create a medical clinic in a poor rural area (Albert Schweitzer), or renew a language thought to be dead (as in the case of Hebrew a century ago and the linguist Philip Lieberman). Such life missions can come to be life-saving and life-giving. Missions sometimes also can turn into monomanias that sow personal hardship for loved ones. But such callings are very rare, and when they happen, they are unmistakable. For most of the rest of us, going out looking for a calling can cause only confusion.

The Motive of "Honor"

Even though it seldom makes sense to think of a single overriding desire, many of our other desires can usefully be viewed as related to the enhancement of the sense of oneself—that is, to one's own and others' judgments about how "good" a person you are. An unusually strong desire for money often can be understood in this light. Why would a person want much more purchasing power than the person could conceivably use for almost any utilitarian purpose in his or her lifetime?

Often a likely answer is: to show that one is successful and "good," deserves honor for that success, and is better than other people. Why do people drive expensive cars and live in palatial houses? Unusually attractive aesthetics and creature comforts seldom are a convincing explanation.

Indeed, the very economists who are thought to view people as economically motivated—especially Adam Smith and before him Bernard Mandeville—knew that a person's standing in the community was usually a deeper goal once the person satisfied the necessities. Mandeville put it this way:

> The meanest wretch puts an inestimable value upon himself, and the highest wish of the ambitious man is to have all the world, as to that particular, of his opinion: so that the most insatiable thirst after fame that ever hero was inspired with was never more than an ungovernable greediness to engross the esteem and admiration of others in future ages as well as his own; and . . . the great recompense in view, for which the most exalted minds have with so much alacrity sacrificed their quiet, health, sensual pleasures, and every inch of themselves, has never been anything else but the breath of man, the aerial coin of praise.[1]

The desire for money is extraordinarily powerful simply because money is the means to obtain so many other goods, including honor (even titles of royalty and public office can often be bought) and power over other people.

Some Useful Tactics for Sorting Out Desires

Asking yourself the fundamental question "What do I want?" is an example of a suggestion that comes up in several apparently unrelated sections of this book.

Wise Tip #1: Ask "What Do I Want . . . ?"

This is the first among the Wise Habits that will be flagged and labeled in the book.

When you don't know which way to go, ask yourself a "What do I . . . ?" question.

When you are working in scientific research and you feel stumped, ask, "What am I trying to find out?" When you are writing an essay or an advertisement and you just find yourself staring at the blank wall, ask, "What do I want to say?" When you are running around in circles doing a million things and cannot decide what to do next, ask, "What am I trying to do?" (Finding the similarity in these questions is one of the benefits of discussing many different kinds of thinking in a single book such as this one.) Guidance often seems to appear as if by magic when you step back and ask yourself the basic "What do I . . . ?" question.

The aim of this chapter is to determine which desires are most important for you, or for an institution with which you are working. The following are useful tactics:

- Assess your wants *systematically*, devoting a block of time to the task, rather than just doing it hit-or-miss.
- Write down your thoughts, rather than just mulling them in your mind. Writing with a computer is even better than using paper and pencil because the computer makes it easy to revise the items on your list.
- Do not exclude from your original list those desires that you think are presently unattainable. There will be time later on to put your wants into their proper perspective.
- Begin the exploration of your mind with pen (or computer) in hand. You might first try the straightforward approach of writing down your desires in a list, then attaching a priority weight to each desire—say, a number between 1 and 5. Or, you can try imagining some stories that illustrate a conflict between two or more desires, and ask yourself how you would like the story to end; from that story you can draw a conclusion about your priorities. Or you can get outside of your own perspective and pretend you are someone else, and then ask what you (the other person) think your own desires are.

Exercises for school kids under the label "values clarification" purport to help young people sort out the importance of (say) animal rights versus having soft drinks in aluminum containers. Or you may be able to dream up another way of grilling yourself about what is important to you. It can be very instructive to look at the choices you actually make, because they may reveal that a desire is stronger or weaker than you are willing to admit to yourself. Done one way or another, this activity adds up to a process of serious introspection.

It's a Tough Job. Give It Your Best Time and Energy

The process of investigating your wants requires effort. It also requires the courage to see yourself as you are, to admit to yourself truths that may not seem flattering. For example, you may come to realize that you really like very much to take life quite easy, to sit by the sea and look into the distance, though you have always believed that this is not an acceptable way of life. Put this desire on your list. Later you can sort out the conflict between that desire and the desire to live in ways that are more acceptable to the community, or according to some of your other values about hard work and contribution to society.

Making a study of one's wants also can be painful. It hurts to come face to face with the hard truth that some of your strongest desires are incompatible with each other and therefore you must forgo some of them; few people are able to have both the freedom of a bachelor and the satisfactions of married life. (Forcing recognition of the inevitable tradeoffs among desires is one of the jobs of the economist when discussing public policy, and it is one reason that economists are not popular with politicians. Who wants to hear that you can't have your cake and eat it too—you can't have a high level of government spending for social programs and also a low level of taxes, for example—when you wish to make the electorate happy with promises of being able to do both?)

Wise Tip #2: Give Life Search Your Best Time and Energy

The subhead to this section is "It's a Tough Job. Give It Your Best Time and Energy." Here we're talking about sorting out your wants, but there is a general lesson here, too: Often we leave our studies in self-knowledge for our after-hours time, when we are tired and therefore not very productive. As I found out in conquering my depression in 1975 (see the story in my book *Good Mood*),[2] often the solutions come only when you commit yourself to working on the job of remaking yourself just as you commit yourself to other tough jobs.

Prepare your materials and schedule, get a good night's sleep, and tackle the work fresh in the morning—day after day, if necessary. Don't fool yourself that other work is more important and therefore deserves your prime time. Figuring out your life deserves your prime time and strength, and until you devote yourself to the job, you may continue to suffer from the lack of knowledge you seek and need.

Analyzing other people's wants with them can be valuable practice for sorting out your own wants. With the benefit of the objectivity that is possible when discussing someone else's problems, you can learn about the confusions from which we all suffer in sorting out our desires, and understand how we all resort to a variety of mental gimmicks (such as procrastination) in order to avoid the work and pain associated with the process.

The Human Condition: Dealing With the Conflicts of Wants

After preparing your list, inspect it for incompatibilities among your wants—between leisure and making a lot of money, perhaps, or between deepening your personal education and getting ahead on the job. When you ask and answer which wants are more important to you, you have information to improve your priorities.

We can form and indulge our preferences for entertainment, say, and our tastes for types of restaurants or when to sleep and wake, solely with regard to ourselves and those close to us. But the choice of one's basic values must also depend upon the human consensus, because values are (by definition) intertwined with our basic beliefs about humanity and human life. Some values are inherently better in a moral sense than are others, just as values should have a higher priority than tastes and other preferences, according to one's hierarchy of beliefs. (This is analogous to the hierarchy of laws in a society, starting at the bottom with local ordinances—about, say, garbage collection—and proceeding upward to the overarching Constitution and its concern with the most fundamental issues of the governance of society.)

Though you ought to give some weight to the values of other persons and groups when choosing your own values, there are still major choices to be made, because there always is far from perfect consensus in any community. Some criteria may be useful in making these choices. I suggest the following criteria that reflect my own values:

- *The extent of universality* throughout humanity, as the value for the preservation of life and the sanction against murder are universal. Universality is connected to the morality attributed to a value.
- *The enduring quality* of those values that persist throughout human history. Endurance also is a hallmark of those values that are widely considered to represent morality.
- *The breadth of application of values*, that is, some (but not equal) concern for the larger group as well as for the people close to you, a fundamental tension that is discussed in the chapter on loyalties.

Tastes Are Tricky

So far I have talked about tastes as if they are as solid and as easy to determine as your social security number.[3] But there are great difficulties in determining your wants, among which are the following:

You Don't Know What You Want, or What Will Satisfy You

There is no necessary equivalence between what you say you now want, and what will give you satisfaction.[4] Indeed, one of the most famous curses is to wish upon a person that she gets what she has asked for. The wish to be a soldier in battle is a classic example. Winning a big-money lottery sometimes leaves people wishing they had never bought the successful ticket.

Tastes Change With Time

In the case of an individual, the subjective value of money changes with your circumstances; a dollar means less to you as you get richer (a phenomenon which, in economics, goes by the fancy name of "diminishing marginal utility of money"). Goals of making money will therefore change as your circumstances change. To some extent you can even forecast the change, and plan accordingly. When you are young and penniless, you can predict that later in life you will earn much more than you do when young, and a given sum will then mean less to you than at present. This may affect your current decisions about borrowing, and it may affect your planning with respect to the goals of earning additional income and doing community service three decades hence.

Biological changes predictably alter your psychic states. The simplest example is the hormonal differences between a young male of 18 and an old male of 88. (This is not to say that all men's interests in sex follow the same trajectory; indeed, men probably differ much more in the intensities of their sex interests at 58 than they do at 18; about women I am less well-informed.)

In other cases a change in taste may be unpredictable, such as the change in your desire for money if you are unlucky and suffer a financial debacle in the future, or the change in your desire for sports due to an unexpected biological change resulting from disease. Such unpredictable changes in taste make long-run planning difficult, of course.

You Can Change Your Tastes

By choosing to take a college course in classical music, you can alter your musical tastes, perhaps to the extent that you develop the goal of becoming a concert promoter. A young man (mentioned again in the Introduction to part II) who formally analyzed his woman friend as a potential spouse found that his values changed as a result of his close inspection of those values during the cost-benefit study.

Others Can Change Your Tastes

Advertising attempts to change your tastes, though it seldom is able to do so with respect to major matters (even political orientation); it does so mainly with respect to such minor matters as which brand of beer to buy. (Trust me on this, both as a one-time advertising man and as a one-time researcher in the field.) Preachers can alter your desires concerning basic morals and values.

You May Wish to Increase Your Desires Rather Than Satisfy Them

To be without desires is not usually desirable, except perhaps in a situation (such as that sort of suffering discussed by the Buddha) in which you must get rid of desires in order to get rid of pain. Desires provide interest and zest to life, as a fresh love affair or a new interest in music might enliven a retiree.

Do You Really Want to Satisfy Your Desires?

Let's expand on the last point mentioned above. Remember the great adage: Be careful what you wish for, lest you have your wish satisfied. Children can't imagine that they would be made worse off if they get the bicycle or the dog they wish for. And maybe it is better that they get the dog or the bicycle. But for adults the matter sometimes is different. It is not unusual for adults to fall into depression after they have satisfied important wants.

For example, people often find themselves at loose ends after they have achieved retirement, or after they have finished a demanding educational program, or after they have found a marriage partner. Then the central problem of life may become something other than determining and satisfying one's existing wants, and may instead become a matter of developing new wants. Indeed, economist-philosopher Frank Knight remarked that people usually do not want their wants satisfied; rather, they want bigger and better wants. (This view did not fit easily with the received theory of economics, however, as trained economists will understand.)

Indeed, one of the worst things that can happen to a human being is to experience lack of desire for new experiences. This is the terrible mood of the writer of the Bible's book of Ecclesiastes, the feeling that "the salt has lost its savor." Again and again the writer of Ecclesiastes says that nothing in life is worth doing because "All is in vain." (The standard English translation is "All is vanity," which is confusing because the word "vanity" has come to have a very different meaning than when the King James translation of the Bible was prepared; the Hebrew clearly is "All is in vain.")

This is the state of spiritual anorexia. It is akin to the physical form of anorexia wherein a person has no desire to eat, and therefore sometimes starves to death. Unless it is relieved, the spiritual anorexia of wanting no new experience often is followed by death, too.

So be glad you have unsatisfied wants, and don't wish too hard to have them all completely satisfied.

Analyzing the Aims of Organizations

Much the same sorting-out process as described above for individuals is appropriate for nonprofit organizations. (For-profit organizations usually have a single, easily specified "desire": making money.) What are the desires of the various groups with a stake in the organization—the beneficiaries of the organization's activities, the staff, the donors of funds, the community at large? Here the heart of the process is to thrash out and reach some consensus about what should be considered the "desires" of the institution. Those "desires" or "values" can then be combined with ideas about the capacities of the organization in order to set goals for the organization.

Listing *all* the desires before weeding them out is especially important for organizations. In discussions of which policies to pursue, there is a tendency to exclude options from consideration on grounds that they are not politically viable. This often means that the most imaginative and basic changes are ruled out from the start. It is usually better not to exclude possibilities on political grounds until after the first stage of list preparation is complete.

After Organizational Goals Are Reached

After organizations successfully fulfill their original missions there arises the interesting question of what the organization should do with itself. Examples include the March of Dimes after a vaccine was found for polio (infantile paralysis), and the U.S. Department of Energy after it became clear that the supposed "energy crisis" of the 1970s was no crisis at all. And an army tends to remain larger after a war than it was before the war.

An organization that has attained its mission could simply disband, of course. But there is a strong tendency not to disband, one important reason being that the staff members develop stakes in their jobs. At that time the organization must develop a new organizational "desire" and aim. The new aim is likely be related to the previous mission in order to take advantage of the organization's investment (about which see chapters 1–3) in acquiring knowledge relevant to that sort of mission.

In some cases the value of the existing organization may be sufficiently great to benefit society at large if the group finds a new purpose rather than disbanding. Usually, however, continuing to exist is simply a wasteful boondoggle for the benefit of the people involved with the organization.

Summary

Identifying your wants is a crucial first step in reaching your life goals. Conflicts among desires, and changes in desires as we age, are two of the difficult hurdles to overcome.

It is crucial to have desires. Having no unsatisfied desires is one of the worst of situations. We need to create new and better wants.

Notes

1. Bernard Mandeville, *The Fable of the Bees* (Oxford, England: Clarenden Press, 1957), p. 48.

2. Julian Simon, *Good Mood: The New Psychology of Overcoming Depression* (Peru, IN: Open Court, 1993).

3. For a more detailed and scholarly view of this subject, with different emphasis, see the masterly article by James G. March, "Bounded Rationality, Ambiguity, and the Engineering of Choice," in *Decision Making: Descriptive, Normative, and Prescriptive Interactions*, ed. David E. Bell, Howard Raiffa, and Amos Tversky (New York: Cambridge University Press, 1988), pp. 33–57.

4. For more information about the confusion in economic theory about the utility concept, see Julian Simon, *Basic Research Methods in Social Science* (New York: Random House, 1969).

Chapter 2

Assessing Your Resources

Brief Outline

- What Do You Have Going for You?
- The Past Influences the Present
- Taking Stock of Your Resources

What Do You Have Going for You?

What do you have going for you? A strong back? Durable nerves? A half million dollars? A law degree? A well-trained ten-person travel agency? A talent for choosing fine musicians?

The resources—we could just as well call them "capacities"—that you can put to work are the second constituent of your goals. (Your desires, discussed in the previous chapter, are the other element.) You must know your capacities, so that you can estimate the costs of various alternatives. This chapter discusses the process of making an inventory and evaluating the physical and human resources available to an individual or organization. You can expect that if you follow the procedures described in this chapter, you will come to know better one important side of yourself.

Your capacities influence the means by which you work toward goals, as well as the goals themselves. Consider as a homely example that you want a ditch dug in front of your house. You recognize that there are a variety of ways to get the ditch dug: (1) Get a shovel and dig by hand. (2) Hire someone to dig with the equipment you provide. (3) Call a ditch-digging firm. (4) Rent a power digger. (5) Ask a relative to do it. (6) If you are a female, flirt and charm a male to do it. (Few males can pull off the opposite.) The choice among methods depends upon your finances, gender, tastes, and values, and whether your back is strong or weak—that is, upon your resources.

The Past Influences the Present

Investments made in earlier years affect the amount of assets you now own. This exemplifies the concept of "path-dependency" in economics, which boils down to the activities in the past leaving traces in the present state of affairs. Sunk costs influence the course of events. But it is the *result* in the present of the expenditures already made in the past, rather than the expenditures themselves, that matter. Hence it is still true that sunk costs should be considered sunk and therefore disregarded in decision-making. (See part II, chapter 6.)

Your resources are different at various stages of personal and organizational life. At the time you enter college, say, acquiring a knowledge of Chinese will require an expenditure of time and effort unless you are of Chinese extraction and learned the language at home, in which case speaking the language is a resource that can influence your choice of goals at college. After you major in Chinese at college, your mastery of the language is a resource and a sunk cost. Sometimes these sunk costs can feel like a burden to you. For example, you may be a whiz at computers but not want to work on them, yet your boss may ask you to do it anyway if she knows of your ability. Another resource that can feel like a burden is if your uncle offers you his business, though it does not interest you.

A short way to say all this: Your history influences your possibilities. This is why only a few firms bid for a given government contract; only those few firms have the resources to do the work at a reasonable price. Everyone recognizes this simple fact in practice, but academic theory has too long omitted the influence of history from consideration.

Taking Stock of Your Resources

Your job is to take stock of the situation to which your history has brought you. Mature persons are likely to have had training, experiences, and even careers that are different from their present situations. Very often you will find yourself circling back to incorporate those forgotten parts of your life into what you do now, to your great benefit. For example, I find that the research I did a quarter of a century ago on libraries and library materials turns up occasionally in my current work on very different subjects. Often it is useful to delve into your background to remember forgotten experiences and skills that are relevant to the present. I have frequently been startled at the strong connections that appear between (1) people's discoveries and new activities, and (2) such pieces of people's pasts as having been an Eagle Scout, or a prison guard, or on welfare. As part of your resource inventory, it is important to review those earlier parts of your life and give them the prominence in the inventory that they deserve. These experiences are rich sources of ideas and skills.

Accountants and lawyers can easily detail your physical and financial assets—the stocks, buildings, machines, land, etc. that you own or lease. Your organizational and personal human resources are more difficult assets to assess. Here is a checklist:

1. Look yourself over. You may have unexpected abilities that friends and relatives will mention to you if you ask, or that testing services and counselors may help you identify. But don't be too sure that the professionals are right; treat what they say as interesting hypotheses rather than as facts.
2. Determine what you are doing now. If you are assessing your resources as part of an organization, find out what people are doing within the organization.
3. Find out what else has been done in the past.
4. Ask people what they can do that they are not doing now.
5. Ask individuals what their *group* can do that it is not now doing. Keep in mind that an established organization in existence is an important asset that is more than the sum of the individual abilities of the people who work with the organization.

When I was in graduate school I worked part-time analyzing the advertising for Chicago's famous Carson Pirie Scott department store. I found that the advertising copy was quite inconsistent. When I asked the top managers what kind of a store they thought Carson's to be, there was absolutely no agreement among them, and also no knowledge among them of how much they all disagreed on this. Finding the common theme and orienting the advertising around that theme promised to increase the sales potential of the store as a whole. In many business situations, analyzing the nature of your customers, and of your products, can be an effective tactic.

Are You Being Reasonably Objective About Yourself?

When assessing yourself, remember that you are likely to have a biased view of your capacities, either upward or downward or both ways at once. Many studies show that most people are overconfident in most kinds of situations, especially where their ability to choose correctly is little better than chance. But in some situations—especially those where their judgments really are very accurate—people systematically under-estimate their abilities (see Plous for a brief review).[1] And having a high IQ (please notice that I did not write "high intelligence") does not lead to less overconfidence. *Item:* I once read that 95 percent of people sur-veyed judged themselves to have a better-than-average sense of humor. Unless the survey was restricted to professional comedians, there is a serious discrepancy between people's judgments and the actual state of affairs. *Item:* Far more than half my students, year after year, raise their hands when I ask "Is your judgment better than that of the average per-son?" *Item:* A recent poll found that among drivers, "37% found their own driving to be 'excellent,' while only 2% felt other drivers are as adept."[2] And Baruch Fischoff says [in *Against All Odds*][3] that surveys in many countries find that about 80 percent of people with driving li-censes say they drive with greater-than-average skill.

This self-regarding bias is so pervasive, and it affects so much of our important behavior, that it might well be included in part IV, chapter 15, on important errors. But there are gains from this bias in helping a per-son be optimistic about the future and feeling in control of her/his fate. The gains might outweigh the losses from the errors it induces. Adam Smith asserted that it is better to think a bit too much of yourself than a bit too little, because other people are likely to take you at your own estimation.[4]

Remember that it is important to identify your weaknesses as well as your strengths.

Appearance and Reality of Your Capacities

Sometimes you need to learn what other people *think* you are and can do as well as what you *actually* are. A singer may think that she is a blues singer whereas others think that she is a country-and-western singer. If she learns that discrepancy, she can either alter her offerings to better fit people's picture of her, or she can try to alter their picture of her to fit what she thinks she is. Either change could help her get singing jobs.

As every salesperson and lawyer understands very well, your stock of acquaintances and friends is an important resource. Businesses sometimes forget, to their woe, that the goodwill of their customers is their most important asset. And it is important to analyze the nature of your customers and acquaintances.

When you are young, it often is wise to *try out* a variety of activities in order to learn your abilities—jobs with people and jobs without people, and so on.

"Know thyself," the man said. He knew what he was talking about, especially from the point of view of setting the direction of your life and your organization.

Notes

1. Scott Plous, *The Psychology of Judgment and Decision Making* (Philadelphia: Temple University Press, 1993), chapter 19.

2. *Wall Street Journal*, August 17, 1989, p. 1.

3. Baruch Fischoff, *Against All Odds Video Recording: Inside Statistics*, produced by the Consortium for Mathematics and Its Applications (COMAP) and Chedd/Angier, in cooperation with the American Statistical Association and the American Society for Quality Control (Washington, DC: Annenberg/CPB Collection, Santa Barbara, 1989).

4. Adam Smith, *The Theory of Moral Sentiments* (London: H.G. Bohn, 1853).

Chapter 3

Choosing Goals and Criteria of Success

Brief Outline

- The Inputs Used in Setting Goals
- The Benefits of Wise Goal Selection
- The Benefits of Setting Goals
- The Goal-Setting Process
- Summary

How many books and articles should I write? How much of my time should I spend writing, and how much with family, friends, community, students? What should I say if my department asks me to teach an additional course?

If I am to arrive at a well-reasoned answer to questions such as these, I must know what my *goals* are. I also need to know various goals for their use as criteria for my personal cost-benefit analyses.

This chapter discusses the information and knowledge that can help you formulate goals well, and it describes some procedures for setting the goals. You can expect that you will have a clearer idea of how to go about setting your goals after you read the chapter, but you must also expect that the process itself will be one of the great challenges of your life—a challenge that recurs again and again as the course of your life changes with the passage of time.

The Inputs Used in Setting Goals

Two sets of considerations bear upon one's choice of goals— capacities and desires. From your capacities you can deduce what is *possible*. Your desires tell you how *valuable* the various possibilities are for you. For example, you might have extraordinary talent as a poker player, but according to your values, making a fortune at poker playing is of little worth because it benefits no one else and hurts the losers. You therefore might exclude professional poker playing as a life choice. Similarly, you might decide against being a musician, despite the high value you place on making music for others and yourself, because you think you have too little talent to create great music or make a decent living at it. In contrast, your considerable capacity to lead people—to motivate them, direct them, and achieve high performance and morale with them—might fit with your high value on contributing to the welfare of the local community, implying that a career in firefighting or crowd management might be a wise goal.

Knowing the uses of goals helps us set our goals. (1) A goal can focus your attention, mobilize your resources, and motivate you toward specific attainments. (2) A goal also serves as a chart for your progress. Measuring your progress assists you in making further plans and in maintaining enthusiasm rather than becoming either complacent or despairing. (3) To the extent that we follow plans rather than just drift into things—though drifting with the tides is not always bad—goals influence how we allocate our lives—what we do with our time and energies. In this sense, goals are indistinguishable from life choices.

The Benefits of Wise Goal Selection

Wise goal selection enables you to make a contribution to the community as well as to satisfy your desires. You thereby gain the satisfaction of using your capacities productively. Indeed, arriving at appropriate goals either by thinking the matter through or by trial and error is an important element in achieving happiness. People frequently learn to trim down overambitious goals that they fail to achieve and which therefore cause them mental distress. Sometimes people learn to scale up from overly modest goals that afford too little sense of satisfaction that they are using their capacities sufficiently, and too little sense of reward from the product of their efforts.

A goal should be sufficiently difficult that it will present a challenge and stretch your abilities. But it must not be unattainable or seem unattainable. If it seems unattainable, you may give up before you begin. (T.S. Eliot said the same of a poem—it must be easy enough to understand, but hard enough so you cannot understand it immediately.) If a goal is unattainable and you go after it anyway, the consequent failure may cause you pain and diminish your energies.

Sports in which the aim is to win against another person are not a good model for goal-setting in the rest of your life and business. In my experience, a person usually does best in work and personal life by trying to *do well with respect to one's capacities and values* rather than by trying to do *better than another person or organization*. A better sports model is trying to make good shots or a low score in golf, or a fast time in running relative to your personal history, or making cleanly executed throws in judo, no matter who wins the match.

Some people believe that the motivation to defeat others increases one's chances of winning various kinds of contests, including business competitions. It is hard to test this sort of proposition, though it is probably true that different people are best motivated by different mental schemas. Research by Scott Armstrong using several different techniques has shown, however, that using one's own firm's profits as a criterion—that is, focusing on one's own *absolute* performance—is more effective than focusing on a firm's share of the market—that is, focusing on one's *relative* performance.[1]

The Benefits of Setting Goals

Some people need specific goals more than others. I do not benefit from a tight agenda or a set of deadlines for the work I am doing. Specific goals just disturb me. For some people, though, goals prevent floundering or procrastinating.

Making a written inventory of your capacities and your desires can help you set goals by forcing you to make your thoughts more objective and more cogent than they are likely to be if you just let them float around inside your head. Discussions with other people also help you systematize and discipline your thoughts. Those two simple suggestions —which apply to every other kind of heavy-duty thinking, too—are all that I can offer. But if you follow these suggestions, they may be all the advice you need. Conversely, you should avoid just stewing endlessly with the same old elements if you seem to be making no progress. Talk and write—these are powerful tools.

The Goal-Setting Process

How does the process of goal selection resemble the process of cost-benefit analysis? Capacities are related to costs, but in an inverse fashion: The greater your capacities, the less your costs in accomplishing a particular object. And desires are related to benefits; an objective "benefit" has no meaning to you unless you desire it.

Choosing a goal is like a cost-benefit analysis in which the costs are fixed in advance—by your capacities—and your task is to choose the alternative that will provide the greatest benefit for the specified cost structure. Here again we see a link between two types of thinking that at first glance do not seem to have anything in common—one of the themes that runs through this book.

Choosing goals involves other goals and values. For example, should the goal of a youth group be simply for the kids to have a good time, or should it also be to make a contribution to the community?

Choosing goals involves an entire hierarchy of goals—the very long-run and fundamental goals, the sub-goals that are part of the larger effort, and the daily sub-sub-daily goals.

Setting Goals for Organizations

For a nonprofit organization, goals are constrained by the organization's history as well as by its present composition and program. The organization should aim to clarify its options so that those persons with a stake in the organization—its beneficiaries, staff, and donors—can thrash out the issues and reach some consensus about what the goals should be. Often, a key issue is how broad or specialized the organization should be—whether it should aim at many goals or just a few. For example, should your state university attempt to offer a very wide range of programs or should it attempt to concentrate upon a few programs in which it already is strong?

What should a nonprofit organization do when it achieves its goal, as chapter 1 noted was the case with the March of Dimes when polio (infantile paralysis) was conquered? The organization could disband, of course. But that might be a waste of an expensive investment in organization.

Setting Goals for Others

Setting goals for other people is a difficult business. For example, the centrally planned Soviet economy had to set goals for each factory in order to evaluate performance. But it is almost impossible—perhaps just plain impossible—to set goals that will do what they are intended to do. For example, if the goal for a nail factory is set in terms of a *number* of nails, the manager will produce only small nails because they require less raw material and less work per million. If the goal is shifted to a *weight* of nails, the manager will make only large nails because they require less work per kilogram. If the goal is set as some *combination* of these two attributes, there must be some formula to trade off shortfalls or overages in the goals on the two dimensions. And it will still be possible for the manager to shave on quality unless that is made part of the goal system. This goal-setting problem is one of the best arguments for private enterprise wherein profit is an efficient overall goal.

When others set goals for you, you must consider whether your resources enable you to achieve the goals. When I was a young officer in the Navy, I was responsible for getting the decks, sides, and seamanship gear shipshape for a major inspection following a period in the shipyard. My divisions were grossly undermanned but I did not recognize that fact fully, nor did I know how to argue for more resources. The result was a poor inspection grade followed by my painful firing from a job that I liked very much. A sensible manager learns how to fight for resources to meet goals or to point out that the goals cannot be met with existing resources.

Summary

To summarize: Your goals should be set with an eye to your capacities. But they should not be set *only* with regard to your capacities and the personal rewards to them. The effects on other individuals and communities may matter, too. Some goals are better than others, according to some hierarchical scheme of values (including yours).

Note

1. J. Scott Armstrong and Fred Collopy, "The Profitability of Winning," *Chief Executive* (June 1994): 60–63.

PART II

INTRODUCTION
TO EVALUATIVE THINKING

Psychiatrist to patient: "Do you find it difficult to make decisions?"
Patient to psychiatrist: "Yes and no."

Brief Outline

- What Is in Part II?
- The Role of Comparison
- What Is Cost-Benefit Analysis?
- The Limits of Cost-Benefit Analysis: To What Is It Applicable?
- The Steps in a Cost-Benefit Analysis
- When to Use Cost-Benefit Analysis, and What You Get Out of It?
- Exercise

What Is in Part II?

The following chapters consider a series of problems encountered in cost-benefit analysis, plus solutions for the problems. The interrelatedness of activities is one cause of difficulty. Chapter 4 shows how the tool of tabular analysis and the consideration of each combination of activities handles the difficulty of interrelatedness. The spreading out of consequences over time also causes difficulty in decision-making. The mechanism of time-discounting and present-value calculation, discussed in chapter 5, deals with that difficulty. Then there are pitfalls in dealing with cost. Chapter 6 points out the pitfalls, and provides a surefire simple framework that avoids the cost pitfalls and leads to sound decisions. Uncertainty is a third major cause of difficulty in decision-making. Chapter 7 presents the intellectual machinery that enables you to deal with uncertainty in a systematic fashion. And chapter 8 provides a set of devices that helps you allow for risk in your decision-making. The presence of more than one goal, and conflicts in goals and preferences among the participants in an organization or within an individual, are another source of difficulty in decision-making. Chapter 9 shows ways of handling that difficulty.

This introduction to part II will be much longer than the introductions to the other parts. The reason is that some readers may dismiss the material in part II as being "only" the type of thinking that is used in business, and therefore is not relevant to nonbusiness aspects of their lives. Not so at all, this introduction argues. The same decision-making problems one faces in business arise in all other aspects of one's life, but they are obscured in other parts of life because they are overlaid with many more complexities than arise in business. Business decision-making is a peculiarly simple arena for choice, even though business decisions can be plenty complex. And that simplicity is the reason for discussing these procedures in the context of business, though they apply elsewhere just as well.

The Role of Comparison

Comparing alternatives is a fundamental activity of human life. Both a subsistence farmer in Africa and a corporate farmer in Minnesota must compare alternative crops in order to decide which crop to plant. A teenage girl compares two boys who ask her to the prom. The United States compares the consequences of invading a fractious Central American nation versus dealing with it in another fashion. We must compare to stay alive, and we compare frequently so as to live better, though sometimes we make life worse by comparing too often.

At the core of every evaluation lies the process of comparison. And the heart of every comparison is a consideration of the benefits and costs of each alternative being considered. Cost-benefit analysis is the formal apparatus for comparing alternatives.

Economists like to refer to their discipline as the science of choice. And they often use Lionel Robbins's famous definition: a set of principles for allocating scarce resources among competing means. But choice can also be seen more simply, as just the selection among alternatives without any explicit statement in advance of the resources available to you.

What Is Cost-Benefit Analysis?

Cost-benefit analysis is the art of sound decision-making for personal, business, and public decisions by systematically comparing the goods and the bads that you can expect with various alternatives. Some additional examples of situations in which cost-benefit thinking surely is appropriate are:

1. What price should a concert promoter set for tickets to a concert? The price for a lifetime subscription to the Chicago Opera? For a new perfume?
2. Should United Airlines sell its chain of hotels? Should Marriott Corporation buy the Wag's chain of restaurants?
3. Should Zebus Inc. buy the big new computer that it needs, or should it rent it instead?
4. Should the federal government place a dam across the Colorado River at Happy Canyon?
5. Should athlete Bo Jackson choose to play professional football or baseball, or both?
6. Should schoolchildren be given annual X-ray examinations if leukemia might be caused thereby?[1]

The Limits of Cost-Benefit Analysis: To What Is It Applicable?

Values, ethics, creation of precedents, and complex social balances must sometimes enter into the decision-making along with the monetary costs and benefits. Among such cases in which narrow cost-benefit calculations are relevant, but probably do not constitute the *entire* criterion, are these decisions:

1. Should the federal government ban cigarette advertising from magazines and newspapers?
2. Should the local electric utility contribute money to the local public radio station?
3. Should Lana go on to college after she graduates from high school?
4. Should Filipino physician Anthony emigrate to the United States?

In the above four cases, though a narrowly economic calculation would omit key elements of the situation, a wider cost-benefit analysis that includes nonmonetary costs and benefits may be an appropriate aid to decision-making.

There are also situations where some may feel that the decision-maker should simply "do the right thing" and damn the calculations, whereas others may feel that the decision-maker should at least know the balance of economic costs and benefits as well as consider the ethical elements. These are some examples:

1. Should Molinari Painting fire the bookkeeper who has worked for the firm for thirty years but is no longer efficient or pleasant?
2. Should a popular magazine accept cigarette advertising?

Although the analytic framework of cost-benefit thinking suits a wide variety of situations, sometimes it produces results that are foolish or worse. Some decisions are simply a matter of taste, and trying to apply cost-benefit analysis obviously would be wacky. For example, one does not explicitly evaluate costs and benefits when choosing a prayer to read at your wedding.

There also are situations where cost-benefit analysis can cause damage because the most important benefits (or costs) are affected by the making of the cost-benefit calculation. Some types of such inappropriate situations are as follows:

1. *When loyalty and commitment are central.* In a love relationship, the other person might regard the analysis as inappropriate. ("Do you simply compare having me with having a new car?") If you make a cost-benefit calculation, rather than simply acting on the basis of commitment alone, you may alter your partner's commitment to you. It is as if there is an implicit agreement not to make cost-benefit calculations, a contract of friendship or till death do us part, and if one doesn't seem to live up to it, as a consequence the other may not also.

Symbolic gestures are a related category of activities that are negatively affected by cost-benefit analysis. If someone thinks that you coolly evaluated the personal pros and cons before deciding to say "I'm with you," the meaning of the gesture may reduced.

2. *Ritual behavior, religion being a vivid example.* Should you read this prayer or not, observe this sabbath rule or not? The religious person suspends such decision-making, perhaps as an implicit contract between the person and his God, or simply as a decision that, *taken as a whole,*

the body of rules is good. Making a cost-benefit analysis of one part or another would be inconsistent with the already made decision to accept the entire package. The wholeness of the overall package commitment is a key element in the package.

3. *When the process of decision-making and control is inconsistent with the act and its pleasure.* In sexual love, for example, the exercise of rationality and studied choice is inconsistent with the pleasure of spontaneity, and may even make performance impossible. In the case of music, evaluating a symphony is likely to affect how you perceive it, and hence can affect your enjoyment.

Aside from these categories, however, just about all other decision-making seems appropriate for cost-benefit analysis—even life versus death (the decision to commit suicide is a straightforward cost-benefit analysis to some terminally ill people), and war versus peace (though the decision is never a simple one).

Before you enter into a relationship, even decisions about such issues as love and faith may appropriately be analyzed with cost-benefit thinking (though I do not urge it). Hardheaded calculation of benefits and costs may well be called for when deciding whether to marry a particular man, or to convert to a particular religion and accept its obligations. It is only *after* one has entered into the relationship that such thinking may be inappropriate.

(Sometimes prudence might dictate doing your cost-benefit analysis discreetly. A graduate student once proposed doing his cost-benefit term paper on whether to marry the woman he was going with. I suggested changing the topic because each student was required to present his project in class, and word might reach his woman friend with distressing results. He insisted, however, on the grounds that she worked in a city eighty miles away, and he went ahead with the topic. His assessment was positive, he proposed, and she accepted. What happened thereafter I know not. With hindsight I still think this was an unsound choice of class project, and perhaps as the teacher I should have vetoed it—but on what grounds? What would you have done in my place?)

You should use cost-benefit analysis when making such business decisions as how much a firm should spend for advertising, rather than using "sales target" or "goal" thinking. The latter sort of thinking is usually a lazy replacement for the hard work necessary to do a sound cost-benefit analysis. Don't get taken in by the claim that certain kinds of business decisions "don't lend themselves" to cost-benefit analysis.

Decisions of nonbusiness enterprises are sometimes less amenable to cost-benefit thinking. A nonprofit institution such as the Catholic Archdiocese of Washington has multiple goals rather than the single goal of making as much money as possible, and it must answer to a variety of groups and individuals both within and outside of the Church. All this makes some decisions more complex and cost-benefit analysis less applicable (though this would not be true when the archdiocese is deciding whether to buy or rent a computer). Nonprofit institutions also may find it difficult to measure and value the resources they use, and the goods and services they provide.

Individuals' life decisions typically are the most complex, because elements of cost-benefit analysis that can be objectively measured by a firm or even by a nonprofit institution—the rate at which future events are to be discounted, for example, and the nonincome value of a college education—must be specified by the individual on the basis of personal taste and judgment.

The limits of cost-benefit thinking will be discussed at greater length in chapters 5 and 6.

The Steps in a Cost-Benefit Analysis

These are the steps in a cost-benefit analysis:

1. *Identify the consequences* of the given action in each period in the future.
2. *Classify the consequences* into positive and negative—the goods and the bads, incomes and outgoes, costs and revenues—and state each of them numerically. If a consequence is uncertain, state it as a probability.
3. *Apply an appropriate weight* to each individual consequence. The weights will be different for different time periods.
4. *Combine the weighted consequences* for the given alternative into a single summary number—technically known as the "present value."
5. Compare the summary number for the various alternatives being considered, and choose the alternative that has the highest present value.

The chapters that follow discuss in detail how these steps are executed.

When to Use Cost-Benefit Analysis, and What You Get Out of It

Please do not conclude from the neat, orderly look of the above set of steps that most evaluative thinking follows this model. Most judgments are snap decisions without formal analysis. The decision-maker somehow consults her or his "intuition"—a seemingly mysterious brew of accumulated mental material that actually is neither mysterious nor "irrational"[2]—and quickly arrives at an answer.

Indeed, formal cost-benefit analysis is done in only a tiny fraction of the decisions we make; the process costs too much time and thought. Systematically working down the series of steps must be reserved for the tough decisions when intuitive thinking seems inconclusive, or when the decision-maker asks someone to perform a formal analysis as a check.

Making good intuitive decisions about when you need, and do not need, to make formal cost-benefit decisions is a valuable skill. It follows that bright, young graduates often err grievously in their contempt for higher-level managers who do not often bother with fancy analytic techniques. It also follows that experienced managers should not be so complacent of their intuition that they scorn a formal analysis of the important decisions.

If we could record the lightning-quick operations that occur inside our heads when we think "intuitively," we probably would be able to deduce a series of controlling instructions analogous to the program of a computer engaged in what is called "artificial intelligence"—say, a program that develops a medical diagnosis and treatment for a patient with a complex and exotic disease. From the outside the computer looks mysterious, but inside the black box, the operations are quite logical and unmysterious.

The information used in cost-benefit analysis is always imprecise, sometimes ridiculously crude. And the more important the decision, the less reliable is the information that is likely to be available, because very important decisions arise infrequently. The machinery provided later for dealing with uncertainty helps us deal with lack of information. Yet imprecision necessarily remains.

Our desires and goals also are imprecise and often muddled. Sometimes it seems as if we first make our decisions, and only afterward decide which goals fit the decisions. The organization buys an airplane because the CEO thinks it should have one, and then tries to figure out what to use it for. The messiness of decision-making is not a sound reason to forswear cost-benefit analysis, however, any more than the complexity of human relations is a reason to be a hermit.

Careful and imaginative cost-benefit thinking often reveals conclusions quite opposite to "common sense." For example, at first thought it makes sense that vaccinating all children in the United States against smallpox is good. But vaccination programs across the United States typically resulted in 6 to 9 fatalities each year, plus 400 to 500 "serious complications." And the United States did not suffer any cases of smallpox from 1949 to 1971. Hence the U.S. Public Health Service recommended in 1971 that routine smallpox vaccination be ended.[3]

Cost-benefit analysis is not the whole of managerial thinking, by a long shot. Developing the ideas for alternatives to evaluate is a crucial element, of course, and must be discussed separately (part III, chapter 10). Much managerial energy goes into fitting together the resources of an organization—both the people and the physical assets—so that they will meet particular needs and accomplish particular goals. An example is scheduling the operations in constructing a skyscraper. This sort of problem-solving is a matter of techniques rather than evaluation, more akin to engineering than to business. The book begins with cost-benefit analysis because the principles are particularly clear and the methods are generally applicable.

Exercise

Read up on the boxer Muhammad Ali's decision not to go into the Army during the Vietnam War because it was against his religion. Compare that option to going into the Army and simply letting the Army use him to give boxing exhibitions. What were the benefits of not making his decision spontaneously, without calculation?

Notes

1. George Beadle, 1959. "Ionizing Radiation and the Citizen." *Scientific American*: vol. 201, no. 3, pp. 219–232.

2. The concept of intuition deserves demystifying. At the present state of science, we do not know what goes on in any particular intuitive state. It is probably a rapid selective cycling and recycling through the above series of steps, together with various processes of gathering information and ideas from one's memory and applying values to them, done so fast that we cannot have a clear record of what is

happening. To put it differently, intuition is the rapid and unsystematic employment of selected aspects of the various thinking processes described in this book, plus some others that are not in the book. Daniel Isenberg, in "How Senior Managers Think" (*Decision Making: Descriptive, Normative, and Prescriptive Interactions,* ed. David E. Bell, Howard Raiffa, and Amos Twersky [New York: Cambridge University Press, 1988], 525–539) distinguishes five functions for the rapid unsystematic process we call "intuition": (1) "Sense when a problem exists." (2) "Perform well-learned behavior patterns rapidly," for example, to run through a checklist of causes why the equipment broke down. (3) "Synthesize isolated bits of data and experience into an integrated picture," that is, to make a set of connections. (4) "A check . . . on the results of more rational analysis," that is, to examine the conclusions of formal studies in the light of one's general experience. And (5) "Bypass in-depth analysis and move rapidly to come up with a plausible solution," the process this section focuses upon (pp. 530–531).

3. *New York Times,* April 2, 1972, p. 14E.

Chapter 4

Evaluating Simple Alternatives

- How to Price What You Sell
- How Many Alternatives to Consider
- Combination Alternatives
- Exercises

In the introduction to part II, these questions were among those posed as candidates for cost-benefit analysis:

Should Lana go on to college after she graduates from high school? The *Wall Street Journal* published a cost-benefit analysis of the decision-making situation of young people who are currently working and are considering going back to school for an MBA. The sound decision turns out to hinge on the cost of the capital (the rate of interest) the person must pay to borrow money for the tuition and to make up for the forgone earnings, and the expected difference in earnings with and without the MBA degree. The analysis is no more complex than the situations considered in this chapter and the next one.

Should Filipino physician Anthony emigrate to the United States? Should Filipino lawyer Moreno emigrate? Immigration statistics show a large influx of foreign physicians but the entry of only a small number of foreign lawyers. Cost-benefit analyses for the two types of persons make clear why this happens: It takes longer to retrain a lawyer in the U.S. system than to retrain a physician.

Should the federal government ban cigarette advertising from magazines and newspapers? This was the first cost-benefit analysis I ever did—in 1964, following the surgeon general's report showing the health effects of cigarette smoking. The subject again was in the news in the late 1990s, and the same sort of cost-benefit analysis is relevant.

This chapter shows you how to analyze the simplest "maximizing" decisions. This simplest case reveals the bare bones of the choice-making apparatus. It also highlights the information needed to make even these simple decision choices rationally. (The only less-complex decision hinges upon sheer preference, such as whether to take vanilla or chocolate.) But once you have this simple framework in mind, you will meet a surprising number of situations that you understand better with the aid of this framework.

The essence of all businesslike decisions, whether made for a firm or an individual or a nonprofit organization such as a government, is (1) constructing a list of relevant alternatives based on your experience and imagination; (2) sensibly estimating the consequences—the costs and benefits, the incomes and outgoes—that you expect to follow upon each alternative choice; and (3) calculating which alternative will leave you with the largest "profit," that is, the excess of income over outgo.

This type of decision is called "maximizing" because the aim of the analysis is to find the alternative that produces the most (or the least) of something. In the first case below, the quantity to be maximized is profit, and the decision-maker is assumed to be a business. But the decision-making unit could just as well be a nonprofit enterprise such as a hospital or an airport.

This promise may help motivate you to study this chapter and the others in part II: If you master the ideas in chapters 4 to 9, you will have mastered the most important ideas found in an entire two-year master's course in business administration. I present these in a closed-circuit television program called "The One-Day MBA" that has been beamed to engineers and others at Fortune 500 companies since 1990, making the same promise I make to you—with a money-back guarantee of the hundreds of dollars each student pays the university consortium—Consortium for Mathematics and Its Applications (COMAP)—for attending. And no one yet has asked for his or her money back. In fact, when the consortium chose a single program for their anniversary celebration, this was the program chosen.

The cases we shall take up here are simple because they all take place *entirely within a single short time period*—a year, say, or even a day. Activities that fit this description include promoting a concert or a symphony tour, and selling baseball hats outside a stadium. But in most business situations, a decision today will have consequences many years into the future, either through long-lived investment in buildings and equipment, or through the goodwill created in long-term customers. This complication of multi-periodicity will be dealt with later.

Also, unlike most business situations, here we assume that we *know with reasonable certainty* what will happen following the decision we make, rather than being uncertain about the results. (Chapter 7 tackles the fascinating issues that arise when we must explicitly grapple with the uncertainty that pervades most human decision-making situations.)

Analyses outside of business—and for many situations within business, too—have the added complication that there are multiple goals rather than the simple goal of maximizing profit. Another nonprofit complication is that the results may not be measurable in a single index such as money. In later chapters we will grapple with these complexities.

Even in a short-run no-uncertainty situation, however, there may arise the difficulty of choosing the best *combination* of variables within our control—price, quality, location, production method, advertising, service, and so on. Developing our technique that far is the subject of this chapter.

How to Price What You Sell

An enterprise must decide the price to charge for its product when it goes into the market. And an individual must decide what price to set on his or her services when the person looks for work. How should you go about it?

The following analyses in this chapter—and all others in part II—can be handled conveniently and easily with any standard computer spreadsheet program such as Excel or Lotus or Quattro Pro. This modern device is wonderfully flexible in enabling you to experiment with variations of the analysis so that you can consider the effect of a change in one element on the other elements, especially on the measure of output (such as profit, in the case of a business) in which you are interested.

You are promoting a basketball game in Bloomington, Iowa, an off-season exhibition featuring a team of professional players playing against a team of recent all-star college graduates. You have rented the 12,000-seat arena for $16,000, and you are committed to pay the teams $2,000 apiece. If you charge just one price for all tickets with no reserved seating, what price should you set?

Assume that you can expect to sell the following numbers of tickets at the prices shown (if all other conditions stay the same) (see Table 4.1).

Table 4.1

Price ($)	Tickets expected to be sold
14	11,200
16	10,000
20	7,900
24	6,200
28	5,400
32	4,000

Table 4.2

Attendance	Expected nonentertainment expenditures ($)
4,000–5,999	3,400
6,000–7,999	4,000
8,000–9,999	6,800
10,000–12,000	8,000

Assume also that your expenditures for nonentertainment labor and other purchases will depend on the number of tickets that you sell (see Table 4.2).

You want to "make" as much money as possible from this operation. That is, you would like to maximize the amount left over after you pay all the expenses. Therefore, it is straightforward common sense to put all your costs and revenues into the columns for price, quantity, and expenditures in a spreadsheet table like Table 4.3.

You then calculate Sales Revenue by multiplying Price by Quantity, and Present Value (PV) by subtracting Expenditures from Sales Revenue. This can be done with paper and pencil, but spreadsheet users will do so by putting computation formulas into the Sales Revenue and PV cell ranges. From here on, we will usually not mention the details of the spreadsheet computation, and proceed as if we were still using paper and pencil.

Here it is worth mentioning that though the spreadsheet was originally developed for business computations, it is now in wide use for

Table 4.3

Price ($)	Quantity	Sales revenue ($)	Expenditures ($)	Present value ($)
14	11,200	156,800	56,000	100,800
16	10,000	160,000	56,000	104,000
20	7,900	158,000	54,000	104,000
24	6,200	148,800	54,000	94,800
28	5,400	151,200	52,000	99,200
32	4,000	128,000	52,000	76,000

computations in science and other lines of work. The spreadsheet is now so ubiquitous that it is taught routinely to students in many U.S. high schools for its use in everyday personal life as well as for work. And the terms "table" and "spreadsheet" will be used interchangeably below.

From Table 4.3 you can conclude that your profit will be greatest at a ticket price of either $16 or $20. We might also note that expenses will be somewhat less at a price of $20 and an attendance of 7,900 than at a price of $16 and an attendance of 10,000, and hence this more refined analysis suggests $20 may be better. The conclusion is only as sound as your estimates of the numbers used in the table, of course. Part III, chapter 13 sets forth methods for making sound estimates.

You might now consider whether there is some price between $16 and $20 that would produce *even more* profit. Therefore, supplement the existing table with an analysis of, say, $18. You can do this in an instant with a spreadsheet by substituting $18 for one of the values you no longer wish to consider—say $32. You could also refine the analysis by considering even finer gradations of prices, but practical decision-makers are usually satisfied with the analysis of a few round-number prices.

When I first began to study business economics, a mathematics instructor asked what I was learning. I mentioned this topic of setting a price so as to maximize profit in the simplest possible situation. He then asked me if the correct answer could not be arrived at by simply looking for the price with the biggest difference between income and outgo. I said yes, that's true in a simple situation, but in a more complex situation you need the more powerful intellectual machinery of the "marginal-revenue-marginal-cost analysis," a name that conjures respect and even fear in those who have encountered it in Economics 1.

My response was wrong. The marginal analysis using higher mathematics is *not* helpful in complex price-setting problems any more than it is necessary—or even useful—in the simple case we're dealing with at the moment. Hard as it may be for some readers to believe, the simple spreadsheet we constructed above cannot be excelled by any other method of analysis. Extension of the same sort of common-sense table will produce the best possible decision in all other business situations, too, as we shall see.

Indeed, the marginal analysis, even using calculus rather than just spreadsheets, cannot handle complex problems nearly as well as can this sort of tabular analysis, even with just paper and pencil. Hence, economics teachers have to stick close to this sort of simple case to illustrate the marginal analysis because problems much more complex than this one are too tough to handle with "advanced" methods. But with the simple tabular method, we shall do more complex problems as easily as rolling off a log.

This is only the first of several important issues discussed in this book in which the conventional wisdom as widely taught in even the best universities is flatly wrong—unnecessary, confusing, or even yielding unsound conclusions. (Of course, it is prudent to proceed with caution when you come across such a far-out unconventional view. But if you do not at least check it out for yourself, you will close off progress for yourself and for society.)

Constructing Table 4.3 immediately raises difficult questions such as: How do you judge how many seats you will sell at various ticket prices? How sure can you be of your estimates? Might you make more money by charging different prices for different parts of the arena? And what about buying some advertising to sell more seats? We will be dealing with these and other questions one by one.

For some flavor of the complexities of price-setting—except that the viewpoint here is that of the buyer rather than the seller—here is a vignette from deal-making between television interviewer David Frost and Richard Nixon's agent Irving "Swifty" Lazar:

> I was utterly confident that my interest in the enigma of Richard Nixon would also be reflected by the public's interest in him as well. And, as an independent, I had no corporate bureaucracy to consult. I went ahead and placed the call to Swifty Lazar. I had no corporate bureaucracy to supply any future backup either, of course, but that was not a consideration in

my mind at the time—only the overriding thought of being first in the race to question Richard Nixon about his years in the White House.

I was glad that I was dealing with Swifty Lazar. Noted for his legendary ability to enter a revolving door behind you and come out in front, Swifty believed in getting right to the point. He wanted $750,000 for his client for a maximum of four one-hour shows. The main competitors— later revealed to be NBC—were currently at $300,000 and on their way to $400,000 for two hours, and would not guarantee more than two hours. That seemed to me to be a heavy rate per hour—and an underestimate of how much Nixon had to offer, both in terms of information and public interest. Others might not agree, but I was sure there was more—much more—than two hours of potentially riveting television in Richard Nixon. I said I was thinking of a maximum of $500,000 for a minimum of four hours. Before returning to the question of a fee, however, I ticked off the points I regarded as mandatory. . . .

Within days, the word came back: The response was not unfavorable. Swifty, God bless him, felt "duty- bound" to tell me that the "rival offer" was now $400,000 for two hours, and then returned to his magic figure of $750,000. I said I could not really go beyond my original figure unless I had more time on the air. We compromised at $600,000 plus 20 percent of the profits, if any, for four ninety-minute shows, with $200,000 of that to be paid on signature.[1]

The key difficulty here is assessing what the other parties will do. Soon we will tackle that difficulty.

The same sort of spreadsheet as used above handles decisions about whether to locate a factory in one city or another, and whether to adopt a new production technique. You need only insert the expected income and outgo (expenditure) for each alternative, and choose that alternative with the highest profit.

How Many Alternatives to Consider

How many alternatives should you consider? It is impossible even in principle to consider *all* possibilities. And in most situations it is feasible to consider only a very small number of them. The fact that the pricing spreadsheet (Table 4.3) analyzes only even-dollar prices is not a drawback of the method; It is only a reflection of reality, wherein firms and even countries—for example, Saudi Arabia when it sets prices for petroleum—choose among only even-dollar or half-dollar prices. A cost-benefit analysis of the pricing process itself would undoubtedly show that worrying that you might do better with a penny more or less in such a case would not be worth your time—and indeed, such a cost-benefit analysis is itself not worthwhile (probably).

Combination Alternatives

Let us now illustrate the technique with three examples slightly more complex than the basketball pricing case.

The spreadsheet method enables you to easily evaluate the effects of two factors at once. Let's say that you wish to simultaneously choose the best price *and* the best amount of advertising. First compare the effects of various amounts of advertising at one of the prices to be considered, as in the top panel of Table 4.4, then at another of the prices, as in the bottom panel. Then choose the best *combination* of a price and an advertising level from the table as a whole. This technique enables you to compare any sets of combinations you wish to consider, using as many subtables as are necessary. Lest you worry that the amount of arithmetic will be inconvenient, the personal computer does all calculations for you in a jiffy.

The following example of a combination alternative illustrates the power of this method. Setting prices for a "line" of two or more related products has long been thought an intractable problem. The core of the problem is that the price of one product affects the sales of the others. For example, the price of the U.S. Postal Service's two-day delivery affects the sales of its overnight service, and vice versa. But the spreadsheet method cracks the problem with ease. Or, for the case of A&P supermarkets' line of three coffees—Bokar, Red Circle, and Eight O'Clock—the analysis is shown in Table 4.5. The results for each line of three prices are compared to the results for each alternative line of prices. Simply choose the line with the largest net revenue after expenditures have been allowed. The key is not to think separately about the individual elements in a line. Rather, because the sales of each product affect each other's, and because the firm is ultimately interested in its overall profit and not in the individual product's results, we consider the combined *results* for each alternative. This all-together technique makes simple almost any analysis of several activities that affect each other such as a structure of discounts.

After looking at Table 4.5 you may conclude that the analysis is indeed simple, but the data to support the analysis may not be easy to

Table 4.4

(a) Analysis for price = $2

Advertising Expenditure ($)	$Q_{t=0}$	$S_{t=0}$ ($)	$A_{t=0}$ ($)	Production expenditures, $B_{t=0}$ ($)	$E_{t=0} = (A_{t=0} + B_{t=0})$ ($)	$(S_{t=0} - E_{t=0})$ ($)
0	1,000	2,000	0	1,000	1,000	1,000
1,000	4,000	8,000	1,000	3,800	4,800	3,200
2,000	6,000	12,000	2,000	5,000	7,000	5,000
3,000	6,500	13,000	3,000	5,300	8,300	4,700

(b) Analysis for price = $2.50

Advertising Expenditure ($)	$Q_{t=0}$	$S_{t=0}$ ($)	$A_{t=0}$ ($)	Production expenditures, $B_{t=0}$ ($)	$E_{t=0} = (A_{t=0} + B_{t=0})$ ($)	$(S_{t=0} - E_{t=0})$ ($)
0	750	1,875	0	750	750	1,125
1,000	3,000	7,500	1,000	2,900	3,900	4,600
2,000*	4,500	11,250	2,000	4,000	6,000	5,250
3,000	5,000	12,500	3,000	4,500	7,500	5,000

*Indicates the price-advertising expenditure combination with the highest expected residual.

Table 4.5

	Alternative 1($)	Alternative 2($)	Alternative 3($)	Alternative 4($)
$P^A_{t=0}$	1.00	0.90	0.80	
$P^B_{t=0}$	0.80	0.80	0.60	Etc.
$P^C_{t=0}$	0.60	0.70	0.90	
$Q^A_{t=0}$	900	1,200	1,300	
$Q^B_{t=0}$	1,400	1,350	1,500	
$Q^C_{t=0}$	1,300	1,200	1,000	
$S^A_{t=0}$	900	1,080	1,040	
$S^B_{t=0}$	1,120	1,080	900	
$S^C_{t=0}$	780	840	900	
$E^A_{t=0}$	630	804	665.50	
$E^B_{t=0}$	896	864	870	
$E^C_{t=0}$	754	732	670	
$V_{t=0}$ $(S_{t=0} - E_{t=0})$	520	600	634.50	

come by. Very true. One of the advantages of this tabular method, however, is that it focuses your attention on the needed data, whereas if you get caught up in a complex mathematical analysis of a decision-making situation, your attention is likely to be deflected from the data. In this case, the data are relatively easy to come by, however, once the spreadsheet makes clear what you are looking for. The supermarket chain need simply conduct experiments with different lines of prices in different store locations.

Lest you think that this tabular analysis is small-time stuff, rest assured that exactly this decision method is used for the very biggest businesslike decisions—for example, whether a firm should start an operation in Africa or should instead invest in deep-sea mining of metals, or whether a government should or should not spend billions of dollars for a canal or a supersonic airplane. (The name "cost-benefit analysis" was first used for such public investment decisions.) Such analyses are, of course, more complex than figuring the expenses for the ushers and arena rental involved in your pro basketball game, and the spreadsheet therefore will have more entries in it. But the method of analysis is exactly the same. And in such a complex situation, not even the bravest economist tries to use fancy mathematical marginal analysis. The formulas just cannot handle the real-life details of a cost-benefit analysis of whether to build a dam or undertake a deep-sea mining operation.

So, if the simple table is good enough for such multibillion-dollar analyses, should it not be good enough for you in your daily life or business decision-making?

You may think that this framework is obvious and uncontroversial for making decisions about price-setting. Incredibly, it is not so. This framework implies that the basic analytical framework of microeconomic decision-making—the marginal analysis—is useless and confusing; and indeed, it is. But economists are so wedded to that contorted method, because of an interesting series of twists and turns in intellectual history, that they continue to teach it to students of business.[2]

After we learn about present-value analysis in the next chapter, we can extend the spreadsheet analysis to decisions that cover many years rather than just the immediate period.

Exercises

This illustrates the general strategy for choosing the best alternative under any set of business circumstances: (1) Write down all the distinct combinations of possibilities, that is, each alternative that you wish to consider. (2) Estimate all the incomes and outgoes that are expected with each alternative. (3) Choose that alternative with the highest residual of income over outgo. For example, if you want to consider a variety of prices—$99.95, $119.95, and $129.95—as well as a variety of discounts (2 percent off for payment within 30 days, or 3 percent off for payment within 30 days, or 3 percent off for payment within 60 days), examine each separate combination—say, $99.95 and 2 percent–30 days. Of course, you might find it laborious to examine each combination that you could dream up. But good business sense will almost always allow you to narrow down the alternative to a manageable few. About the only situations in which this is not true are some technical decisions such as how to split crude oil refining into auto gasoline, airplane gasoline, heating oil, and so on, and advanced mathematical techniques are available to aid such decisions.

Notes

1. David Frost, *I Gave Them a Sword* (New York: Ballantine, 1978), pp. 10–12.

2. Modern economics follows in a line from the English economist Alfred Marshall. The original geometric analysis done by Marshall showed only curves for supply and demand, and the analysis applied to *agricultural markets*, as wholes. In such cases, the independent variable is the weather, and hence it makes sense to put the quantity supplied on the horizontal axis, and the dependent variable price on the vertical axis. For manufactured goods, however, price is the appropriate independent variable, especially when one is making the analysis for the firm rather than the industry. But economists were stuck with the old tradition. And when they came to add the additional machinery known as the marginal analysis for price-setting purposes, they found themselves making the analysis with respect to quantity rather than price, which has tied generations of students into knots. The ironic part is that the great French economist Cournot (Augustin Cournot, *Researches into the Mathematical Principles of the Theory of Wealth* [Homewood, IL: Irwin, 1838, 1963]) had the analysis quite straight in 1838, but his great book never affected the later mainstream of analysis. For more details, see Julian L. Simon, "Unnecessary, Confusing, and Inadequate: The Marginal Analysis as a Tool for Decision Making," *American Economist* 25 (spring 1981): 28–35.

Chapter 5

Weighing Present Versus Future
Benefits (and Costs)

Brief Outline

- The Concept of Discounting for Time
- Rent Versus Buy (Zero Salvage Value)
- How Sharply Should You Discount Future Events?
- Summary
- Exercises

- Should you go to graduate school and postpone earning income until two years from now, at which time you could expect a higher income than otherwise? Or would you be better off working for the next two years rather than going to school?
- Should your trucking firm buy a loading device that will cost you a pretty penny this year, but which will reduce labor costs for at least five years?
- Should the federal government build a dam in Happy Canyon? The difficulty in making such a decision is that the taxes required to pay for it would be levied now, while the benefits would only gradually accrue over many decades and even centuries.
- Should you tell a lie which may get you out of a jam for the moment, but which may have ill consequences on your reputation and conscience in coming months and years?

This chapter shows you how to take into account both the present and the future, in a manner that sensibly weighs their importances. Combining present and future is reasonably straightforward in business situations, but the same machinery can be adapted for personal and other nonbusiness situations. This is a tough and important task, but I promise you that you will soon understand how to handle it.

The Concept of Discounting for Time

Most important decisions have consequences in the future as well as in the present. In each of the above examples, the decision requires weighing benefits and costs that occur in different years. A given amount of money does not have the same value when you possess it now compared to getting it in some future year. Nor do nonmonetary consequences have the same value for us if they will occur far in the future as if they were to occur now. If this idea is not immediately obvious to you, ask yourself whether you would be willing to lend a hundred dollars to me now, and then get back from me the same amount five years from now. (If the answer is yes, please express the money to me as soon as possible.)

Please notice that your reluctance to lend me money and get back the same amount later—an interest-free loan—has nothing to do with inflation; we could easily modify the arrangement to allow for inflation. Rather, you will not consider this a good deal because having the use of the money for the next five years has a value for you as well as for me, just as having the use of a farm for the next five years has value and the renter therefore pays for the right to do so.

The concept of *time-discounting* enables us to handle all the above examples. With the discounting device we can appropriately weigh the incomes and outgoes in various future periods, and then add the set of them into a single overall sum, which is called the *present value* of the stream of future incomes and outgoes. This is the core idea in making decisions about investments and other actions taken in the present that will have ramifications long into the future. Time-discounting is the single most important and powerful idea in all of managerial decision-making.

Think of time as a *measurement*. Indeed, the fundamental idea underlying Albert Einstein's theory of relativity is that, as he put it, "we understand by the 'time' of an event the reading [position of the hands] of . . . clocks."[1]

Indeed, time is the *most important* measurement because the length of the period during which an event takes place measures how much pleasure or pain we will experience. Furthermore, the time distance into the future measures how important the upcoming event is to us now.

John Locke viewed humans' relationship to time as the characteristic that most distinguishes us from the animals. He spoke about "the great Creator, who [gave] to man an ability to lay up for the future as well as supply the present necessity," though before we get too proud of ourselves, we should notice that the squirrels are pretty good at saving, too.

Now let's get specific about how time-discounting operates. The full name of the concept is "discounted net present value." The *discount factor* is the proportion of a sum next year that makes it equal in value to a smaller sum today. That is, if the appropriate one-year discount factor is .80, a dollar one year from now is worth 80 cents today, and a dollar two years from now is today worth .64 (that is, .8 x .8) of a dollar. The *cost of capital* (sometimes confusingly called the "discount *rate*") is the side of the coin opposite from the discount factor. It is the proportion of the sum *this year* that you must pay to have the use of the money until next year. If the price of using 80 cents for a year is 20 cents, so that you will pay back a dollar next year, the cost of capital is 25 percent. That is, a *cost of capital* of .25 corresponds to a *discount factor* of .80. These are two names for the same idea.

> *The definition of present value*: Present value of a given alternative *equals*
> (Expected revenue from the given alternative in the first year)
> *minus*
> (Expected expenditures on the given alternative in the first year)
> *plus*
> (Expected revenue in the second year, multiplied by the one-year discount factor)
> *minus*
> (Expected expenditure on the given alternative in the second year, multiplied by the one-year discount factor)
> *plus*
> (Expected revenue from the alternative in the third year, multiplied by the two-year discount factor—that is, the one-year discount factor multiplied by itself)
> *minus*
> (Expected expenditure in the third year, multiplied by the two-year discount factor)
> *plus*

(Expected revenue in each subsequent year, each multiplied by its appropriate discount factor)
minus
(Expected expenditure in each subsequent year, each multiplied by its appropriate discount factor)
plus
(The expected market value of nonmonetary assets at the end of the decision horizon, discounted to the present)
minus
(Market value of nonmonetary assets at present)

Let us work an illustration showing how the present value is computed. Please notice how the choice of the discount factor can affect which alternative should be chosen as best (see Table 5.1).

Consider a situation in which an owner of a new patented item has a choice of selling the item gradually over a period of, say, three years (after which time we assume demand falls to zero because this is an item people buy only once), or of tooling up in a hurry, selling them all at once in the first year, and then closing up the business. Assume that the revenues and expenditures under the two alternatives are as follows:

where $P_{t=0}$ is the price of $Q_{t=0}$ is the quantity that is expected to be sold.

If the appropriate discount factor is .95, the present values of the two alternatives will be as follows:

$V_{1,T=0} = (\$50,000 - \$20,000) = \$30,000$
$V_{2,T=0} = (\$20,000 - \$13,000) + (\$20,000 - \$5,000) \times .95$
$+ (20,000 - \$5,000) \times .95^2$
$= (\$20,000 - \$13,000) + [(\$20,000 \times .95) - (\$5,000 \times .95)]$
$+ [(\$20,000 \times .95^2) - (\$5,000 \times .95^2)]$
$= \$7,000 + (15,000 \times .95 + (15,000 \times .95^2) = \$34,787$

With a .95 discount factor, alternative 2 is clearly better, yielding the higher present value. But now consider the results if the appropriate yearly discount factor is .50 rather than .95:

$V_{1,T=0} = \$50,000 - \$20,000 = \$30,000$

Table 5.1

	$P_{t=0}$	This Year (First Year) $Q_{t=0}$	$S_{t=0}$	$E_{t=0}$
Alternative 1 (i.e., i = 1)	$5	$10,000	$50,000	$20,000
Alternative 2 (i.e., i = 2)	10	2,000	20,000	13,000
	$P_{t=1}$	Second Year $Q_{t=1}$	$S_{t=1}$	$E_{t=1}$
Alternative 1 (i.e., i = 1)		0	0	0
Alternative 2 (i.e., i = 2)	10	2,000	20,000	5,000
	$P_{t=2}$	Third Year $Q_{t=2}$	$S_{t=2}$	$E_{t=2}$
Alternative 1 (i.e., i = 1)		0	0	0
Alternative 2 (i.e., i = 2)	10	2,000	20,000	5,000

$$V_{2,T=0} = \$7,000 + (\$15,000 \times .5) + (\$15,000 \times .50^2) = \$18,250.$$

If a .50 discount factor is appropriate, the first alternative is clearly better and should be chosen.

The unrealistically high and low discount factors for the examples in Table 5.1 were chosen to bring out the point that the appropriate choice often depends upon the discount factor used in the calculation.

Another example: Fenster says that if you will lend him $10,000 to help start a print shop, he will pay you back $1,800 per year for the next ten years. He will pledge his house as security and (based on his character, as well as on the value of the house), you figure that there is almost as little risk of not getting the money back as with a U.S. government bond. You want to decide: Is the loan a good deal for you?

If you discount the future at 90 percent from year to year, then the $1,800 payment one year from now is presently worth (.9 x $1,800) = $1,620, the second year's payment is presently worth (.9 x .9 x $1,800) = $1,448, the third year's is presently worth (.9 x .9 x .9 x $1,800) = $1,303, and so on. The sum of these discounted payments is $10,551. And if you subtract your original $10,000 investment, the *net present value* of the deal, figured at a 90 percent discount factor, is $551. Since the present value is positive, you should accept the offer if the 90 percent discount factor—equivalent to a 11.1 percent "rate of return" or "cost of capital"—is appropriate.

Consider still another example, comparing the alternatives of buying versus renting a machine as seen in Table 5.2. The present value of purchasing is –$10,000 at any discount factor, because the purchase takes place immediately. The present value of renting, however, depends upon the discount factor. With a discount factor of .8, purchasing is the better alternative. With a discount factor of .5, however, renting is the better alternative.

Rent Versus Buy (Zero Salvage Value)

Present value of buying:
PV of $10,000 today = –$10M
Present value of renting:
PV of $4,000 each year for 4 years =
$-\$4,000 + (-\$4,000d) + (-\$4,000d^2) + (-4,000d^3)$
At .8
$= -\$4,000 - \$3,200 - \$2,560 - \$2,048 = -\$11,708$
At .5
$= -\$4,000 - \$2,000 - \$1,000 - \$500 = -\$7,500$

One more illustration: In many business situations the price in the present period has an effect upon sales in future periods as well as upon sales in the present period. For example, customers may be induced by a low price now to begin a long-continuing habit of purchasing for a given brand of beer. Or, a low price of natural gas now may bring some customers to buy gas dryers and refrigerators, which will lock them into buying natural gas during the life of those appliances. This is the case of a supermarket chain entering the prescription drug market:

> Giant . . . keep[s] prices low on many popular drugstore items and on prescriptions, all to build market share. The higher market share is ex-

Table 5.2

	This Year (First Year)	Second Year	Third Year	Fourth Year
Purchasing	−$10,000			
Renting at discount factor = .8	−$4,000	−$4,000 x .8 = −$3,200	−$4,000 x .8² = −$2,560	−$4,000 x .8³ = −$2.048
Renting at discount factor = .5	−$4,000 = −$2,000	−$4,000 x .5 = −$1,000	−$4,000 x .5² = −$500	−$4,000 x .5³

pected to pay off in the long run for Giant after new shopping habits are established and some of its prices are raised.[2]

Trial offers similarly cause sales in the future to be higher than they would otherwise be at the prevailing future prices.

More specifically: Say you are considering a low introductory price for your newly opening pizza shop—$6.95 for your basic pizza in contrast to the $8.95 you expect to charge after the first two-month introductory period. The purpose of the introductory price is to acquaint a large number of customers with your excellent product. You estimate the number of customers acquired in the first two months with the $6.95 price, and then you estimate the number you expect in the rest of the first year, in the second year, and so on, at your $8.95 price. Each subperiod has a separate set of columns in your table. Then you also make estimates of customers for the first year, second year, and so on, assuming you do *not* set a low introductory price. The number of customers after the first two months will be lower (at least for a while) in the no-introductory-price alternative, because you will have brought in fewer customers in the first two months. The question is, will the extra revenue from the extra customers later on outweigh the cost of getting them with the low introductory price? Computation of the profit for each alternative will reveal which is preferable.

In all these cases, the spreadsheet analysis presented in chapter 4 is expanded to contain sets of columns not only for the present year but also for several future years. And the incomes and outgoes in those future years must be discounted so that the alternative with the highest present value may be correctly chosen.

The concept of present value is the appropriate *definition of profit* in business decision-making. The *accounting* concept of profit is another matter altogether, because the aim of accounting is to assess what happened in the *past* rather than to make choices for the future. Only in the simplest case—when everything happens in a single period and the activity being analyzed is the only activity of the firm—is accounting profit equal to present value.

The computation of the present value of an investment has a long history. English and Dutch lenders, and insurers such as those at Lloyds of London, have for hundreds of years used the technique to adjudge how much to charge for loans and insurance. Indeed, calculating the net present value of each alternative is the appropriate way to compare *any* two courses of conduct whose consequences will continue to be felt into the future. Other examples include deciding whether to give up the pleasure of smoking now in order to extend the likely length of your life, and figuring whether it makes sense to buy aluminum siding for the house in order to avoid the need for painting in the future. The fundamental notion of discounting future incomes and outgoes, and then summing these discounted flows to calculate a present value for each alternative, is always at the heart of the matter. This big idea is indispensable in making almost any decision that has economic ramifications, and for many noneconomic decisions, too.

How Sharply Should You Discount Future Events?

Just *how much* allowance you should make for having the dollar now, rather than in one or ten years, is a very tough question. The answer must depend upon your circumstances. If the decision concerns an individual rather than an organization, the appropriate discount factor also depends upon personal preferences.

A discount factor represents the combination of two elements: (1) An adjustment for "pure" *time preference*, which allows for the fact that a dollar in hand now is worth more to you than even a sure-fire dollar a year from now. This is shown by the fact that interest is paid to you on even a "risk free" government-guaranteed bond when there is no inflation so that someone else can have the use of your dollar from now until a year from now. (2) An adjustment for *risk*, because financial markets as well as individuals value opportunities inversely to their risk. Risky loans pay a higher rate of interest than otherwise similar risk-free loans, and risky stocks sell for lower prices relative to their expected payouts than do less risky stocks.

The Discount Factor for a Publicly Held Corporation

For a corporation whose stock is traded in a public market, the appropriate discount factor is an average of the prices that the firm has to pay for the various classes of capital it uses in the business. For example, if half of the firm's funds come from bonds that pay lenders 10 percent a year, and half comes from stocks that return 20 percent a year to stockholders, the overall cost of capital is 15 percent, and the discount factor is roughly .87.[3]

The Discount Factor for Entities Other than Public Corporations

There is continuing controversy about whether or not government programs should attribute a lower value to a given benefit to be received by a citizen a century from now, say, than to the same benefit received by a citizen now. That is, should a discount factor be used in calculating the value of government investment in a dam or a recreation area? Whatever the morality of the matter, discounting is universal practice. It is woven into the fabric of all our governmental decision-making and will certainly continue so in the future. Less settled is what the government discount factor should be.

The appropriate discount factor for government agencies and nonprofit organizations cannot be established as objectively as for a business. Politics may enter in, as well as subjective judgments. My own belief—which many economists share—is that government and nonprofit institutions should use the same investment criteria—that is, the same discount factor—as do private business activities with the same degree of risk.

The most difficult choice of a discount factor arises when making personal decisions. For activities that affect your economic situation, you can sometimes find guidance in the cost for you to borrow money. For example, when you reflect on the decision about whether to postpone earning and continue in school, you can ascertain how much the bank would charge you for a loan to go to school. (And, indeed, you should always consider the possibility of borrowing to finance such activities, rather than limiting yourself to waiting until you have saved the necessary money. Too often I have seen students err by working for several years at the minimum wage to fund schooling, instead of borrowing and later being able to repay out of much higher income and therefore less cost in work time.) Interestingly, individuals usually can obtain capital at lower rates than can businesses, suggesting that loans to individuals are generally less risky than business loans.

For decisions about activities that do not mainly affect your economic situation—for example, comparing the pleasure of smoking now versus the possible shortening of your later life due to the smoking—taking future events into account in a reasonable fashion is extremely difficult. Even if you can estimate the expected shortening of life—about five years for the average smoker, or five to nine minutes per cigarette smoked—you are faced with a complicated risk assessment; a *particular* person might lose twenty years of life or none. For comparison, is the pleasure of ten minutes smoking worth ten minutes of nonlife in the *present*? If it is, you might ask yourself at what rate you would have to discount lost life in the future to make a balance against ten minutes of smoking now. If that discount would be very high, you might say to yourself that the loss *then* does not mean enough to you *now* to quit smoking. You must also factor in the immediate pain involved in breaking the hold that smoking has upon you. But this sort of analysis is so difficult that one is not likely to actually do it. Indeed, I have never seen a satisfactory analysis for such issues.

This much is clear and obvious: The older you get to be, the larger the weight it is sensible to assign to the present relative to the future. Also, the greater the risk you presently face—in wartime battle, for example—the lower the weight you are likely to place upon possible future consequences.

It sometimes is useful to imagine what you would think *then* of the calculation you are making *now* if you were to reach a point, say, at which you are told that you are about to die from lung cancer due to smoking. Perhaps the greatest contribution of the concept of time-discounting in such situations is to help you *think explicitly* about how much weight you wish to put now upon a given event that will occur well into the future.

People sometimes make choices that seem inconsistent in light of time-discounting. The most dramatic example is having a house painted, or going to the dentist, and then committing suicide a week later. The

likeliest explanation is not a gross inconsistency in present-value calculation, but rather the presence of several conflicting desires that are only
alternately in the person's mind and are never brought into mental relationship with each other. We will discuss such cases later with the help
of the concept of multiple selves.

Also interesting is when people pay to be compelled to do something—for example, when they pay a bank to force them to save—or
when they do things tonight that they will hate themselves for tomorrow. Both kinds of cases are explained by people applying a much lower
discount factor from the immediate present to the near future than from
one future period to another. (Whether or not it is *sensible* to have such
a "kinked" structure of discount factors is another matter.)

Of course there are great difficulties in factually assessing the likely
far-off consequences of today's decision. How will you like being a
physician if you make the investment of going to medical school? How
good a musician will you be if you undertake long training to be a concert pianist? We will tackle these problems of prediction in part II.

Summary

Explicitly allowing for time differences in events is hard mental work.
But it is all-important. The present-value concept is the appropriate technique to use.

Additional Reading

Chapter 2 in my *Applied Managerial Economics* contains a more lengthy
discussion of the subject matter of this chapter.

Exercises

1. What are your thoughts about the following newspaper clipping in
light of the concept of present value?

> We know what the Redskins would do. They have done it 16 of the last
> 19 years, counting the 1987 draft. They'll trade the pick, take the player
> and run.
> "Traditionally, a second-round pick this year is worth a first-rounder
> next year," Gibbs said.

2. And about this clipping from a Sunday supplement story:

It is my Social Security number.

I got it in 1941, four years after the program began, when I went to work as a copyboy for the Associated Press in Chicago.

Since then, I have paid $20,490.63 in payroll taxes. If I retire at age 67, I'll get at least $9,480 a year. That means that, in a bit more than two years, I'll get back all the money I put in during 43 working years. (I was in the Army in World War II and paid no taxes then.) What's more, I'll keep collecting $9,480 or more each year until I die. With a life expectancy of 79, I can figure on getting a sort of bonus of at least $142,200. All gravy. Not a bad deal.

3. And this news report:

BIRMINGHAM, June 21—Heisman Trophy winner Bo Jackson, the No. 1 pick in the NFL draft, announced today that he had signed with baseball's Kansas City Royals, shunning a reported $7 million deal with the Tampa Bay Buccaneers.

Jackson said that one consideration in his decision was the possibility of injury in football.

"My knees are my bread and butter," he said. "They have never been injured, and I don't feel like going under anybody's scalpel."

4. How would you compare the following two modes of auto purchase?

In a lease, the customer's monthly payments are lower than they would be for the same car bought on credit. But the lessee doesn't own the car, which is returned to the dealer when the lease expires—normally after four years.

Consider a moderately equipped [auto X] that would sell for $11,288. [The manufacturer] calculates that the standard lease on the car would be $229 a month for 48 months, or a total of $10,992. With a 5% tax on the monthly payments, the cost would total $11,542.

If a person were to buy the car with the standard minimum down payment of 13%, or $1,481, and finance the rest at 11% for 48 months, the monthly payments would be $253, or a total of $12,144. Including the down payment and lost interest earnings on that amount, as well as 5% sales tax, the buyer's cost would be $14,840, compared with the lessee's $11,542.

5. Do the ideas in this chapter cast any light on the common observation that it is easier to get a commitment from a person to give a talk half

a year or a year in advance, than it is a week in advance? And that a person often accepts an invitation a long time in advance and later comes to wish it had not been accepted?

Notes

1. Albert Einstein, *Relativity* (New York: Crown, 1921), p. 24.
2. *Washington Post*, July 30, 1990, Business, p. 28.
3. This is not strictly true. The discount factor for a particular decision hinges on the extent of the risk involved in the activity being analyzed. Even more precisely, the analysis should consider the change in risk for the enterprise as a whole and not just for the single activity.

Chapter 6

How to Think About Cost

Brief Outline

- Nonbusiness Costs
- Opportunity Cost
- Nonmonetary Costs Other Than Time

Should you indulge yourself in having a couple of beers each day, or a chocolate sundae from time to time, if your doctor tells you that such a pleasure may shorten your life? How about smoking, if the best research shows that each cigarette costs, on the average, five minutes of life? The shortening of your life, if it will occur, is indeed a cost, and the expected effect must be considered a cost when you make your decisions about eating, drinking, and smoking.

The subject of cost goes far beyond money costs. The most interesting and important costs relate to life itself—how long your life will be, how you will use the time that may be available to you, and how healthy you will be to enjoy that time.

Even business costs are difficult to understand. You'd be surprised how many businesses do not know which of their branches are profitable and which are not, simply because they do not have a sound idea of the costs being incurred by the various branches. And not uncommonly, the next step is bankruptcy. You may think that producing estimates of costs is the work of accountants, and that you can get the necessary answers from them. But providing cost assessments for decision-making is not their responsibility, and what they do provide is seldom immediately relevant for decision-making. Figuring your costs is one more example of topics covered in this book where the answers seem easy to obtain, but are not.

Nevertheless, this chapter does promise you that by the time you finish it, you will understand how to go about figuring your costs in business or personal situations, and you should be able to avoid the disasters that too often come upon people in the absence of this knowledge.

Nonbusiness Costs

The life-span costs mentioned above are very difficult to think about clearly. The loss of five minutes of life may well have a different meaning if it is at the end of a life of seventy-eight years rather than at the end of a life of thirty-eight years. To avoid such complications, we will mainly consider examples from business, because money costs are simpler to deal with. But the underlying principles are the same.

Most time costs do not affect length of life, though. Rather, they are a matter of spending time on one activity or another.

The main difference between business-expenditure costs and life-span costs is that you have a limited lifetime to allocate, whereas the sources of payments of expenditures are not fixed from the outside. And in business both the costs and the expenditures are easily measured in money terms, whereas the benefit of being at your sister's wedding (or, thought of another way, the cost of missing an airplane flight for the wedding) cannot so easily be figured in money terms. This is a major complication in personal decision-making.

Sometimes, however, even nonbusiness costs are easily comparable. For example, you can easily compare bicycling to the airport to beat the traffic versus taking the car. Or you can compare taking the bus versus the more expensive cab by considering the time saved against the amount of time you have to work to pay the extra expense. But these are unusually easy cases to deal with.

A last general comment before we get down to business: Generally one thinks of costs as a negative factor. But costs also have a crucial positive role in making life meaningful. Many philosophers have noticed that if life were never to end, it would be unbearably dull. There would be no penalty for a mistake, because you would always have time to do it over again. And if there were no penalty for mistakes, there would be no exultation in success. Similarly, Navy liberty time ashore is so delicious for a sailor partly because you know it will end exactly at 3 A.M. tomorrow morning.

Will life become less exciting as people become more affluent and no longer have the excitement of the cost constraint of a limited stock of purchasing power, and will that absence also remove a key discipline from life? Perhaps people will always find a substitute constraint and discipline. This may explain the current interest in physical fitness.

The negative elements related to an alternative—call them "expenditures" when they are monetary and "costs" otherwise—are remarkably easy to deal with conceptually. But they are often difficult to handle *psychologically and organizationally*, which often causes firms and individuals to reach disastrously wrong decisions.

Pitfalls and Distinctions

There are two major pitfalls in dealing with monetary expenditures: (1) not ignoring "sunk" expenditures, and (2) not allowing accounting notions of overhead and depreciation to get in the way of clear thinking. We'll consider the two errors in that order, and then show how to deal correctly with costs. Finally, the chapter will touch on the vexing matter of nonmonetary costs.

First let us make some distinctions, while noting that it is everyday practice for just about everyone—this writer included—to use language in a sloppy way here. The term "costs" or "cost" is more general than the term "expenditures," which properly refers to the *actual outlays* you will make, in the period in which you will actually pay them out. When making decisions, you should attach expenditures to the period in which they will actually be paid out. More generally, when making decisions, the concept of costs can be dispensed with entirely, working only with expenditures. Though I, as others, slip into using the two words interchangeably, it would be best to leave the word "cost" to accounting work and to economists' analyses of the economy and markets, neither of which is within our scope here.

A variety of cost concepts are frequently used in talking about business: variable cost and fixed cost, incremental cost, marginal cost, and opportunity cost. These concepts sometimes are useful for shorthand figuring. But they also can confuse the issue, and you can get along very well without them. You cannot go wrong by working only with total costs, in the fashion described below.

Sunk Costs

A sunk cost—which really should be called a "sunk expenditure"—is an outlay that *has already been paid out*. An expenditure that has been paid out *should not be allowed to affect any subsequent decision.* That is the most important cost-related lesson in a nutshell.

The rationale for ignoring sunk costs becomes obvious in the case of Farmer Jones. His operations were identical last year to his neighbor Smith except that Jones spent $10,000 on some research and development to try to improve productivity, whereas Smith did not make such an expenditure. Unfortunately, Jones's R&D was useless, and Jones's crop is just like Smith's. If Jones tries to "recapture" his R&D expenditures by charging a higher price for his grain than the market price, he won't sell his grain at all. His only viable option is to consider the sunk costs sunk, ignore them even if he cannot forget them, and sell at the same price as Jones. The same would be true for Smith if he spent a bunch of money last year for new equipment, whether the equipment was useful or not. When it comes time to sell your product, get the best price you can, and that's that.

Someone may ask: How will you ever recover your investments? This question fails to distinguish between the beforehand (ex ante) investment-time decision and the afterward (ex post) selling-time decision. Jones's decision to spend the $10,000 for R&D may have been perfectly sound when he made it, and if the research had been successful he would have increased his production by more than $10,000. But the ex post decision must be made on the basis of how things actually turned out, and not how they were expected to turn out. Similarly, it may have seemed sensible to bet on a horse that, it turned out, stepped in a hole and broke its leg during a race, but afterward all you can do is tear up the losing ticket. (Distinguishing between the situations ex ante and ex post the decision is very often helpful to clear thinking.)

Exactly the same sunk-cost logic applies to the price at which you buy an asset. Afterward, your selling decision should be independent of whether you can "recover" some or all parts of that sunk cost. After the deal is consummated, the purchase of a truck is sunk to a truck dealer, and the price she paid is irrelevant to the price she should resell it for. She should simply sell it for the highest price she can get. If that price is below what she paid for it, and she insists on getting a price equal to her purchase price, she will not be able to sell, and she will lose the whole of the possible sale price.

The lesson about ignoring sunk costs is easy to understand logically. But it is very hard to put into practice for psychological reasons. Many people become bewitched by the prices they pay for a stock or a piece of real estate. The thought of selling for less than they paid is painful, and therefore they hold on beyond the time they would otherwise sell, to their detriment.

Furthermore, accountants tell managers that they *must* allow sunk costs to enter into subsequent decisions, to the great detriment of those decisions. A small but (to me) painful story illustrates how accounting-cost notions can lead to the wrong decision. One day, I asked an executive of the firm that had published a book of mine why the firm did not continue with a mail-order advertising campaign that had just been tested to sell the book. He told me that the advertising campaign was not profitable. I was curious, and we examined the figures.

The test showed that the firm could expect to sell copies at the mail-order price of $8.95 for an average advertising expenditure of about $3.00 per book. (This was many years ago when prices were lower.) I said that in view of the production expenditures necessary for printing additional books—only about $1.25 or $1.50 per copy, because the book had already gone through two printings, plus small expenditures for handling and mailing—the advertising campaign clearly seemed to promise a profit. But the executive said no, we had to add in the "overhead" of several dollars, which meant that the advertising campaign would be below the break-even point.

When asked what the "overhead" charge was for, he replied that it was the standard charge the firm's accountants insisted be applied to all such decisions. He said the overhead covered executive salaries, editing, physical plant, and so on. He agreed with me that additional advertising for this book that had already been produced would not increase the firm's need for editors, and so on. Nevertheless, he insisted on including that overhead charge in the calculation, and hence the campaign was not continued. The result was that both the firm and I wound up a lot worse off than we could have been—a bad decision because of bad reckoning—not considering sunk costs as sunk.

Allocating Over Time and Among Activities: Don't

A difficulty in business decision-making is that accountants supply most of the routine data in business and nonprofit organizations. Accounting concepts, however, are not suitable for decision-making, especially the concepts of depreciation and the allocation of overhead costs. The business of an accountant is to look backward, to "account for," in order to audit for honesty and to apportion credit and blame for profitable operation, as well as to determine how much money the business earned (or lost) in the prior period. The concepts of depreciation and overhead allocation are crucial in making those assessments of what has already happened. But decision-making must always be forward-looking, and the backward-looking accounting concepts are not helpful and may be misleading.

The appropriate procedure is to treat expenditures perfectly symmetrically to the treatment of revenues, as integral parts of the cost-benefit analysis. The sound operating rule is as follows: Write down the total revenues and total expenditures for the firm in each period, for each alternative that is being considered. (The term "total" means the total for *all* the firm's activities and not just for the changes being contemplated.) Then choose that alternative that leaves the greatest excess of total discounted incomes over total discounted outgoes. More precisely, choose the alternative that produces the highest present value for the firm as a whole. Whenever there is the slightest doubt about the nature of costs—more generally, whenever you are making a profit calculation for any kind of decision in business—you should put aside shorthand concepts such as incremental costs and go the confusion-free route of conducting a total-cost, total-revenue analysis for each alternative.

Consider the example of the movie theater's Christmas Eve decision. As of the day before Christmas, the situation was as follows:

	$P_{t=0}$	$Q_{t=0}$	$S_{t=0}$	$E_{t=0}$	$V_{t=0}$
Shut	—	—	—	—	—
Open	$2.00	$50	$100	$60	$40

The V of staying open is higher, as of the day before. For additional interest, let us also see how the situation would have looked as of almost a *year* before, the preceding December 31, when the lease was signed for the year's rent and insurance:

	$P_{t=0}$	$Q_{t=0}$	$S_{t=0}$	$E_{t=0}$	$V_{t=0}$
Alternative of being closed Christmas Eve, results for whole year	Various	Yearly (not necessary to know)	$50,000	$41,000	$9,000
Alternative of being open Christmas Eve, results for whole year	Various, and $2.00 Christmas Eve	Yearly plus Christmas Eve	$50,100	$41,060	$9,040

From the standpoint of the year before also, taking the whole year into account, it is better to operate on Christmas Eve than to stay closed.

The point is that you must understand correctly the alternatives as they face you at the particular moment of decision—and the alternatives can and often will appear very different at different moments.

Given the rules that (1) costs to which you are committed must be considered as committed for all alternatives, and (2) expenditures should be indicated when they actually will be paid, the following point is seen to be important: A crucial part of any cost estimation is to ascertain just *which* expenditures you are committed to for various periods in the future, from the vantage point of the moment when the decision is being made.

In practice, you do not need to include data about most of the firm's other activities. You only need to record the actual data about activities that will be affected by the decision at hand. In the example above, you do not need to know the theater's other revenues for the year. Nevertheless, it is important to indicate in tables with Xs or Ys or whatever that there are revenues and expenditures that are the same for all the alternatives being considered, in order to be sure you do not overlook the possibility that they might be affected. Simply overlooking other possible changes frequently causes shorthand reasoning about costs to go wrong.

Opportunity Cost

Opportunity cost is an important and sometimes useful concept, but it is slippery. The core of the idea is that the relevant cost for an alternative is the benefit you would receive if you adopted the best *other* alternative. For example, if someone offers you $50 for a day to help move some furniture, your opportunity cost depends on what you would otherwise do during the day. If it is a day when you would otherwise work as a gardener and earn $40, then your opportunity cost is $40, and it pays you to accept the furniture-moving alternative. If you would earn $60 as a gardener, then $60 is your opportunity cost, and you should turn down the furniture-moving job. Quite the same analysis would apply if you own the theater business in the example above, and you must decide the value of your own time if you will have to be at the theater to keep it open on Christmas Eve.

So far, the notion of opportunity cost boils down to the proposition that you should consider all the alternatives and choose that one with the highest present value. In a business setting, therefore, the concept of opportunity cost adds little or nothing to our thinking.

But what if you get $60 a day working as a gardener Monday to Friday, and the furniture moving will be on Saturday? Or, what if you must consider the value of your own time in keeping the theater open Christmas Eve when otherwise you would stay at home? What you earn as a gardener is irrelevant—unless you can get gardening work for that Saturday. But if you would otherwise not work on Saturday, is your opportunity cost zero? No, because your time has value to you as leisure. The worth of the time as leisure is known as your "reservation price." It is an opportunity cost that you assign on the basis of your tastes. If you are terribly bored and would move furniture for nothing just to get out of the house, then your reservation price is indeed zero. But if it would take $100 to get you to give up your Saturday at the beach, then $100 is your reservation price and your appropriate opportunity cost. In practice, you can only know your reservation price by noticing how much it takes to induce you to work rather than not to work.

In brief, your reservation price is the appropriate opportunity cost to be assigned to a nonmonetary input—usually your own time—in an otherwise monetized cost-benefit analysis such as the decision about whether to keep the theater open on Christmas Eve.

Nonmonetary Costs Other Than Time

Nonmonetary outlays of effort, emotion, reputation, and personal relationship present special difficulties. Businesses have the advantage that money is an all-purpose measuring rod that compensates all activities and makes their comparison easily possible—at least in principle. But many business costs are not obvious, sometimes because they are not paid for directly, or because they affect the firm only indirectly. An example is the attention of the top management. Many firms have long lists of projects that they are quite sure would bring a high rate of return on the capital invested in them. Nevertheless, many or most of these projects will never be undertaken, because every project requires some of the attention of top management, some of their time and mental energy. This attention is in very short supply and cannot be increased easily, if at all. A small project may require almost as much attention as a big one. Hence, management rations its supply of attention, giving it to projects with the biggest *total* potential return rather than those with the highest *rate* of return.

Attention is probably the resource that most inexorably limits the growth of active firms. Consider a firm that has embarked on a policy of growth by merger. As it grows, it may continue to enjoy solid or improved credit, to improve its reputation, to increase its pool of knowledge. Its greater organizational size creates problems, but many such problems can be avoided by maximum decentralization. Why, then, does the firm not grow even faster? One reason may be insufficient opportunities for merger or purchase. But, more probably, top management may not be able to devote attention to more new alternatives. The need for close attention by the owner is also the chief reason that farms do not grow much larger than they are in the United States and elsewhere. This important hidden effect should not be omitted from the reckoning.

Many personal decisions involve costs that are hidden, difficult to quantify, or difficult to admit to. And in the absence of a monetary measuring rod, evaluation can be very difficult, as we have already seen in the case of valuing your own leisure time.

Let us say that you are mulling a decision to move from Chicago to Atlanta for a new job. The differences in present salaries, and perhaps even in future salaries, are easy to compare, as are differences in living expenses, because they are expressed in money. But what about the cost of giving up the garden into which you have put so much sweat and devotion? Of leaving your old friends, and of the effort of making new friends? And the possible hassle of political difficulties in the new job?

You could attempt to assess the cost of giving up the garden in Chicago by estimating how many hours it would take you to build a new garden like it, or one that would be equally satisfying to you, at your new Atlanta home. This procedure would at least provide a numerical measure that might help you judge the cost quantitatively. You might go even further and put a money value on the hours of time required to construct the new garden, and you could then directly weigh that cost along with the differences in salary and living expenses. Converting other measures to the common measuring rod of money in this fashion can often be helpful.

The cost of leaving your old friends and of making new ones is even more difficult to handle. You could ask yourself: How big a sum of money would it take to make me feel that the gain would be equal to the loss of the old friends? But the very process of trying to place a monetary value on friendship may be so odious to you that you will not do it, and perhaps wisely so. In that case, about all you can do is to make a list of the various nonmonetary costs and benefits and perhaps rank them according to their importance to you. The exercise of making the ranking can help you clarify for yourself how much weight to give to the various elements. But that may be as far as systematic cost-benefit analysis can go in such a situation.

Some costs may be even more difficult to think about because you do not choose to admit to yourself how large they are, or you do not choose to inquire. What if you are secretly in love with a married person with whom you have never even talked outside of the office? You do not wish to acknowledge to yourself that you care a lot about that person, and that you hope circumstances might change in the future to make it possible for the love to come to fruition. Here I abandon you to the wilder shores of human decision-making, with hardly a hint of a suggestion about how to proceed. (You might try flipping a coin to decide the matter, then observing whether you are disappointed at the outcome.)

Everything said in this section about nonmonetary costs applies equally to nonmonetary benefits. Indeed, the two may be seen as opposite sides of the same coin. Not enjoying a benefit can be thought of as a cost, and not incurring a cost can be thought of as a benefit.

After you have arrived at sound concepts of how to think about cost, you are left with the difficult job of actually estimating the expenditures for the alternatives you are considering. That task is discussed in chapter 7.

Chapter 7

Allowing for Uncertainty

Brief Outline

- The Concept of Probability
- Allowing for Uncertainty When Comparing Alternatives

*Uncertainty, in the presence of vivid hopes and fears,
is painful, but must be endured if we wish to live
without the support of comforting fairy tales.*
—Bertrand Russell,
A History of Western Philosophy

Will Chip Lohmiller's kick from the 45-yard line go through the up-rights? How much oil can you expect from the next well you drill, and what value should you assign to that prospect? Will you be the first one to discover a workable system for converting speech into computer-typed output?

Today's actions often continue to affect events many years later. This preservation of consequences constitutes a difficulty in decision-making. Chapter 5 showed how the mechanism of time-discounting and present-value calculation deals nicely with that difficulty.

Interrelatedness of activities is another difficulty in making decisions. However, the mechanism of tabular analysis with the spreadsheet and the consideration of each combination of activities handles the difficulty of interrelatedness with ease, as we saw in chapter 4.

Now we come to uncertainty, a third major difficulty in decision-making. When reading the business examples in previous chapters, you certainly realized that you usually cannot know with reasonable certainty just how many sales you will make at each possible price. And often the expenditures you must make at each possible level of sales are quite uncertain, too.

This chapter presents the intellectual machinery to deal with uncertainty in a systematic fashion when valuing and comparing alternatives.

The intellectual machinery of probability that enables you to deal with uncertainty is the second of the two great tools you need to make decisions, whether in business, in some other sort of enterprise, or in your personal life. (The concept of present value, which you learned about in chapter 6, is the other great tool.) If you can handle these two simple tools with skill and good sense, you will be able to deal with almost any decision that can be handled quantitatively. Or, to put it differently, once you master these two simple tools, you have most of the concepts you can gain from a two-year graduate course in business administration—that I promise you.

The Concept of Probability

The central concept for dealing with uncertainty is *probability*. Mathematicians and philosophers have wrestled long and hard with the concept of probability and its proper interpretation for use in formal mathematics. For decision-making, however, the following uncontroversial interpretation suffices: A probability statement is always about the future. To say that an event has a high or low probability is simply to make a forecast. But one does not know what the likelihoods really are for future events, except in the case of a gambler playing black on an honest roulette wheel, or an insurance company issuing a policy on an event with which it has had a lot of experience, such as a life insurance policy. Therefore, we must make guesses about the likelihoods, using various common-sense gimmicks.

All the gimmicks used to estimate probabilities should be thought of as "proxies" for the actual probability. For example, if NASA Mission Control simulates what will probably happen if a valve is turned aboard an Apollo spacecraft, the result on the ground is not the *real* probability that it will happen in space, but rather a proxy for the real probability. If a manager looks at the last two Decembers' sales of radios, and on that basis guesses the likelihood that he will run out of stock if he orders two hundred radios, then the last two years' experience is serving as a proxy for future experience. If a sales manager just "intuits" that the odds are three to one (a probability of .75) that the main competitor will not meet a price cut, then all his past experience summed into his intuition is a proxy for the probability that it will really happen. Whether any proxy is a good or bad one depends on the wisdom of the person choosing the proxy and making the probability estimates.

A probability is stated as an arbitrary weight between 0 and 1. Zero means you estimate that there is no chance of the event happening, and 1 means you are sure it will happen. A probability estimate of .2 means that you think the chances are 1 in 5 (odds of 1 to 4) that the event will happen. A probability estimate of .2 indicates that you think there is twice as great a chance of the events happening as if you had estimated a probability of .1.

There is no essential difference between the sort of probability that the life insurance company estimates on the basis of its "frequency series" of past death rates, and the salesman's seat-of-the-pants estimate of what the competitor will do. No frequency series speaks for itself in a perfectly objective manner. Many judgments necessarily enter into compiling every frequency series—in deciding which frequency series to use for an estimate and choosing which part of the frequency series to use. For example, should the insurance company use only its records from last year, which will be too few to give as many data as would be liked, or should it also use death records from years further back, when conditions were somewhat different?

In view of the inevitably subjective nature of probability estimates, you may prefer to talk about "degrees of belief" instead of probabilities. That's fine, just as long as it is understood that we operate with degrees of belief in exactly the same way as we operate with probabilities. The two terms are working synonyms.

A probability estimate for an event that occurs many times—such as the likelihood of death of a man in the United States during his fiftieth year—is easy to interpret. But the probability of a one-time or first-time event, such as the likelihood of success of the first mission to Mars, is harder to interpret. I view the latter as representative of that category of events that have *some* similarity to the event that was to be forecast, with the extent of similarity judged on the basis of analogy and theoretical reasonings.

Allowing for Uncertainty When Comparing Alternatives

The Concept of Expected Value

Consider these two alternatives: (1) a thousand-dollar bill in hand, or (2) a 50 percent chance of two thousand-dollar bills and a 50 percent chance of nothing. It is intuitively clear that if you were to be given a choice between these two alternatives on (say) 5,000 occasions, you would be equally well off whichever you consistently chose. The concept of *expected value* enables us to evaluate and compare the two alternatives formally, leaving aside (for now) any feeling of pleasantness or unpleasantness about the certain and the uncertain choices.

The *expected value* is the combination of the value of each outcome weighted by the probability that the outcome will take place. That is, the expected value is the weighted average obtained by first multiplying the value of each outcome by its conditional probability, and then summing. It is the same as the present value in the single-period context where no discounting need be done. An example: Conditional on the fact that someone offers to gamble double-or-nothing for a dozen apples, using a fair coin, the expected value is:

(1) Outcome	(2) Probability	(1) x (2) Expected Payoff
No apples	.50	0 apples
12 apples	.50	6 apples
		Expected value = 6 apples

An expected value can be calculated meaningfully for payoffs measured in apples, dollars, happiness points, or whatever. But please notice that expected value is not synonymous with *worth*. Twice as much money does not necessarily mean twice as much pleasure or utility to you. For example, a 50–50 chance of $1,000 may be worth less to you than a sure $500. We'll deal later with that complication.

If you wish to know the present value of an expected value of a set of outcomes at some *future* time, you may discount the expected values just as if they were sums of money, just like any other present-value calculation discussed earlier. But of course this does not take into account the fact that there is uncertainty and risk in the expected value of a set of possible outcomes, as compared to a sum for sure. This matter will be handled later.

The value of a business opportunity is the sum of all the possible outcomes of an alternative choice, each weighted by the probability that it will occur. For example, the expected value of a one-in-ten chance that you'll get $100 if you sing in a contest, plus a nine-in-ten chance of getting nothing, equals (.1 x $100 + .9 x 0) = $10.

This does not mean that the value *to you* of this contest opportunity is $10. If you need money badly, and this will be your last day on earth, having a one-in-ten chance of $100 may not be worth to you ten times a sure prospect of having $10. Or the chance of $1,000 may be worth more, if you desperately need $100 for a ticket out of hell. But over the long run of a good many alternatives in the operation of a business or a life, the expected value is a reasonable way to compute the values of opportunities. Later, we will see how to modify the expected value to take into account the special circumstances of the disadvantages of risk for an individual (and for firms, too).

We operate on the basis of expected value literally all the time. When you decide whether to take an umbrella in case of rain, you are implicitly taking into account the probability of rain, together with the costs of carrying the umbrella and of getting wet if it rains and you do not take the umbrella. Without an explicit calculation, your implicit intuitive solution will often be in error. For example, consider that the chance of rain is one in fifty, your valuation of getting wet is –$10, and your valuation of carrying the umbrella is –$1. The expected value of carrying the umbrella is –$1, and the expected value of not carrying the umbrella is .02 x –$10 + .98 x $0 = –$.20. So the expected value of carrying it is much more negative (less positive) than not carrying it. If you do this calculation for yourself, you may well find yourself not carrying an umbrella in many situations where you would otherwise have carried it for lack of thinking clearly about the matter. (Indeed, an analysis is only useful if it often leads to conclusions other than those you would have arrived at in the absence of the analysis.)

Another way to do the same calculation: State your values of carrying the umbrella and of getting wet if it rains and if you have no umbrella, then figure backward to the probability of rain that would make it worthwhile to take the umbrella—that is, the probability that would balance the expected values of the two alternatives. I will leave it to you to check that the probability must be 10 percent (.1), or greater for carrying it to be worthwhile, given the valuations in the paragraph above.

The concept of expected value is at the heart of all insurance. The insurer estimates the probability of the insured-against event—say, the probability of death of a man during the year he is aged fifty-five in the United States at present—and then multiplies that probability by the value of the insurance to obtain the expected value of the loss. That expected value plus its operating expenses forms the basis for the insurance company's calculating the price it will charge for that insurance policy. The expected-value concept is also at the heart of all prices of wagers with bookmakers (in the states and countries where that is legal, of course!).

Another example: The concept of expected value underlies the decision to accept an offer of a settlement in a lawsuit about a patent of yours. Assume that the company you are suing offers you a $200,000 settlement. You figure that you have a .6 chance of winning $1 million in court. (Leave aside for now the complication that you do not know for sure how much you would be awarded if you do win.) The expected value of continuing the suit to a trial is $600,000, and you should therefore turn down the offer unless you are willing to pay a lot to avoid the risk of losing (a matter that will be discussed in the next chapter).

In such a case, unfortunately, the calculation of expected value to a lawyer working on a contingency basis will differ from the client's expected value, because the lawyer will take into account the costs of her time if the settlement is not accepted. In contrast, the client does not pay those costs, and the appropriate calculation for you therefore does not include them. Hence the lawyer sometimes has a stake in your accepting a settlement even when it is not in the client's interests. (This discrepancy between interests of people on the same side of the table occurs in many circumstances. For example, it is usually in the interest of a publisher to set a higher price for a book than is best for the author.)

The choice of a price to bid in a closed auction is another important application of the concept of expected value. The decision hinges on the probabilities of winning the auction at various prices you might bid. The higher your bid, the more you would gain if you win the auction, but the lower the chance of winning because some competitor is more likely to underbid you. You should evaluate alternative bids according to their expected values, which you calculate as the probability of winning multiplied by the gain if the bid is won at that price.

Table 7.1

Bid ($)	Probability of Winning	Bid – Expenditure ($)	Expected Value ($)
20,000	.1	20,000 – 16,000 = 4,000	400
19,000	.3	19,000 – 16,000 = 3,000	900
18,000	.5	18,000 – 16,000 = 2,000	1,000
17,000	.8	17,000 – 16,000 = 1,000	800

Consider, for example, that you are in the painting business, and your town calls for bids on painting the town hall. You figure that the work will cost you $16,000 if you get the job. The bid prices you are considering, and the probabilities you estimate for winning the auction at each of those prices, are shown in columns 1 and 2 in Table 7.1.

The expected value for each price is calculated by multiplying the probability of winning by the difference between revenue and expenditures if you do get the bid. The bid price with the highest expected value in column 4 is the best alternative.

When risk is ignored in a present-value calculation, an expected value in a future period may be treated just like a certain income or outgo. In that fashion the complications of both futurity and uncertainty may be dealt with at once, as long as no decisions need be made in the future. (If they will be, we must resort to the more complex machinery of the decision tree, which we tackle below.)

The Decision Tree

The situation is more complex when there will be a *sequence of choices* rather than only one choice. Consider calculating the expected value of this gamble: You flip a nickel. If it falls on its head, I'll give you $240, and you will also get a chance to flip a dime. If the nickel does fall heads and you do get a chance to flip the dime—a chance you may reject, of course—I'll give you $250 if the dime falls on its head, but you must give me $300 if it falls on its tail. If the original nickel flip falls on its tail, you get $150 from me plus a chance to flip a quarter. If you get the chance and choose to flip the quarter and it falls on its head, I'll give you $150, but if it falls on its tail, you must give me $100.

Would you pay $200 for this gamble, which is diagrammed in Figure 7.1? It looks easy to evaluate at first, but you soon see how puzzling it is. The heart of the difficulty is that you cannot evaluate the choice of taking the deal *now* unless you know what you will choose to do *after you see whether the coin falls on its head or tail.*

Curiously, even though all the necessary elements of knowledge to solve this problem were available 300 years ago, it was only in the past half-century that the solution was discovered, a powerful mathematical technique known as "decision-tree analysis" or "backward induction"— or more frighteningly, "dynamic programming."

The way out of the impasse is to start at the *farthest-away* point in time and figure the expected values of the *farthest-away* sets of outcomes. Then you decide which alternatives you would choose in the next-to-last period if you reach those points, and so on, all the way backward to the present. When this process is complete, and only then, you can choose a first-period alternative.

The steps in a decision-tree analysis require only simple arithmetic, and can be easily learned when you need to do so. In perhaps nine of ten cases, the greatest value of the decision-tree analysis is not the formal calculation, but rather the exercise of forcing yourself to clarify your thinking on paper.

Consider, for example, the picture of the decision about choosing a college major (Figure 7.2). You will find it very difficult to decide on the probabilities, costs, and benefits to put into the picture. You can avoid making these quantities explicit if you avoid putting the analysis on paper. But a sound decision requires that you *do* make these quantities explicit. And in most cases, the process of making your best guesses about these quantities reveals the best decision without formal analysis.

The value of paper, pencil, and picture-making is brought out by this famous puzzle: A man points to the image of a person and says, "Brothers or sisters have I none. That man's father is my father's son." The puzzle is hard for most of us to solve in our heads. But drawing simple pictures usually reveals the answer immediately. Try it.

Before you can assess its value to you, you must know the chance that an event will occur. But the relevant probability is not obvious in

Figure 7.1

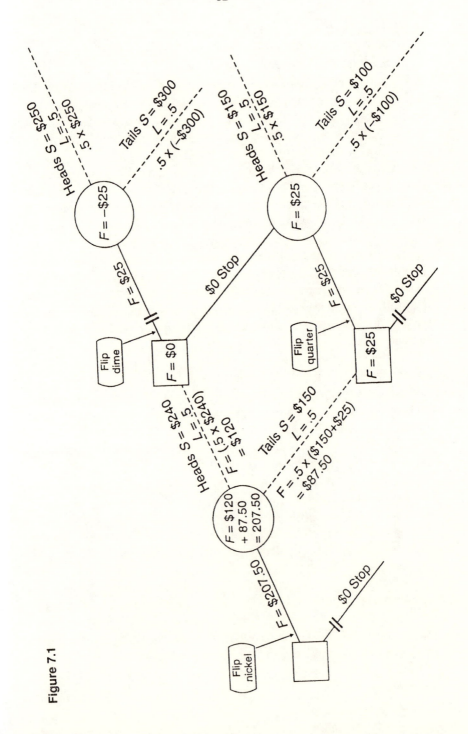

Figure 7.2

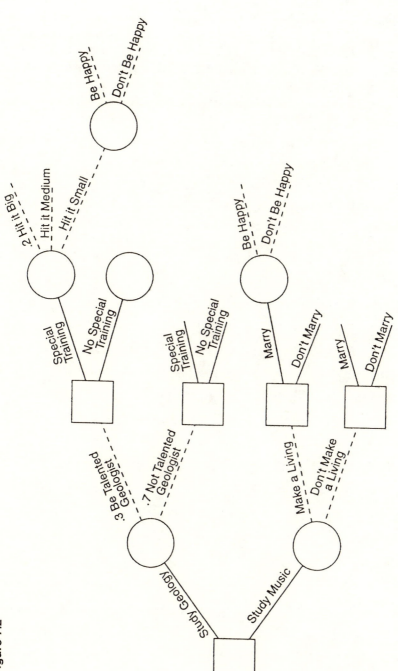

many circumstances. First there is the problem of assessing even the "simplest" likelihood—for example, the likelihood that it will rain on Sunday. (Estimation of probabilities is discussed in chapter 8.) Then there is the complication that several probabilities may interact, such as the probability of rain on Sunday *and* your favorite football team winning the game, a complex probability. Complex probabilities are dealt with in chapter 9.

Chapter 8
Dealing With Risks

Brief Outline

- Understanding Insurance (and Gambling)
- Possible Criteria for Assessing Risk
- Risk in a Business Setting
- Summary

Have you ever bought insurance on a house or car? When you do so, you are paying the insurance company to assume the risk of there being damage in connection with your car or your house; if damage occurs, the insurance company indemnifies you. This arrangement removes or reduces your risk of a large loss. If there is no damage, you pay the insurance company anyway. On balance, you and the rest of the insurance company's customers are willing to pay in more than the company pays out in damage claims so that you can shift the risk *away* from you to the insurance company. And the insurance company profits by taking more revenue from premiums than it pays out to claimants (in ordinary times).

Now consider someone who gambles in a casino. Each day the casino takes in more than it pays out to winners (unless it is a very unusual day). In this case, unlike the case of insurance, the customer pays the casino for a shift of risk *toward* the person.

How can it be that in one case a person pays to reduce risk, and in another case the same person pays to increase risk? This chapter throws light on this puzzling apparent paradox, as part of learning how to deal sensibly with the risks that enter unavoidably into our lives. I can't promise to remove risk from your life—and, indeed, life without risk would be so dull as to be unlivable, probably. But the chapter does promise to tell you how to grapple with the unavoidable risks of life as well as possible.

Understanding Insurance (and Gambling)

People sometimes enjoy the experience of uncertainty. Some are even willing to pay for the thrill of gambling in a casino. More commonly, though, uncertainty is a negative consequence that people are willing to pay insurance premiums to avoid.

There are several reasons why a person may prefer a sure outcome to a set of uncertain outcomes. You may dislike the shivery feeling of worry about what will happen. Or you might imagine yourself feeling regret or unpleasant surprise or disappointment if facing a particular outcome that you could avoid by insuring against it.

In contrast to these subjective matters that differ from person to person, there is an important objective fact that influences choice in risky situations: The financial market will generally pay you to bear uncertainty in the form of variability of results. That is, the more variable the expected returns from an investment, the greater the payoff. For example, riskier securities such as stocks pay (on average) a higher return than do less risky securities such as government bonds. Looking in the other direction, insurance companies will reduce the possible variability in your stream of income by selling you guarantees that if a catastrophe should occur to you, you will be recompensed; you pay them a premium to assume risk for you.

Insurance does not enable you to avoid *feelings* of disappointment or surprise or regret aside from financial loss. Sometimes it might be possible to arrange for another individual to shoulder bad feelings for you, however. For example, you might arrange in advance for someone else to take responsibility if a decision should have an undesirable outcome, or for someone else to take the phone call and deal with the consequences if a catastrophe should occur. But your feelings are mainly yours to be borne alone.

Learning About Your Own Desire to Avoid Risk

The strength of your desire to avoid risk is likely to depend upon your economic and life circumstances, and upon the size and nature of the risky outcomes. For example, your desire to purchase life insurance is likely to be different when you have young children than when you no longer have children of school age. For another example, you may feel no need to insure against the first $500 of loss in an auto accident because that loss would not disrupt your life. But to avoid larger possible losses, you are willing to pay an insurance premium that costs more than the expected value of the loss, because such a loss could disrupt your life badly. For a third example, you are more likely to quit your lawyer job and join a partner in hanging out a shingle after you hear that an unknown Aunt Tillie died and left you a hefty bundle.

Now that we have in hand the mechanism of expected value for analyzing uncertain choices *without* consideration of risk, we are ready to allow for risk when we do not feel neutral about uncertainty but instead prefer to avoid it.

A preference for certainty over uncertainty may be thought of in various ways: (1) You prefer to have a thousand-dollar bill rather than a 50–50 chance of $2,000 or nothing. And you would be willing to accept a smaller sum for certain rather than the "expected value" ($1,000) of the alternative with an uncertain outcome. More generally, you are not indifferent regarding payoffs with different probabilities but the same expected value. That is, you prefer a .5 chance of $10 to a .05 chance of $100. (2) You would not pay twice as much for a given probability of winning twice as much. That is, you might be indifferent between $9 and a 50–50 chance of $20, but you would prefer $900 to a 50–50 chance of $2,000. And (3) an idea that often has been intertwined with the above ideas about uncertainty concerns the different meanings of sequential increments of the same amount of money. That is, the second thousand dollars does not seem to give as much good feeling as does the first thousand dollars; twice as much money often is not "worth" twice as much to you. This is the famous idea of "diminishing marginal utility." But though this idea seems intimately related to the above ideas about uncertainty, and though it has often been considered interchangeable with them in theory, the relationship is not obvious.

In practical terms, we want to know which choice we should make in a particular risky situation, such as purchasing insurance or opening a law office or choosing among investment opportunities in three countries that differ greatly in political stability. There are two steps to a sound decision: (1) Understand the nature of the risk and how it fits into the rest of your life (your business). (2) Use appropriate devices for allowing for the cost to you of assuming the risk or the benefit of avoiding it.

In the simple two-choice yes-or-no examples mentioned above, you should first try to gain a clear idea of the basic notions of probability and expected value, next consider the choice in light of your entire economic and noneconomic life circumstances (and especially your present state of wealth), and then choose according to your enlightened preferences. The last step sounds vague, but we will look at some techniques to make it less vague.

Sometimes it helps, for example, to consider a hypothetical set of other choices and ask yourself what you would do if you faced them. You can then look for consistent patterns in your preferences that will help you make your choice. You can also ask yourself such questions as: How much would it take to make me twice as happy as an extra $1,000 would?

Illusions, paradoxes, and apparent self-contradictions abound in the risky choices people make even when the choices are relatively simple. Often people's responses depend upon how the issue is posed—for example, whether the same amount is seen as a loss of what you have, or a nongain, both of which are objectively identical but subjectively very different. Hence, risky choices have fascinated economists, statisticians, and psychologists during the last decade or two. But these peculiarities need not detain us here. It comes down to the fact that your willingness to accept $900 (or $800 or even $700) rather than a 50–50 chance of $2,000 is of the same nature as your choice to use public transportation and save money rather than buy a car.

The "Certainty Equivalent" of Your Uncertain Prospects

The $900 (or whatever) that you will accept in exchange for the 50–50 chance of $2,000 or zero is called the "certainty equivalent" of the uncertain opportunity. It corresponds to the risk-adjustment portion of the discount factor discussed in chapter 5. The extent to which the certainty equivalent is less than the expected value of the uncertain opportunity— that is, the difference between $900 and $1,000 in this example—is a measure of the extent to which you are *risk averse*. Scholars in finance and economics have done a great deal of advanced theoretical thinking about risk aversion, but as yet no one has developed convenient ways of applying this work to everyday life for individuals. So we continue to bumble through these decisions, often making them differently than we would if we were to spend the effort necessary to think them through in a satisfactory fashion.

Possible Criteria for Assessing Risk

These are some of the competing principles used in risk analyses, each associated with a different criterion goal for optimization:

1. *Maximization of "utility."* The utility principle is the oldest and the most widely used device to allow for risk, especially among finance specialists, perhaps because it lends itself better to mathematical analyses than do the others. It aims to maximize your "utility"—that is, the supposed satisfaction that you might achieve from the resulting sums of money. It systematically takes into account that twice as much money will not give you twice as much satisfaction, the appropriate adjustment depending upon your wealth and the extent of your dislike for risk. All this has little or nothing to do with the concept of utility that Jeremy Bentham proposed in the eighteenth century, and from which the term originally comes. When you apply this principle, you reduce somewhat the expected value of the alternative you choose in order to reduce the variability among possible outcomes.

2. *Minimization of regret or disappointment or unpleasant surprise.* These related principles aim at reducing the chance that you will end up feeling badly about the outcome. For example, if someone first tells you that you have won a lottery and then two minutes later tells you that it was an error, you are likely to feel worse than if you had never heard either message. (Similarly, hearing from a doctor that you do not have a disease that you thought you might have had is likely to send you out in a particularly pleasant mood.) You therefore choose in a fashion by which you reduce somewhat the expected value of your choice in order to reduce the chance that the outcome will be one that will make you feel regret, disappointment, or unpleasant surprise.

3. *The mini-max principle.* This principle applies to some situations that are head-to-head games with one or more other players, in which you expect them to actively try to outfox you and where your loss is their gain. This is unlike most situations in life (and in business), where your relationship with the relevant groups of individuals (such as impersonal customers) or with nature (for example, when you are drilling an oil well) is not gamelike because your "opponent" is not actively trying to out-

fox you. The mini-max principle is a very complicated mathematical strategy for obtaining a combination of relatively large gains while taking the chance of relatively small losses, by attempting to avoid the worst situation that your opponent might force you into. This principle may be appropriate for some very specialized games and perhaps occasionally in war. But, to my knowledge, it has never been found appropriate in everyday life, despite all the inflated claims made for it. It is a classic example of the adepts of a fancy mathematical technique succeeding in a massive snow job on people who do not understand the mathematics but are so insecure about their ignorance that they take it on faith that there *must* be something of value inside the mysterious mathematical black box—something worth paying a high fee for. Unfortunately, cases like this are not rare in the world of "scholarship."

The choice among these principles for dealing with risk depends upon your taste. But if your goal is to maximize profit in business, you will not make *any* allowance for risk other than that warranted by market (rather than personal) considerations. The techniques for utilizing the other criteria can be left aside here—and, indeed, may not ever be appropriate in any practical situation, I would argue, despite the theoretical discussion of them.

Risk in a Business Setting

Lending or investing money is a common situation in which risk is a crucial issue. When a bank lends working capital to an individual or a firm, the interest rate depends upon how risky the bank deems the loan—that is, the bank's estimate of the chance that the borrower will default. Similarly, the bonds of firms that are unstable or have little collateral must pay higher interest rates than do bonds of firms that are more solid. The stocks of firms whose prospects are very uncertain sell at a lower price relative to the firm's earnings than do the stocks of firms whose earnings are stable and seemingly assured from year to year. And the rate of return to preferred stocks is on average higher than the rate of return to bonds, because in case of a bankruptcy the preferred stocks would lose their value before the bonds would. (Common stocks are riskiest of all in this respect.) This structure is equivalent, from the point of view of the person supplying the funds, to a lower discount factor for a more risky situation. (Chapter 5 discussed the mechanics of using the discount factor and introduced its interpretation.)

The Power of Diversification

You can go beyond making a single risky choice by arranging your "portfolio" of risk-taking activities so as to reduce the total risk. For example, instead of investing all your wealth in a single stock, you can diversify among a set of stocks. A life insurance company greatly reduces its risk by selling a great many insurance policies rather than just one. The prospect that any single individual will die this year is very risky, but the rate of death among (say) a thousand people of the same age is known in advance with high probability, being affected only by the small chance of a major catastrophe. And the insurance company forestalls some of that risk with a clause that protects the company against war loss, which will greatly increase overall risk.

Almost any diversification reduces the overall risk even while keeping the returns the same. But it is not possible to eliminate *all* risk with diversification. In the past few decades, the study of finance has worked out a variety of devices for "portfolio analysis" to take maximum advantage of diversification. The most important element in a diversification program, however, is to remember to do it.

Summary

People pay to *increase* their risk when they gamble. But aside from situations where risk is exciting, people generally are risk averse and are willing to pay to *reduce* risk—as when they buy insurance.

Various mental devices can help you assess your risks and deal with them, such as comparing your actual situation with hypothetical gambles with varying odds.

There are several principles for optimizing—maximization of "utility," minimization of regret or surprise, and the mini-max principle. Trying to maximize your utility is the most reasonable criterion in almost all everyday situations.

Diversifying the situation in which you are involved—as, for example, in buying a variety of stocks rather than just one—can reduce your risk without reducing the benefits you gain from the activities.

Chapter 9

Reconciling Multiple Goals

Brief Outline

- Try to Proceed Between the Horns of the Dilemma
- When You Really Must Choose Among Goals
- Summary

You like long vacations, but you also like to make a good living—what balance in your schedule should you strike between the two desires? Or, you want to help your daughter improve her baseball skills, but you also want the rest of the Little League team that you coach to feel that you are treating everyone fairly—how should you handle those two competing aims? You want to buy a new boat, but you also want to help bring over an immigrant family from the old country—which desire should get how much of your money?

Cost-benefit analysis as presented in chapters 4 to 8 presupposes that you have a single criterion of success on which to compare the various alternatives. In ordinary business situations, money profit—or, more accurately, present value—serves as the goal and hence the criterion of success. Profit is a wonderfully convenient criterion because in business most relevant elements can be reduced to money. But in most situations in your personal and work life, you have more than one goal in mind, which complicates the analysis.

Many—even most—of the chapters in the book promise that you can improve your thinking and your sense of well-being with the devices set forth in them. This chapter can promise you help, too, but conflicts among serious wants almost inevitably bring sweat and tears. Being able to eat your cake and have it too is an unusual resolution of true conflicts among desires.

Even in business decisions, profit often is not the sole criterion. The welfare of employees, the community, and the nation as a whole may also be goals for a business. Nonprofit organizations not only have the complication of multiple goals, but also none of their goals usually can be stated in monetary terms. An individual, too, has many wants, and often desires conflict with one another. The most obvious example is the conflict between the desire for leisure and the desire for the fruits of labor.

We must find a way, then, to choose the most satisfactory course of conduct reconciling our multiple goals. But the task is difficult. And as is generally the case, the more difficult the problem, the less applicable the technical devices available to us. The devices that this chapter is able to offer are quite rough in operation and do not lend themselves to numerical calculation, unlike the previous chapters. We could entertain ourselves with some fancy mathematical schemes, but, in my experience, these formulas tend to confuse and hide the problem rather than clarify it and make it easier to handle.

Try to Proceed Between the Horns of the Dilemma

Before you get into heavy-duty thinking about how to resolve a difficult conflict between two desires, it always makes sense to exercise your imagination, seeking a resolution that will satisfy both desires. If there is one bicycle and two people who must get from point A to point B, consider whether both of you can ride at once—one on the seat and the other in back on the tire guard or in front on the handlebars or the horizontal tube-support in front of the rider. The material progress of civilization consists in large part of finding ways to use resources more efficiently—often for more than one purpose at a time. An example is handling the conflict between more production of copper at a mine and more ugly and dangerous slag heaps. Imaginative engineers and managers have found ways to make the slag heaps valuable assets rather than costly waste dumps, and hence one can increase production and gain from both the copper and the slag.

Romantic conflicts are often tough or impossible to resolve by finding a way between the two horns of the dilemma. A woman marrying both of the men she adores is unlikely to work (unless she is a sea captain or a long-distance trucker). Even for a boy to take two girls to the dance is seldom a happy resolution. But few situations are as intractable as romantic conflicts of desires. So ransack your brain for third-way solutions before you confine your thinking to deciding between the two conflicting courses of action.

When You Really Must Choose Among Goals

First We Must Specify the Goals

In many situations we cannot immediately specify the goals. Every one of us has said, "I don't really know what I want."

Sometimes the situation is even more complex: "I want not to want" may sound illogical, but it has a very real psychological meaning, and a very important role in human life. People who are addicted to alcohol or smoking or gambling may want very much not to suffer the pangs of the desire, and they often pay for promised cures of those desires. After marrying, a person may strongly want not to desire a connection with a former lover or a new heartthrob. Much of Eastern philosophy focuses on methods for reducing one's desire through meditation and other spiritual exercises.

Before we can proceed with choosing among alternative courses of conduct, we must clarify what we want to accomplish—if anything. That is, we must decide which goals are relevant and what the criteria of success will be. These convoluted matters will be left for future chapters. For the moment, however, let us assume that we know our goals. This chapter will tackle only the problem of reconciling multiple goals when they are known.

Business Analysis Is Easiest—but Still Tough

Let's begin with a business example. Consider a business whose owner believes that she has an obligation to pay her workers "decently" even if this means paying more than necessary to have their services. She also wants to make as large a profit as possible, consistent with her other goals. And she wants to ensure the survival of her business. How should she decide how much to pay the workers?

Let the owner consider a wage that is, say, 5 percent, 10 percent, or 15 percent above the market wage. She can calculate the effect upon her profit, her personal wealth, her capacity to invest in expansion, and the size of the cushion that will protect the survival of the business. She can then ask herself whether paying 5, 10, or 15 percent above market is worth forgoing the purchase of a new computer system, say, or a 20 percent decline in the survival chances of the business for the next five years, or the calculated reduction in her personal wealth.

This is the method of *trade-offs*. You consider how much you must reduce your movement toward one goal when you increase movement toward another goal. Then you choose the combination you most prefer. The decision is similar in nature to the individual's decision about whether to make a donation to charity.

Some other business examples include the decision about whether to finance a program to retrain workers whom the firm must cut off the payroll because their old skills are not needed; whether to clean up a slag heap created by the firm's mine even though the law does not require the cleanup; and whether to give money to the town to build an outdoor swimming pool.

Sometimes the firm may consider that these actions are simply good business in the long run, as General Motors considered it good business not to set the highest feasible prices for its cars after World War II when autos were in short supply. But this is not a problem in multiple goals. It can be handled just as advertising or pricing or other multiple-variable alternatives are handled in chapter 4; it would be phony to characterize the case as charitable or altruistic.

Nonprofit Organizations Are More Complex

Nonprofit organizations face multigoal problems more difficult than those faced by for-profit firms. Consider, for example, a foundation that has taken as its mission the research in the fight against two diseases, malaria and stroke. How should it allocate its resources between the two? It can ask itself how many people can be protected against malaria if it spends $1 or $2 or $4 million on malaria, and ask the same question for stroke. Then it can ask whether one person protected from stroke is worth two persons protected from malaria, or three or four. Finally it can allocate its resources so that the highest number of "worth" units are achieved. Here again we are using the method of trade-offs.

This brief description skims over enormous difficulties such as: How soon can the benefit of the research be expected to begin? What actions would other foundations and government agencies take if this foundation did more or did less? How should the various bad effects of a disease, such as disability and death, be weighed? A satisfactory full-scale analysis of this decision could take months. Hence, most decisions on these matters are made without much thought at all, which also is not a good alternative.

In multigoal situations, I suggest you at least compose a written statement of the problem, adducing all the relevant available facts and numbers, and making explicit the procedure you are using to balance the several goals. Then use that statement as the basis of discussion with at least one other person. This procedure is likely to turn up aspects of the decision that you may overlook if you don't put the matter on paper. And explicitly stating the procedure you are using to deal with the several goals together is likely to help you make sense of that process.

Another example and method: If the U.S. Postal Service were a private firm, it could set the prices for first-, second-, third-, and fourth-class mail simply with reference to the single goal of maximizing profit. But the price-setting decision is much more difficult for the publicly owned U.S. Postal Service, which has a responsibility to provide service to every home in the country at the same price, as well as to make enough money to (almost) break even. But because it is a government monopoly, it cannot raise prices sky-high if that would seem grossly unfair, even if that would increase profits. And its *relative pattern* of prices must seem sufficiently fair to the various classes of customers that they do not create political trouble. These are all difficulties that a private firm does not face.

One way to handle a problem like this one is to first arrange the conditions to meet the necessary "constraints," such as the socially determined upper limit on price for the government Postal Service, and afterward to maximize profit (or another criterion). In the case of the Postal Service, this means meeting the constraints by making the commitment to serve every home, and also setting an upper limit on the price of first-class mail, and then choosing the other prices in such fashion as to bring in the most "profit"—that is, revenue minus expenditures.

This is the general method of what the mathematicians call the *constrained maximum*. First you arrange conditions to meet all but one goal, and then you use ordinary cost-benefit analysis to choose the best alternative available within those constraints.

A convenient way of handling multiple goals—the way that we often go about it without noticing exactly what we are doing—is by "satisficing." *Satisfice* is Herbert Simon's useful term for trying to do as well as you can in a practical way, rather than try to "optimize," which implies aiming for the best possible theoretical state of affairs. When you satisfice, you specify a level of attainment of each goal that would leave you reasonably well satisfied, even if the goal is not fully attained, and then you seek to achieve those levels jointly. If you cannot manage to reach a satisficing level of each goal, you then consider where you might trim with the least pain, and keep trimming around until you have selected a combination of levels that are jointly attainable. This method does not seek to *maximize* your satisfaction, because maximization is an ideal beyond our mental capacities in most cases. Satisficing is a helpful approximation or "heuristic," the latter a fancy term for a rule-of-thumb.

Please do not lament, or consider it an imperfection, that our mental capacities are limited. Our intellectual limitations constitute an inevitable state of affairs that must be recognized by anyone who wishes to view the world realistically and deal with it effectively. This idea will reappear again and again in this book. It was at the heart of the vision of human nature urged on us by David Hume, the greatest philosopher of the eighteenth century. There is a delicious irony in the wonderfully rational Hume using his powerful powers of reason to analyze and convey to us the limits of reasons, and the implications for sensible social and political institutions.

Less realistic views of human nature that aim for the very best conceivable state of affairs have great intellectual charm. But they also can be a delusion, a snare, a waste of resources, and a danger.

Sometimes the problem of multiple goals is so vexing that you can only surmount it by breaking up an organization into separate activities. The health research foundation may decide that it can best do justice to malaria and stroke by setting up a separate foundation for each. And the clash of goals for the Postal Service may be so severe that the public can best be served by narrowing the U.S. Postal Service's goals to serving only those classes of customers who would not be served by private enterprise, and then allowing private enterprises to legally deliver mail to all who want to pay for their service.

Sometimes social goals conflict so sharply that the only possible resolution is a trial of strength among the contending groups. (Hopefully, this trial is through politics rather than weapons.) For example, the National Park Service had to decide whether to (1) spend $365,000 to corral and airlift 400 wild burros out of Grand Canyon, or (2) kill them at a cost of $30,000, or (3) simply leave them as "pests which erode the environmentally fragile canyon" and deprive other animals of food.[1] The money to capture or kill the burros could be used for many other purposes either by the government or by taxpayers. People's differing values for the burros, the canyon, and other human purposes lead to different decisions, and there is no single "rational" solution. Inevitably the decision in such a situation will arise out of politicking and negotiation by environmental groups, animal-rights groups, federal bureaucrats, and other interested parties.

Chapter 3 tackled the issue of deciding what your goals are.

Summary

Dealing with multiple conflicting goals is a tough task. Clarifying the goals is a first necessary step. You can sometimes solve the problem by avoiding it—finding an ingenious alternative path between the horns of the dilemma, thereby satisfying all the competing goals.

If the dilemma cannot be avoided, you must find trade-offs that will balance the goals in a sensible fashion. You should try to satisfice rather than seek a theoretically optimum policy.

Note

1. Associated Press, *CU-News Gazette*, May 23, 1980, p. B-6.

PART III

GETTING USEFUL IDEAS AND KNOWLEDGE

Brief Outline

- Three Kinds of Knowledge
- The Relative Smallness of Any Person's Knowledge
- Start by Immersing Yourself in the Raw Facts
- Obtaining the Various Sorts of Knowledge

How do you fix a flat tire on a bicycle? Why does the rider stay upright on the moving bicycle, rather than immediately falling to one side or the other? And how can you make a bicycle much easier to pump?

The subject of part III is increasing your stock of existing knowledge and new ideas. There is considerable overlap between those two categories. Someone else's idea becomes your knowledge when you learn of it. And you may think up an idea all by yourself but years after it was published widely and already is common knowledge. Still, it is often useful to distinguish between the processes of producing new ideas and of obtaining existing knowledge.

You need knowledge and ideas to help you operate the machinery of your life and your enterprises more efficiently. You also need ideas about new alternatives for your personal or professional life as the raw material for cost-benefit evaluation. And you also must know how to eliminate from consideration ideas that are unpromising, so as not to waste valuable time making unnecessary analyses. Chapter 10 discusses how to create and how to eliminate ideas.

Three Kinds of Knowledge

Knowledge can usefully be categorized as (1) *tacit*—such as knowing how to ride a bicycle, (2) *applied*—such as knowing how to fix a bicycle, and (3) *abstract*—such as understanding why the rider and bicycle don't fall down.

The relative importance of these kinds of knowledge to you is subject to argument. Surprising to me, some writers say that tacit knowledge bulks larger than other knowledge. I cannot think of a way to measure the relative importance of tacit and other types of knowledge, however.

The Relative Smallness of Any Person's Knowledge

Neither you nor I nor anyone else can contain in one head more than an infinitesimal part of the knowledge possessed by all 6 billion of us on earth. If you lack information of a particular sort, then it is quite possible that someone else has that knowledge, and there is some chance that you can manage to transfer it into your own store of knowledge.

The world's knowledge is produced by many different people. Soichiro Honda (of motorcycle and auto fame) said this about ideas: "Where 100 people think, there are 100 powers; if 1,000 people think, there are 1,000 powers." This is equally true of knowledge. One implication is that when you are in doubt about something, it makes sense to talk it over informally with some of the people you happen to meet casually in the locker room, on the job, wherever. Someone is just likely to know what you need to know.

(Of course, the person with whom you raise the topic may give you an uninformed opinion, rather than solid knowledge, which can be worse than useless. Even a person with the reputation of an expert can make unsound statements. Distinguishing between reliable and unreliable statements is a topic we will consider in chapter 11.)

A famous article entitled "I, a Pencil" by writer Leonard Read dramatized the wide dispersion of knowledge by showing how no one person in the world has nearly enough knowledge to produce a simple pencil. Making a pencil requires being able to produce the gum in the eraser, the carbon that does the writing, the tree that provides the wood, and the metal that holds the eraser. Production requires knowing how to shape the carbon into a narrow cylinder, saw and paint the wood, and print the label on the pencil. It also requires transporting the eraser gum from

Malaysia, the wood from Finland or Oregon, the paint from who knows where. No single human being, even if he or she were to spend an entire life trying to learn all the skills necessary to produce a standard pencil, could succeed in doing so. Furthermore, many other people must know how to carry out the various procedures necessary to sell and distribute the pencil after it is produced. Yet all this knowledge that the pencil manufacturer requires is possessed by average individuals widely dispersed all over our planet.

Start by Immersing Yourself in the Raw Facts

Before we rush on to more "sophisticated" methods of getting ideas and knowledge, I wish to emphasize and re-emphasize and emphasize again that every knowledge-acquiring venture should begin with a slow and wide-ranging look at the actual raw material or circumstances in which you are interested. It is certainly true that our perceptions are conditioned by the innumerable categories—call them theories, if you wish—that already exist in our minds, some of which may even be present at birth. But these categories do not wholly constrain us from seeing new things in new ways and then developing new categories. The only way to break out of the old categories is to saturate yourself in the raw experience you wish to work with and learn about.

Let's be specific, as befits the point I am trying to make here. If you want to know how to keep the beach umbrella on your porch from being blown over in the wind, look at how other people protect their umbrellas; look at other items that are protected from being blown over; sit down and look at your umbrella and its immediate surroundings; and so on. Perhaps put the problem aside for days and weeks as you give yourself a chance to reflect on it again and again. Do not simply ask an "expert" at the office for a solution, or just look it up at the library or on the Internet, though you certainly should do those things, too, if you do not come up with an adequate solution. Or, if you want to understand race relations in the United States and you are white, you might live with a black family for a while, or even darken your skin, as journalist John Griffin did, and then live as a black for a spell. Only this kind of first-hand experience can save you from the incredible blunders that "theorists" too often make when they draw their ideas solely from the body of abstract knowledge.

Keep in mind the old legend about the Greeks who were debating the number of teeth in a horse's mouth, using all manner of assumptions and deduction. One of their number eventually suggested that they look at a horse's mouth. The reaction he met in the legend is too often what happens in highly educated circles even today: The others shunned him on the grounds that he was a crude intellectual boor. (Lest you laugh at the horse-teeth legend as just a joke, please know that Aristotle—according to most judges, the clearest and strongest thinker among the ancients—thought that women have one less tooth than men have.)

Obtaining the Various Sorts of Knowledge

Tacit Knowledge. There is no mystery about how you gain tacit knowledge: You practice, learning from both your errors and your successes, whether the knowledge is riding a bicycle or learning the proper manners in a new culture. Book knowledge of the principles may help. A skilled practitioner can often speed your learning. But practice is essential. No one can learn to swim without getting into the water. That's about all that can be said at a general level about acquiring tacit knowledge, and therefore we shall simply leave it at that.

Applied Knowledge. Developing applied knowledge also needs practice, and practical teachers can help you learn. But knowledge of the abstract principles can be important or even crucial in developing applied knowledge. This is more and more the case as modern science develops. In earlier times, a person could learn how to build houses with only on-the-job training. Nowadays many construction workers must understand such principles as those of electricity and heat flow to do a competent job.

Abstract Knowledge. As its name suggests, abstract knowledge is further away from the specifics of a particular situation, and it is comprised of general principles. These principles make up the body of knowledge found in print in libraries. Imagine that the domain of knowledge is a jungle maze containing millions of books and magazines, and billions of pieces of knowledge, with a secret code to its paths and contents. Your problem is to wend your way through this maze so that you arrive at the pieces of knowledge that you seek for a particular purpose. This is a formidable intellectual challenge, though the search engines available on the Internet are changing the nature of the information-seeking process. The series of links jumping from item to item as you search the

Web makes vivid the linkage within the domain of knowledge that you wish to explore.

Chapters 11 and 12 teach about acquiring applied and especially abstract knowledge. The first place to turn for knowledge is where the knowledge may already exist. Chapter 11 tells you how to mine libraries and experts. Chapter 12 presents the basic principles of scientific research that apply when you must create reliable knowledge on your own.

The scientific method may be thought of as simply using all the capacities of your mind as systematically as possible. But a checklist of the important issues to keep in mind, and the order in which you should consider them, can be useful. Violations of these same principles are much the same as the errors we make in drawing everyday conclusions, as will be discussed in chapters 14 and 15. And many of the same principles are the converse of the logical fallacies that have been known to philosophers since the Greeks. This is a nice example of how the same principles of thinking appear in several different contexts.

The entire business of creating ideas, obtaining relevant information, and evaluating the alternatives is a back-and-forth process, rather than a neat series of steps, even though it is necessary to neaten up the process when presenting it here on the printed page. These ideas are discussed in chapter 13.

Now on to the methods of gaining knowledge.

Chapter 10
Getting and Eliminating Ideas

Brief Outline

- How to Get Ideas
- Eliminating Ideas
- Summary

How can you arrange the Thanksgiving holiday so that the family will avoid the usual painful hassles that lessen the pleasure of being together? Where can you get good advice about how to market your new voice-transcribing computer system? How should Russia make the transition from a planned and centrally controlled economy to a market-based economy?

This chapter is about both creating and eliminating ideas. I promise you that after reading the chapter, you will realize that you can systematically increase your flow of ideas when you need them and will know which techniques can help you do so.

How to Get Ideas

Creating a set of alternatives usually requires only that you do a work-manlike job of collecting the obvious possibilities, without ignoring any important alternatives. *Example 1*: A family building a new house considers how to deal with the heat of summer. They need evaluate only (1) a central air conditioning system; (2) window air conditioners, (3) fans, (4) desert coolers, (5) moving away and building the house in a cooler climate, (6) building the house underground, (7) sweltering. They can collect all of these ideas plus a few other variations by asking friends and commercial heating-and-cooling agencies. *Example 2:* What should the United States do about an American clergyman seized and held hostage in Libya? The president orders up a menu of alternatives from the Joint Chiefs of Staff, the State Department, and the National Security Council. A satisfactory list is likely to contain only rather obvious possibilities, though an unorthodox alternative or two may also be included. *Example 3*: If you are the president of General Motors, what should you do about foreign auto imports? You can (1) produce abroad, (2) diversify into nonauto products, (3) leave the automobile business, (4) improve quality, or (5) automate. That's about it.

The Key Step

The key step in developing a good list of alternatives is to search widely enough so as not to miss any *obvious* possibilities. Overlooking, and therefore never even considering, an obvious important possibility is the most frequent defect in the process of idea collection. This pitfall usually can be avoided by sitting down with pencil and paper and then discussing the situation with others who have general and specific knowledge of the matter at hand.

The vital point is to *actually carry out a systematic search*. You must *stop, look, and listen* rather than simply proceeding with existing alternatives, or limiting yourself to that set in hand plus perhaps one other idea that struck your mind by happenstance. Happenstance imagination is wonderful, but it should be supplemented by a system to help you avoid overlooking the obvious, as well as come up with ideas that are not obvious.

Keep Looking

Keep on looking for a better idea, too. The third-floor attic of our house was to be renovated to make it a study. The contractor was delayed several months by other jobs. During those months, my wife, the carpenter, and I found several important ways to make the renovation much more valuable, ideas that we would not have had if the contractor had come on time.

Another example: The four shelves of the little plastic cart that carries my writing tools, clipboard, message pads, and other miscellany around my workroom with me were slipping out of the side rails. What to do? One day I thought of extending the little lips on the rails by using tape. No good. Two days later: tape on the shelf edges. No good. Next day: old nails under the shelf edges to make them protrude more. No good. Then pulling in the side rails with string or wire. No good. Then a week later: pushing out the sides of the shelves with sticks. No good. Then a yardstick ruler down each side of the cart to make the rails extend farther inward. Might work. So I made a note to buy some pieces of wood. But I put off getting them. And two days later I went into the basement and noticed two old metal curtain rods. Perfect! They are stiffer than wood, and easily extend to the exact length. And that did it.

Have a Prepared Mind

This example also shows the importance of having a "prepared mind," as some have called it. The curtain rods came into my mind as a solution to the cart problem because my thoughts were directed toward the problem, and I had identified various possible lines of solution—push in, pull out, build up edges, stick something under or through the edges, and so on. Ideas don't enter unless your mind is open for business.

Let the Ideas Evolve

Ideas evolve, as the cart solution did. Once I collected a sample of the little yellow gummed date-stamp slips in the back of the University of Illinois library books. Some had been there since the system began early in the twentieth century, and the old ones still remained even though the system had been computerized. They all look basically the same, but there are dozens of small variations in placement and language of the instructions. When the stock was about to be reprinted, the person in charge at the time had undoubtedly ordered a small improvement. And the improvements added up over the years to a more efficient little slip. Too many people think that progress comes from Newtons and Einsteins, people who are supposedly geniuses. Certainly they are important. But the small creative contributions of many of us are indispensable to progress.

Often the greatest benefit of a new idea is to provoke re-examination of the present situation plus a review of the options. This often causes a shift to something other than *either* the present alternative *or* the idea that struck you by chance.

Clarify the Problem

A frequent pitfall in creating ideas is not having a clear idea of the main problem. Developing a terrific set of alternatives to handle an irrelevant situation may evoke others' admiration for your imagination, but it does not improve your situation or induce much continued demand for your services.

Experience Can Help or Hinder

Extensive and varied experience helps you produce a long and good list of alternatives. But long experience sometimes closes the mind to new ideas. If that idea were any good, I would have seen it already, you think.

Imagination, Of Course

Imagination is the second element in producing ideas. A newly imagined idea often arises from a sense of dissatisfaction with the existing situation. If you don't itch, you won't scratch, someone said. This was literally my situation once. My body itched for no apparent reason. Then I noticed it was just my upper body that itched, and especially my neck and shoulders. I first thought the itch might be due to a sweatshirt I'd worn earlier while doing dusty work. But a shower and a clean shirt did not solve the problem for long, so I ticked off that possibility. Then I thought it might be due to the synthetic material in the shirts I was wearing; again experimentation showed it not to be so. (But were these experiments really conclusive? Perhaps the itch was slow to develop and slow to go away, but let's leave that aside for now.) Then I noticed that the itch became most apparent upon waking in the morning and from my afternoon nap, so perhaps the sheets or pillow might be the cause, but again it was not so. Then . . . surprise! My hair was too long! The dander on my head was making me itch. The reason that this was so surprising is that I am thoroughly bald, and it never occurred to me that the tiny fringe around my skull could be producing enough dander to cause an itch.

What I arrived at in this case by imagination, a physician would have arrived at from experience. A doctor undoubtedly would have a mental list that includes dander from hair, especially in the year the incident occurred, when doctors were seeing many cases of long hair. Similarly, when a virus is going around town, a physician quickly spots its particular symptoms. But when an exotic tropical disease arrives, even skilled physicians may not recognize it for some time.

Necessity and Invention

The general principle underlying itch-and-scratch is that necessity is indeed the mother of invention. The Nobel Prize–winning economist and philosopher Friedrich Hayek may well be right that "Man has been impelled to scientific inquiry by wonder and by need. Of these wonder has been incomparably more fertile."[1] Much basic knowledge is created in noncommercial settings, influenced only indirectly by economic needs and priorities. But as Hayek goes on to note, "Where we wonder we have already a question to ask." The need of the community, interpreted in the widest sense, often is the cause of the questions in thinkers' minds. This implies that you should give full sway to your "divine dissatisfaction." Ask yourself: What is not perfect enough here that we can improve?

Brainstorming

The group activity called *brainstorming* can speed the flow of ideas. Brainstorming is a procedure for unlocking the compartments of your mind and breaking down the barriers against the free flows of images, associations, comparisons, analogies, metaphors, and other nonroutine aspects of thought. The technique was first used by advertising copywriters when stumped for new ideas about how to promote a product. It can be used in any context, however, and its principle can even help an individual working alone.

Brainstorming works by letting you express the "crazy" thoughts that you would otherwise censor because you think they might sound foolish. Your wild idea can be the seed of someone else's not-so-wild idea. When you brainstorm, you shut off the monitor that criticizes silly ideas, and you let 'em rip. The critical thinking takes place later.

These are the rules of a brainstorming session:

1. Provide everyone with full information in advance about the problem to be addressed. The more you know about the problem, the better your chances of coming up with a good idea.

Luck usually favors the prepared mind. Yet people who walk into the session knowing nothing of the problem sometimes come up with the best ideas because their thinking has been the least limited by past thinking.

2. No one may criticize anyone else's ideas or their own. Suspend all judgment about whether an idea is good or bad. You can tell someone that his/her idea is really wild if you mean that admiringly, but aside from that—no judgments. Just accept what you hear, and rack your brains for ways to improve the idea that you have just heard, or come up with another idea that is even farther out.

3. The wilder and crazier the idea, the more the group should welcome it.

4. Shoot for quantity of ideas rather than quality—just the opposite of ordinary everyday behavior.

5. Try to find a kernel of solid sense in even the wildest idea, and then try to add to that kernel. That is, don't jump from one idea to the other, but try to *enhance each one* before moving on. Even in the brainstorming session there is an underlying discipline, just as there is an underlying control in an artist even when she feels as if her imagination is completely unfettered and her mind on automatic pilot. The trick is to keep the discipline as light and unobtrusive as possible.

The brainstorming group should in advance designate a leader who will (1) make known the rules before the brainstorming meeting, (2) record the ideas that are suggested, (3) shut off any critical thinking, (4) try to get everyone involved, and (5) work toward building up good ideas rather than just rushing helter-skelter from one to the other.

Only after the brainstorming is over should you bring to bear your everyday critical faculties. Only then should you make judgments about which ideas are good enough to pursue and which ones should be dropped.

The Letting-Go Mode

There is considerable similarity between this two-step create-then-criticize procedure and the reports of many artists about how they work—first letting themselves float effortlessly on the currents of imaginative thought and idea production (though still under the control of a hardly noticed discipline, as mentioned above), and only later on subjecting the ideas to critical scrutiny.

Brainstorming also has much in common with the meditation of Asian "religious" thought, which also is a letting-go process. ("Religious" is in quotes because of the great differences between what is called "religion" in the West and the East.) Brainstorming is quite different from meditation, however, in being energetic rather than effortless. You are trying to accomplish something in brainstorming, whereas in meditation you try not to try: This is an important apparent paradox that goes to the heart of the process of creating ideas.

There also is a connection between the letting-go mode of thinking and dreaming—both daydreaming and dreaming while asleep. While dreaming, you do not maintain the same control over your mind that you do when fully awake. There are many accounts of ideas that came to people when asleep, though always when the mind had been prepared while awake. One of the most famous is the story of Friedrich August Kekule, the father of organic chemistry. One night in a dream he saw a snake with its tail in its mouth. This gave him the idea that the structure of benzene is six atoms of carbon arranged in a ring, which turned out to be what the *Encyclopedia Britannica* calls the "most brilliant piece of prediction [ever made in] organic chemistry."

Letting go is one of the fundamental elements of many disparate branches of thinking—scientific and practical idea-getting, art, religion (mysticism in Western religion is related), and some therapeutic devices to fight the sadness of those who suffer from depression.

Generating ideas requires that you prepare your mind well. But you must also keep yourself from being wholly absorbed by what is known. The ideal is a delicate balance between enjoying the fruits of past work and yet being sufficiently free so that you can depart from past work to new ideas of your own.

The Power and Complementarity of Opposites

The paradoxical combination of thorough acquaintance with existing knowledge *along with* keeping yourself unencumbered by what is already known illustrates another theme that runs through many kinds of thinking: You need both of two opposed principles—in this case the opposed principles of discipline and freedom.

People often wonder about the oriental martial arts: How can the students be so rigidly regimented in their training and yet have the spontaneity to play well? There is no satisfying logical answer. Yet the outcome is beyond doubt: The method works. And many great innovative artists such as Leonardo da Vinci and Pablo Picasso have insisted on the importance of achieving a mastery of the craft of drafting, which requires arduous and precise training. For many great innovators, the skill to execute perfectly with your hands what your eye sees provides the springboard to great departures from the known, rather than being a bar to imaginative departure.

Two other pairs of opposites that influence the creative flow are order-plus-disorder, and ambiguity-with-clarity. We naturally pursue order and clarity, because life is more comfortable in their presence than in the presence of disorder and confusion. And it makes sense to struggle for order and clarity. But at the same time we must recognize that disorder and ambiguity often promote new ideas. ("Necessity is the mother of invention.") This is partly because they constitute states of need—for order and clarity—that induce ideas. Partly they promote new ideas because by their very nature they are states in which there are many and conflicting stimuli contending within your mental playground. It is natural to *compare* two or more contending stimuli. And from that comparison arise ideas, as well as evaluation (as discussed in part I). That is, a *variety* of dissimilar but comparable stimuli is crucial to the production of ideas.

The fish would be the last to discover water, it is said. This explains why immigrants—who have been exposed to two different cultures—are so likely to produce new ideas. Hence it pays to tolerate some ambiguity and confusion, and occasionally even to cause it purposely. Unfortunately, however, most of us feel *so* uncomfortable with confusion and disorder that we do our utmost to get rid of it.

Too Much Knowledge

Too much knowledge—especially too much knowledge of the existing theory—can hamper the production of new ideas. Some people have the happy facility of forgetting bodies of knowledge and hence freeing up their creative abilities. Friedrich Hayek refers to such people as "puzzlers" or "muddlers," and repeats with approval the semi-joke that an educated person is one who has forgotten a great deal. He quotes Alfred

North Whitehead that "muddleheadedness is a condition precedent to independent thought." Hayek writes:

> Their [the muddlers'] constant difficulties, which in rare instances may be rewarded by a new insight, are due to the fact that they cannot avail themselves of the established verbal formulae or arguments which lead others smoothly and quickly to the result. But being forced to find their own way of expressing an accepted idea, they sometimes discover that the conventional formula conceals gaps or unjustified tacit presuppositions. They will be forced explicitly to answer questions which had been long effectively evaded by a plausible but ambiguous turn of phrase of an implicit but illegitimate assumption.[2]

So don't despair if you are not in total command of all the knowledge in your field. Hayek also says that those "whom I regard as eminently 'masters of their subject' . . . seem also to be particularly susceptible to the opinions dominant in their environment and the intellectual fashions of their time." I would guess that he is correct.[3]

A Touch of Intentional Disorder

You can sometimes evoke ideas by purposeful exposure to random or incongruous stimuli. For example, a mechanical contraption called the Think Tank presents you with a random pairing of concepts, between which you try to find interesting connections. This is how an advertising copywriter used the Think Tank:

> First, I twist the dials on the sides of the Think Tank to jumble up the words inside. Second, I copy down six random words that appear in the window of the Think Tank. Third, I spend at least five minutes with each word, using word associations and so forth, that relate to the problem I'm trying to solve. Usually one or more of the words will "trigger" an idea. Here's an example:
> My problem was to come up with some new ideas on how to get more credit card holders for Amoco. I twirled the dial on the Think Tank and the word "water" popped into the window. In a matter of milliseconds my free, stream-of-consciousness thinking was set in motion and led to a unique idea. Water made me think of boats. Boats need gasoline, just as cars do (a good-size cruiser may spend $75 to $100 or more for a fill-up). There are Amoco gas pumps at marinas on the water. Why not send our regular credit card solicitation package with a special letter and special appeal to a list of boat owners?

Figure 10.1

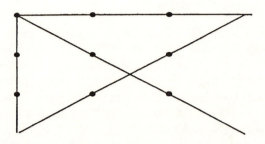

Forced incongruity arises when someone asks a question such as: What happens if we add the best characteristic of your favorite toaster to the mini-tape recorder that we are selling? Incongruity can be useful in education, too. Next time you take a little girl or boy for a walk, ask, Why doesn't that tree fall down? And why doesn't it fly into the air?

Out-of-the-Box Thinking

You may find useful some devices for training yourself to break out of conventional ruts. One of the most famous of these is this puzzle: Consider the nine dots in Figure 10.1. How can you connect all of them with an unbroken series of only four straight lines? The solution is to extend a line beyond the apparent rectangular borders—"outside of the box," in violation of an implicit rule for behavior.

The nine-dot puzzle has become so famous that it is common in the late 1990s for a creative person to be called an "out-of-the-box thinker." But this label can point in the wrong direction. It identifies creativity and idea generation with being good at solving puzzles. But that is more a mathematical facility than the creation of new ideas, because it takes a *given* set of conditions and attempts to "solve" a "problem." Yes, the essence of the nine-dot problem is realizing that a condition that is easy to assume—that one must remain within the rectangle drawn around the nine dots that trace a box—does not necessarily hold.

There is a better model for creative thinking. Imagine that a group of people are given the problem of escaping from a formal box-hedge maze on an English country estate. A maze is a classic mathematical problem. The mathematician would have you use your deductive problem-solving powers to find that path through the maze that leads to the exit with the fewest steps, or in the shortest time. And when set the problem, most students will dutifully set out to do what the mathematical teachers expect, and accept their teachers' judgments about their success or failure.

But another person might proceed differently: He whips out a machete and slashes ports through the hedges directly from the starting point to the finish. Or perhaps she gets a ladder and climbs over. Or swings over on a rope from a high tree. Or simply runs back out the entry point and then around the maze to the end point.

One can guess the grade she would receive from a mathematician for such behavior: "F" for flunk! Why? Because the maze was not "supposed" to be dealt with that way. But who decided what was "supposed" to be done? And was that even stated at the start? More likely the proper behavior was only implicitly specified, and people understood what was wanted because we are so well socialized to work by certain rules, usually deductively.

This analogy reflects on the general value of training in deductive thinking. Ever since the Greek geometers, and probably before, it has been assumed that the possession of the sorts of skills that they taught implied that a person is a "better" thinker. But whom would you prefer to have with you if cast away on a deserted island, or working in a new factory you are setting up—the person who is good at the deductive mathematics of box hedges, or the person who finds another and quicker way to get to the finish point? I do not dismiss the value of the deductive thinker; he may be very helpful in setting up efficient production schemes in a factory. Rather, I am simply saying that the nonformal thinking is not necessarily inferior to the former.

Again, Immerse Yourself in the Raw Situational Facts

One special note about getting ideas for scientific problems to work on: Expose yourself to the world of real events and people. Look out your window as much as in the scientific literature. Certainly this is true in the social sciences, where social problems are perhaps the best source of important ideas. For example, the rampant unemployment of the 1930s stimulated Keynes to write his society-shaking book (for better or for worse). But in the physical sciences, too, interesting ideas may arise from watching the cream mix with the coffee in your morning mug, or watching the raindrops jerk their way down the window, or wondering why the squirrels chase each other in the patterns that they follow. It is also true in art, as poet Wallace

Stevens remarked: "The great well of poetry is not poetry but prose: Reality."[4]

Eliminating Ideas

After producing a flock of ideas, you must quickly eliminate the least promising of them so that you can devote attention to those ideas that warrant closer inspection and evaluation. You cannot afford the time for careful evaluation of *all* the possible alternatives in any situation. Reducing the set to a manageable number is a crucial element of judgment in decision-making.

Sometimes you can safely eliminate an idea on the grounds that others must have thought of it, tried it, and found it to be unsuccessful. For example, a mail-order advertiser can reasonably conclude that a magazine that carries little or no mail-order advertising is not a profitable place to advertise for most products; other mail-order advertisers have surely tried it and found it wanting. (Of course, there may be circumstances that make a generally poor medium a successful one for your given product, but the circumstances will almost surely be very unusual ones.)

On the other hand, a seemingly obvious idea may simply never have been thought of by someone in a position to try it. Consider the little loop on the inside of the wide upper end of men's ties that keeps the narrow end underneath from floating free. Before perhaps 1980, there were no such loops, though obviously there were no technical reasons for not putting them on ties; instead men used tie clips or looked sloppy. Then, after the tie loops, came loops on the tongues of sneakers for insertion of the laces to keep the tongue from sliding to one side, an even more utilitarian improvement. Odds are that the sneaker loops were an emulation of the tie loops. They, too, could have existed years before if someone had gotten around to making the innovation. So do not be too quick to assume that it must have been tried before. (It would be interesting to study the history of those loops as an interesting case of innovation. Incidentally, lots and lots of seemingly obvious topics for fruitful scientific research have never been studied, simply because no one ever got around to it. The limited number of minds in the world limits the amount of knowledge that can be produced in any one period.)

Weeding out ridiculous ideas requires that you have some knowledge of the world about you. Why does the tree not float off into the air? You must understand the force of gravity and the mechanism of the tree's roots holding it in place.

Creative Skepticism About Numerical Statements

You should develop the habit of asking yourself whether the numbers you hear and read make sense, given your general knowledge. For example, a superb self-help book for the asthma sufferer by a well-qualified allergist says on the first page that (1) there are 11 million asthma victims in the United States, (2) "over 50 percent of asthma patients spend greater than 18 percent of their family income on asthma care," and (3) "Over $1 billion is spent each year by asthma sufferers on hospital care, medications and doctor visits."[5] If you know that there are almost 250 million people in the United States, with average family income of more than $25,000 for a total national income of more than $4 trillion, you know immediately that either the $1 billion figure is wrong or (more likely) the 18 percent of family income for half the patients is wrong, or both are wrong, by a huge factor of perhaps 10 or 20. (My guess is that the $1 billion figure is too small, and the 18 percent of income is too high.) The habit of checking ideas against your general knowledge saves you from many such blunders.

Too Little Knowledge When Deciding Against Ideas

Too *little* knowledge can be dangerous, too, when weeding out unfeasible ideas. If you are making fantasy movies in Hollywood and someone suggests having a tree float into the air, it would be useful to know about more than gravity and roots, and to think of helium and balloons painted like trees, before you dismiss the idea of airborne trees as ridiculous. There is always the danger that what seems ridiculous to you may be practical in the mind and hands of another person. For example, for twelve years after I first published my volunteer-and-auction scheme for dealing with airline oversales, everyone in and out of the airline industry said it was a ridiculous idea that could not possibly work. They made fun of the idea and said I lacked the necessary knowledge of the industry. (That's what insiders always say to ideas from the outside. This is the NIH syndrome—Not Invented Here.) When the idea was finally tried, it turned out that the insiders' knowledge was insufficient (in addition to insufficient profit motivation, probably). Now the scheme works beautifully every day of the year. (Remember an airline asking for volunteers when the plane was over-full? That's the idea.) More about this in chapter 11 on experts.

The Concept of Dominance as a Tool for Decision

The concept of *dominance* is a neat logical tool for quickly eliminating ideas. You can sometimes simplify complex choices by finding an alternative that is better in *every* relevant characteristic than another alternative, though sometimes the dominance is not immediately apparent.[6] For example, my excellent colleague W. was considering joining me at institution N—first on a one-year basis to see if he would like it. But he would have had to take a pay cut for the trial year. He therefore tried to balance the better quality of the institution he might come to against the money cost for that year. But then we noticed if he were to come to N for a year and later go back to M, the latter institution would raise his pay on return because of his having been at N. Hence if he visited N and did not like it enough to remain, he would not lose any money in the long run; money therefore was not a reason to reject visiting N. And he would not choose to stay at N after visiting if it did not then seem better than returning. So he did not need to compare coming to N permanently versus staying at M. Instead he needed only to compare staying at M versus visiting at N. And the latter alternative dominated the former because it provided valuable experience about whether he would want to remain, while not having a money cost.

The analysis is shown in two charts. First we see how the decision looked at first, with the numbers in the cells indicating the order in which an institution is desirable on that characteristic:

Original Analysis

Institutional Alternative	Preference	Money
Stay at N	1	2
Stay at M	2	1

Neither alternative is a clear choice because each is preferred on one dimension.

Now let us add the possibility of visiting N for a year, creating two new alternatives:

Amended Analysis

Institutional Alternative	Preference	Money
Visit N, then stay at N	1	3
Visit N, then return to M	2	1
Stay at M	3	2

The second array indicates that visiting N and then returning to M *dominates* simply staying at M, because the former is preferred on both dimensions. Therefore W. could immediately decide to visit N and use that year to decide whether to stay at N permanently—which is what he did. Thus the principle of dominance immediately enabled him to eliminate the alternative of staying at M without more complex analysis.

Here is another example of how one can discover an alternative that dominates another and thereby simplifies decision-making: J. was doing administrative work at university N when university Q offered him a nice position to be entirely a scholar. This was attractive to J., largely because he wanted to stop doing administrative work. But upon reflection he recognized that he also could be wholly a scholar at N—by resigning his administrative job. And at N he could make a better salary, his family would not have to move, and there would be some other advantages as well. That is, being a scholar at N dominated being a scholar at Q. But until he sought to expand the list of alternatives in the search for combinations that would dominate the obvious alternatives, the alternative of being a scholar at university N did not appear on his list.

(How did it come out? In a typically realistic twist, *J. decided that he wanted to go to university Q anyway.* How could this be, if our analysis was correct? The fact is that something was left out of our analysis—J. just felt like moving. And this hidden benefit was only brought to light by the dominance analysis. Well, that's life.)

Often it is possible to expand the set of choices from say, A and B, to some *combination* of A and B, by taking parts of both in sequence. The case of Professor J. above is an example. Another example: Daniel is looking for an apartment. Should he take apartment A or continue looking? Another possibility is to take A for a short while and also continue looking in a relaxed fashion. Of course, there are added costs to this alternative, such as the additional burden of looking and moving again, and perhaps a security deposit. But the added costs may be less than the costs of being locked in with a bad alternative, or having to look for an apartment under pressure.

Muddling Through

Alternatives often fall into two general categories: (1) radical, usually meaning major changes to be implemented at once; and (2) "meliorative," meaning incremental changes to fix one problem after another, implemented gradually. Often you find yourself discussing whether (1) the ideas for radical changes with far-reaching consequences—which by their radical nature require thorough analysis—should be considered further, or (2) the scope of the discussion should be limited to less-global adjustments where no attempt will be made to do an overall analysis. This latter sort of "myopic" adjustment process is known as "muddling through." Muddling through is an inelegant procedure, to be sure, but often it is effective, in considerable part because it permits study and learning from the results along the way.

There are three possible reasons to decide in advance against adopting a radical idea: (1) It is not politically feasible even though it might improve the overall welfare of a situation. (2) The consequences are too unforeseeable. (3) It is possible to reach the radical idea in a series of less-radical steps, allowing for trial-and-error learning along the way.

Political Infeasibility of a Radical Change

There is no doubt that prudence is often a virtue in discussions of policies to adopt. If you urge policies that others think not worth discussing because the political situation renders them beyond possibility of adoption, people may dismiss you as impractical and a waster of the group's time.

Sometimes, however, labeling an idea as politically unfeasible is a device to eliminate the idea by people who oppose it. I suggest that in such a case you say something like this:

> If the rest of you consider the idea sound but politically unfeasible, let us quickly agree in stating that. We can then simply send on the suggestion

to the next stage of deliberation noting that we find it sound but guess that it is unfeasible, and allow the other decision-makers to dismiss it rather than us dismissing it here. Sometimes good ideas are dismissed too early on grounds of political unfeasibility when they really are not unfeasible, or can become feasible in the future. So let us at least pass on our best judgment, along with other policies we recommend as next best and also feasible.

This tactic has the virtue of smoking out the real reasons for opposition, and sometimes the tactic can prevent an idea from being eliminated too early.

Unforeseeable Consequences

The wisdom of eliminating a radical idea on the grounds that the consequences are unforeseeable obviously depends on just how foreseeable the consequences really are. And people differ greatly in their judgments about foreseeability. Karl Marx believed that he could foresee the consequences of proletarian revolution and socialist economy clearly enough to urge with confidence those courses of action. To have opposed those radical social changes on the grounds that their consequences were not foreseeable makes sense in the hindsight of most of the people who have inherited the results of the governments set up in Marx's name in Eastern Europe and China. On the other hand, we never can know all the consequences of a change, and unless we are prepared to move even in the face of considerable uncertainty, we will never move at all.

Anglo-Saxon governments have tended more toward making small ameliorative changes rather than large changes, as compared to France and China. Perhaps this is connected to the supposed greater willingness of the French than of the British to trust in "logic." It would be nice to have that supposition tested by a reliable piece of research. I doubt the existence of most supposed differences in national character, and this one—as well-believed as any—would make an interesting test case.

The issue is somewhat different with respect to societies as a whole than with respect to mechanical systems and small groups. A society embodies spontaneously acting forces for change that prevent paralyzing stasis, as long as individuals have reasonable liberty to act. And a society embodies many patterns of behavior, the consequences of whose disturbance are unforeseeable because the patterns have evolved over generations rather than being the result of design by contemporaries.

But if one goes on patching up an old bicycle tire rather than purchasing a new tire when the patches become many, there is no spontaneously acting force to change the situation independently. Therefore, the penalty for rejecting radical change in favor of only small changes is greater in mechanical matters, and in groups too small to have independently acting centers of initiative, than it is in society at large.

Step-by-Step Implementation

Often it is possible to gain the benefits of radical change while avoiding the hazards of radical moves by embarking on the radical change in small steps, to provide time for evaluation of the effects. This obviously will not work in all cases, however. Sometimes the change must be all or nothing, as with pregnancy and birth; one cannot be just a bit pregnant. But in a surprising number of cases, ingenuity can create sequential alternatives.

Consider an issue dear to me, a major increase in the volume of immigration into the United States. Often the argument rages between (1) those who call for an open door, on the grounds that the effects of present rates of immigration are positive, and (2) those who call for no change on the grounds that the effects of huge increases in immigration are unforeseeable. I advocate increasing immigration in steps perhaps every three years, each new step taken only after there has been a chance to see whether the previous level has caused unforeseen problems of a sort that do not occur with present levels of immigration.

In principle, in many cases a sequential strategy should appeal to both sides because it does not threaten major costs and keeps open the possibility of major benefits. But most people are so sure that they can foresee consequences on the basis of their experience and logic that even a tiny experiment is unnecessary. A painful example mentioned earlier was my idea that airline oversales should be handled with a volunteer auction system. Opponents said it would cause chaos. I suggested a trial for a single day in a single airport at a single ticket counter. But for twelve years I could not induce even such a minor trial because the airlines were so sure they knew what the results would be. (And, of course, they were wrong, as the results at all U.S. airports since 1978 have shown.)

Summary

Having a clear idea of the problem is a crucial first step to finding sound alternatives to deal with the problem.

Good ideas help you identify sound alternatives for action. Sometimes other people will supply good ideas if you ask—as you should. Sometimes you must try to come up with good ideas out of your own experience and imagination.

It is important to collect *all* the obvious sound alternatives without overlooking any. Making a list with pencil and paper helps you avoid overlooking any obvious sound ideas. A systematic search, rather than a hit-or-miss process, is your object.

You must prepare your mind for good ideas by studying the matter thoroughly. You must also give your mind free time to be fallow so that ideas can enter. Devote prime time when you are fresh, rather than when you are tired. And you should learn how to let go and drift on the currents of thought so that new ideas can enter.

Providing a variety of random inputs can lead to a serendipitous solution to a problem.

Notes

1. Friedrich A. Hayek, "The Theory of Complex Phenomena," *Studies in Philosophy, Politics and Economics* (Chicago: University of Chicago Press, 1978), pp. 22–42.

2. Hayek also says of these "puzzlers" that "many of their particular ideas in different fields may spring from some single general conception of which they are themselves not aware but which, like the similarity of their approach to the separate issues, they may much later discover with surprise" (1978, p. 54). This rings true in my own experience. The underlying conception of humankind as improving its state of knowledge and evolving patterns that tend toward group survival has guided my expectations about the effects of population growth upon a wide range of phenomena. See my "Does Doom Loom?" *Reason* (April 1984): 31–34.

3. Among economists, Nobelist Paul Samuelson seems to fit Hayek's description perfectly. Nobelist Kenneth Arrow may also fit the description.

4. *Washington Post Book World*, December 24, 1989, p. 8.

5. Allan M. Weinstein, *Asthma* (New York: Fawcett Crest, 1987), p. xxiii.

6. Economists well recognize a cognate of dominance in the concept of Pareto improvement.

Chapter 11

Experts, Expert Systems, and Libraries

Brief Outline

- Experts
- Expert Systems
- Libraries
- Summary

On what date this year would it be best to plant the field at the northeast corner of the old Reith farm in Champaign County? How should you deal with a set of brand-new boots and tender feet when you find yourself forced to take a long march in them tomorrow? What are the problems to be overcome in disposing of nuclear waste, and what is the best way to overcome them? How much in welfare services do immigrants to the United States use, and how much taxes do they pay, on average?

Knowledge exists that can help you answer these questions. How you may acquire such knowledge is the subject of this chapter.

Look first for knowledge where the knowledge may already exist—in experts, computerized "expert systems" that codify the knowledge of experts, and libraries whose books and periodicals may contain the writings by experts and scholars of the subject. This chapter is about how to take advantage of these sources of knowledge.

The chapter doesn't promise you answers to any specific questions. But it does promise that it will help you know where and how to look for answers.

Three Kinds of Knowledge

The knowledge referred to in this chapter includes both *applied* know-how—such as techniques that will prevent tender feet from getting sore on a long march—and *abstract* knowledge—such as understanding why new skin grows at the rate it does on the feet and on the face. *Tacit* knowledge, such as how to patch up feet that are sore from a long march, must be acquired by experience.

Experts

Obviously it makes sense to start your search for an answer to a particular question by seeking help from people who understand where the relevant knowledge may be located. Experts serve two helpful functions, as subject-matter experts and as librarians. They can apply knowledge that they possess, as when a refrigerator repairperson fixes your machine or a lawyer gets a patent for your invention. Experts also can serve as your guides in the realm of abstract knowledge.

A subject-matter expert can summarize for you the existing knowledge relevant to a routine question, making it unnecessary for you to venture into the library at all. For example, a competent lawyer can tell you how the law of copyright applies to reproducing an advertisement in a book. (If the point is very tricky, however, you need a truly first-class lawyer—an expert "expert." Or you might learn how to do legal research and study the point yourself.) Another example: If you seek a mechanism to help your bank predict whether a borrower will repay a loan, a scholar in finance may be able to quickly provide you an appropriate formula and a copy of the article that describes it.

But Some Experts Are Worse Than Useless

On some questions, however, the "experts" are useless or worse. For example, for decades the consensus of the "energy experts" has been that the price of energy will go up, against all the evidence of history. And for decades their forecasts have been terribly wrong, costing Americans hundreds of billions of dollars in subsidies to "alternative" energy sources that are now unlikely ever to be used, regulations and bad investments in energy-saving autos and other equipment, and in wasted time due to slower auto travel. On this matter, you would have done better to venture into the library yourself and study the problem down to its roots, rather than consulting the supposed "experts," though this obviously would not have been easy to do.

How to Assess the Expertise of "Experts"

People frequently claim to possess knowledge on subjects about which they are ignorant. And they are often willing to charge you high prices for that supposed knowledge. As an industrial folk saying has it, an expert is a guy from out of town. Your problem is to determine if a person does indeed possess valid knowledge. The problem is much the same with respect to both experts and nonexperts, except that the knowledge that supposed experts offer usually is relatively arcane, and therefore it is harder for you to test for quality. The knowledge that a dentist applies to your mouth, for example, is especially hard to rate because it is almost never put to a public examination; even asking another dentist is seldom a satisfactory test.

Here are some guidelines to help you assess whether another person possesses knowledge that will be useful to you:

1. The more *local and specific* the subject, the more likely the answer will be valid. If you want to know whether a given field on a given farm is dry enough to plant as of today, the farmer who cultivates that farm is likely to have very reliable knowledge on that subject. He or she has direct knowledge of the situation through her or his eyes, and probably has had *specific* experience with that field for some years past, plus relevant *general* knowledge of when to plant.

Indeed, even if the farmer is not an accredited expert on agronomy, she or he is likely to have better knowledge about when to plant that specific field than is an accredited expert in an office many miles away. The importance of specific knowledge of this kind, held by people working on a particular farm or in a particular factory or in a particular retail establishment, is one of the main reasons central planning such as practiced in Soviet communism until its breakup in 1991 cannot in principle be as efficient as a decentralized market system.

Our politics often suffer from not distinguishing local from distant knowledge. If you ask Susan whether coworker immigrant Sam is a hard worker who pays more in taxes than the cost of the welfare services Sam's family uses, Susan's knowledge is likely to be very reliable. But if you ask Susan whether immigrants from Sam's country *generally* are hard workers and not welfare abusers, her knowledge is likely to be worse than useless. Hence polls regularly show the inconsistent results that Americans say *positive* things about the immigrants *they know*, and *negative* things about immigrants *in general*. The same is true of poll questions about whether their own neighborhoods are overcrowded, compared to questions about whether the country and planet are overcrowded. Yet reporters and politicians give weight to public opinion that immigration should be reduced because of welfare abuse, and that population growth should be reduced because of overcrowding, in violation of this principle that knowledge about events at large is likely to be less reliable than knowledge of the situation close at hand.

The less local and specific the knowledge, the more necessary are the specialized scientific techniques discussed in the next chapter.

2. The more *formal education* the person has had with respect to a subject, the more knowledge the person is likely to possess. This principle is obvious. The strength of experts' education is in areas of knowledge that require specialized techniques and training. (Of course, dowsers claim that their extensive training with the specialized techniques holding a forked stick make them experts at finding water, but not all specialized techniques and training are proof of valid knowledge.)

Furthermore, as noted in point 1 above, formal education is not always enough to offset lack of local knowledge or lack of experience. Once when I was in the Navy and had just joined a Marine battalion, I needed information about how to prepare for a long hike in brand-new boots. I found that enlisted chief petty officer medical corpsmen (the equivalent of master sergeants) knew more about practical remedies such as painting the tender areas of the foot with protective tincture of benzoine, and standing in a pan of water to wet the boots before departing, than did physicians who had had much more formal education but less experience with this particular problem.

Education and impressive credentials are not solid proof of expertise, as a history of unfounded expert assessments, *The Experts Speak*[1] shows in hilarious detail. Supposedly well-informed persons holding their country's highest political posts often make ludicrously wrong predictions. For example, Benjamin Disraeli, then Chancellor of the Exchequer and later prime minister of Great Britain, asserted that building the Suez Canal was a "most futile attempt and totally impossible to be carried out."[2] And the most authoritative publications and specialists have told us that such innovations as railroad trains, automobiles, airplanes, submarines, electric light, the phonograph, the telegraph, and the telephone were technologically impossible or would never amount to anything even if they could be created. Perhaps most amazingly, the world's best scientists often are utterly wrong—and with confidence!—even about their very own subjects.

The subject of nuclear power is instructive because it is of current interest. These were the assessments of three of the greatest physicists of our time or any other. "There is no likelihood man can ever tap the power of the atom," said Robert Millikan.[3] "There is not the slightest indication that [nuclear energy] will ever be obtainable," said Albert Einstein.[4] And "The energy produced by the atom is a very poor kind of thing. Anyone who expects a source of power from the transformation of these atoms is talking moonshine," said Ernest Rutherford, himself one of the great pioneers in the field.[5]

Even *The Experts Speak*, the compendium of experts' nonsense from which I just quoted, sometimes gets it completely wrong, labeling sound judgment as nonsense. For example, it quotes as nonsense the words of the inventor of the hydrogen bomb, Edward Teller, "What do you think you get more radiation from, leaning up against an atomic reactor or your wife? . . . [Y]ou get just a bit more from [the reactor] than from your wife."[6] Teller is unquestionably correct. He went on to joke that perhaps this meant only that one should not sleep with more than one other person at a time. Also quoted is physicist Dixy Lee Ray, ex-governor of Washington and former chairman of the Atomic Energy Commission, as saying "A nuclear power plant is infinitely safer than eating, because 300 people choke to death on food every year [in the United States]."[7] And she is quite right, because nuclear power has caused zero deaths in the United States, unlike every other energy source, and even the Soviet experience does not tilt the balance the other way. (Do I hear you saying that I have it wrong? Maybe this makes the point.)

In my own trade of economics, the profession passed from a majority of the most respected scholars approving Keynesian theory and policies in the 1950s and 1960s to the vast majority approving quite the opposite sort of theory and policies by the late 1980s and 1990s. So much for trusting in the experts.

Whether the government should *license experts* in a given field is always an interesting question. In some cases, licensing obviously is protection for the incomes of the practitioners. Requiring six months or a year of training in such subjects as electricity and blood chemistry does not improve a barber's skill, and few people would have trouble sorting out the bad barbers from the good barbers without a license on the wall. And if there were no legal requirements to become a physician, private agencies rating physicians might (or might not) soon sell information providing better protection than do the legal requirements. Government licensing of such professions as public relations can appeal only to the most naive members of the public—plus, of course, the practitioners who would be protected from competition. But the fact that an electrician is certified by the state as competent might indicate a somewhat better chance that your job will be done right than if it is done by an uncertified person.

It is also important to recognize when a distinguished expert is opining about matters that are outside the person's field of knowledge. In such cases, you should pay no more attention than you would to any other layperson. Einstein, Bertrand Russell, and Andrei Sakharov are examples of great minds in science who have been remarkably naive—indeed, downright ignorant—about economic systems, yet all have written in praise of socialism. Experts in one field are all too often given forums for their opinions in other fields, and too often they accept the lure instead of steadfastly keeping their public pronouncements to what they know about.

3. The more *experience* the person has had, the more reliable the knowledge (usually). If Susan has worked with immigrant Sam for ten years, her knowledge of his work discipline is likely to be greater than if she worked a week with him. But in some situations, experience may not be enough to offset lack of education. As it is truly said of some people: He has had twenty years of experience—one year's worth, twenty times. And the long experience may lead to the belief that a person *must* know a lot about the situation, even if he doesn't, because otherwise he would be stupid and we both know that he is not stupid, right?

4. The more *immediately testable* the knowledge, the more reliable the expert is likely to be. A refrigerator repairer is likely to be more reliable when she says that she can fix the machine than is a head shrinker who says that he can repair your schizophrenia, or an economist who claims to know when to increase the nation's money supply. One reason that immediate testability is linked to knowledge is that in such cases the expert gets lots of chances to check her or his ideas against the reality of what works and what does not—that is, lots of "feedback" that should improve his or her knowledge. One might also hazard the gener-

alization that the more general the question, the greater the variability among experts.

5. The *more uniform* the results of a procedure, the more reliable the supposed expert. Refrigerators respond more uniformly to treatment than do schizophrenics or economies, for reasons that are fairly obvious but that would be hard to state briefly.

6. The larger the body of *tested scientific knowledge* on a subject, and the *more evidence* that has accumulated, the more reliable the experts are likely to be. There have been many more experiments with drugs to combat high blood pressure than with drugs to increase creativity, and therefore people who prescribe the former are more deserving of credence than those who prescribe the latter. And a physician who says that aspirin will not cause delayed side effects is more to be believed than a physician who says that the newest drug for depression will cause no side effects, because aspirin has been used so widely for so many years.

7. The absence of conclusive scientific evidence that a procedure works, and the presence of evidence that the procedure does *not* work, suggest that no one should be considered an expert in the practice of that procedure. For half a century, studies have shown that the stock market "experts" do not forecast which way the market is going in the short run any better than a flipped coin does. But great is the human desire to feel that the world is not beyond our control, and great is our belief that there just might be magic this time. People therefore continue unabatedly to pay large sums of money for market forecasts in newspapers and newsletters and by stockbrokers. J. Scott Armstrong calls this the "seer-sucker principle": "No matter how much evidence exists that seers do not exist [in a given field], suckers will pay for the existence of seers."[8] (More about this in chapters 14 and 15 on clarity and error.)

It is quite amazing that scientific testing is not conducted even when it is easy to do. Dentists obviously did not test the old method of up-and-down brushing before they "expertly" prescribed it to everyone in the nation, or they would not now be prescribing side-to-side brushing. Whether they have yet tested the latter, I do not know. But which patient would question their expertness on this subject? Much the same was true of the exercises prescribed to millions of back sufferers until a few years ago.

8. *The greater the benefit to the person from simply providing an opinion—distinguished from producing results, as in the case of refrigerator repair—the greater the chance that you will pay for worthless*

knowledge. A racetrack tout has an obvious stake in your believing that the tout has some inside knowledge about which horse will win. So does a stockbroker; if you believe the stockbroker's recommendations, you will buy and sell more stock from her and provide her more profit in commissions. Psychologists and psychiatrists who are "professional clinicians do not in fact make more accurate clinical judgments than laypersons" when predicting violent behavior or determining who is faking mental illness; hence they seem to be of little assistance in court trials.[9] It is not surprising that psychoanalysts did not welcome the tests that showed an absence of proven improvement from their expensive treatments.

You must also worry about the expert's self-interest, or even knowledge itself, affecting the *content* of the information you receive. Scientists who study nuclear fusion obviously desire that U.S. senators and congressional representatives believe that fusion has a bright future if research in the field is well supported. But there is a mechanism operating in the opposite direction in some circumstances; experts often are overly pessimistic about future discoveries in their fields. Apparently this happens because they focus on the subfields in which they work, which have already been opened up (by definition), and they focus away from the possibility of wholly new subfields outside their own.

Check the Track Records of "Experts"

You can improve your chances of getting valuable knowledge from experts if you check the results of those you are considering employing. In some fields, such as economic forecasting, those people identified as experts do no better than chance at forecasting short-run ups and downs, so you do not even need to check out individuals. (Of course, some individuals will *seem* to have successful track records, but this is almost surely due to chance, just as someone in a crowd of ten thousand people each flipping ten coins will probably observe ten heads.)

Journalists seldom check the records of experts. Instead, they usually decide whom to consult on the basis of fame and organizational attachment. Just as a celebrity may be said to be a person well known for being well known, an expert is a person whom others think is an expert. For example, the best-known prophets of gloom and doom with respect to the world's food and natural resources have been wrong again and again. Yet the same people who have been so consistently wrong during the last two decades of concern about these matters continue to be the most consulted of all. Their abysmal forecasting records seem never to be held against them.

Young people often have trouble accepting how wrong experts can be, perhaps because most of the information that children receive is specific and well founded: If you don't wear a hat, your ears will be cold; turn your hips when you hit the ball. Children extend this trust to matters about which knowledge is much less well founded, and the trust is often fostered by the prestige of persons they hear from—honored professors, respected journalists, and so on.

Indeed, it is uncomfortable for us adults, too, to think that some important part of the world around us is unknown and even unknowable. We like to feel that we can master our environment, and it comes very hard to be told that we cannot.

Though this section focuses on experts, the topic blends into the entire subjects of knowledge and of sound thinking. Therefore, many other chapters in the book throw light on experts and expertise, and how to think about them.

How to work with experts so as to effectively transfer their knowledge to you deserves some attention, but there is no space for it here.

Expert Systems

An "expert system" is part of the recently developing field known as "artificial intelligence." Such a system is a synthetic expert. The people who create the program mine and systematize the knowledge of several living, breathing experts into a computer program, which may then be consulted by a user. For example, the MYCIN program combines the knowledge of physicians skilled in diagnosing and treating meningitis and bacterial infections of the blood into a computer file that other physicians can then consult.

Harnessing the Power of Computers

The computer has a wider array of information stored in it than does a single ordinary physician's memory, because the program creators drew upon the knowledge of several top-notch experts. This means that exotic diseases that the ordinary physician would never see in a lifetime are cataloged in the computer, along with a wide range of symptoms that might only occasionally be seen. The computer also has the advantage that it is never forgetful or fatigued. In operation, the computer asks the user a series of questions, each question depending upon the answers previously given, in a sequence resembling the way that a physician ordinarily thinks when making a diagnosis.

A hypothetical automobile-repair example is easier for the layperson to follow than a medical example. The computer first asks you to classify your problem into either (1) car won't start, or (2) some other problem. If you respond with "1," the computer then asks you if (1) headlights are dim, (2) the fuel filter is clogged, or (3) the battery cables are loose or corroded. The computer also asks for information about the starter: (1) no cranking? (2) slow cranking? (3) normal cranking? (4) grinding noise from starter? Depending on which pair of answers you give, the computer asks you further questions, until there is enough information to recommend what to do.[10]

Expert systems are still in their youth. Other successful examples include a program to help understand soybean diseases, another to aid decisions made in oil drilling, still another for geologists' use in prospecting for ore deposits, and a system to make diagnoses in locomotive repair.

An expert system is very specific. It gives you a diagnosis and treatment for a particular person's illness or a particular car's problem. Knowledge in libraries tends to be more abstract. Consider, for example, a formula that helps banks predict who will default on loans. The formula is a general tool that you apply to a specific case by inserting the particular characteristics of the potential borrower.

Libraries

The applied and abstract knowledge accumulated by humankind is collected and stored in libraries and databases. Were the contents of all libraries and databases to be destroyed, progress would be set back thousands of years. The destruction of the Alexandria library caused irreparable loss of classical knowledge. But the widely diffused publication and modern electronic storage of information makes such a loss almost impossible nowadays.

Traditional Libraries

A librarian—an expert on libraries—knows the general rules and outlines of this maze of knowledge, but usually stands on the sidelines while you venture in. Sometimes a librarian knows the specific location of the knowledge that you seek. But more often the librarian knows the directions you should go—which catalogs you should consult and which reference tools you should use. Internet specialists can guide you through the World Wide Web.

Deciding when to go to the library yourself and when to consult experts will depend upon such factors as the utility of the money you would pay to experts, your skill at using the library, the type of question before you, and the degree of expertise of experts. Using a library effectively is a fascinating challenge. It is much more interesting than I ever thought it could be when I took the tour given to new students at the university when I arrived as a freshman.

World Wide Web

In the 1990s the World Wide Web gave a wholly new turn to the process of seeking information. Whereas the middle-aged person usually thinks first of going to the library (or sending someone else there), the younger person often thinks first of searching the Web.

And indeed, the Web can be an amazingly quick and fruitful source of information. By entering a few keywords into the various search engines, and following links from place to place, you can arrive at an amazing variety of material.

Also on the Web are many databases that were formerly available only in expensive reference volumes found at a good city or university library, such as various sourcebooks published by official organizations such as the United Nations and the U.S. Bureau of the Census. The Web also contains original databases of many research organizations.

This resource changes so fast that it is not worthwhile trying to describe the Web further here. The only important fact is: Remember www.

Internet Discussion Groups: Another New Resource

Discussion groups on various subjects on the Internet range from aeronautics to zoology. And you can often post a query there—say, a query on a "listserv" (a membership-only group of people) devoted to permutation methods in statistics—about whether anyone knows of a technique to do a given job. Or you could post a query about possible substitution of repair parts on an open discussion group devoted to motorcycle repair.

Such queries are often an astoundingly quick and easy way to get top-quality information. The potential of this medium for the future of information-getting is very large, though still not known.

Summary

People who have expertise are one important source of knowledge. But supposed experts can be worse than useless if they give you wrong information. Assessing the expertise of supposed experts is a tricky matter, for which guidelines are suggested. Reputation is an insufficient test, though it can often be helpful. Checking a person's track record is most important.

Expert systems are devices in which expertise is compiled into computers in such form that the program answers specific questions that you pose to it in sequential fashion. Medical diagnostic programs have been among the most successful expert systems so far.

It is worth learning how to navigate libraries. Modern computer indexes are a great help.

Notes

1. Christopher Cerf and Victor Navasky, *The Experts Speak* (New York: Pantheon, 1984).

2. Ibid., p. 219.

3. Ibid., p. 214.

4. Ibid., p. 215.

5. Ibid.

6. Ibid., p. 217.

7. Ibid., p. 216.

8. J. Scott Armstrong, "Evidence on the Value of Experts in Forecasting: The Seer-Sucker Theory" (Philadelphia: University of Pennsylvania, Photocopy, 1979), p. 1.

9. David Faust and Jay Ziskin, "The Expert Witness in Psychology and Psychiatry," *Science* 241 (July 1, 1998): 31–35.

10. Paul Harmon and David King, *Expert Systems* (New York: John Wiley, 1985, pp. 110–111).

Chapter 12

Using Scientific Discipline to Obtain Information

Brief Outline

- Who Needs Science?
- Conditions That Require the Discipline of Science
- Steps in a Scientific Investigation
- Summary

Last month, an Atlanta newspaper columnist named Lewis Grizzard came here for a visit. He wishes he hadn't. Reason: Our wondrous, knowledgeable, kind, efficient taxi drivers.

Grizzard took four taxi rides during this stay. The first driver took him to Union Station when he had asked to go to National Airport. The second charged Grizzard $10 to drive around in search of a restaurant that they never found. The third ran up $11 looking for the Key Bridge Marriott—having started all of 200 yards away, in Georgetown. The fourth couldn't locate a rather well-known local landmark, the U.S. Capitol.

When Grizzard got home, he wrote a column that was more like a fragmentation grenade. Conclusion: Washington is the worst taxi city in the country.

. . . So I thought I would go to Atlanta for a day, take as many cabs as I could between my flight in and my flight out, and see whether Grizzard's hometown cabs were worse than ours.

It wasn't even close. [The author goes on to describe nothing but good experiences in Atlanta.]

Ladies and gentlemen, the loser, and still champion: Washington, D.C.[1]

***

Anyone who has ever taken a cab from the Atlanta airport will be exceedingly reluctant to do so again. For years, it has been unusual to find a cab driver at Hartsfield [Atlanta] who could speak English, make change, or find his way around town. And the cabs themselves were, if anything, worse than the drivers.[2]

Who Needs Science?

Casual observation satisfactorily provides most of the information we need for our work and our personal lives. Is it raining? Stick your head outside the door. Can J.J. fix bicycles? Give her your bicycle and try her out. Will the flower plants survive the winter? Put them out on the porch and check when spring comes. No special knowledge is necessary to get competent answers to questions like these.

Indeed, as chapter 10 noted, investigation of *every* question should *begin* with such first-hand observation—actually looking inside the horse's mouth to check out the dental situation. But the investigation should not *end* with first-hand investigation in many cases. In many kinds of situations, the methods of science are essential.

The aim of this chapter is teach you what you need to know as a *consumer* of scientific research in any of several roles—as a manager who must make judgments based on the information that research yields, as a politician who must make policy decisions that require scientific background, and as a citizen who reads newspapers and watches television news and then votes. The chapter does not promise to teach you how to *perform* research; for that knowledge I commend you to my long book on the subject.[3] The chapter does, however, promise to inform you about the basic principles of scientific research that are applicable whenever you must create reliable knowledge on your own.

We All Need Science When There Is Variability

A thrown baseball breaks windows with painful regularity. Sugar unfailingly sweetens the tea. One does not need the methods of science to confirm these connections because they happen the same way every time, or almost every time. Casual observation of the phenomenon suffices.

Many questions cannot be answered with casual observation, however. Is taxi service worse in Washington, D.C., than in Atlanta? A journalist takes a few rides in each city, and writes a column announcing that the service is worse in Washington (or in Atlanta). But he cannot base a valid conclusion on that evidence, and the column is simply amusing foolishness.

Representative Sampling Is the Key

To get a valid answer to the taxicab question, one must take a *representative sample* of rides by a representative sample of customers, and the sample must be large enough to allow for the considerable *variability* from ride to ride. The reporter's haphazard sample of a few rides is quite inadequate. Scientific discipline, and the sampling techniques that are part of it, must be brought to bear in this case.

The representative sample need not be constituted perfectly, nor need it be huge. A show of hands in a class of 200 students asked whether the previous cab ride was bad would provide a much more valid estimate of the proportion of bad rides in one city, and the same one-minute survey in two cities would be sufficient for a much more satisfactory comparison than the journalists' method.

Or consider whether brushing your teeth horizontally is more effective in reducing gum disease than brushing vertically. The important effects do not occur until months or perhaps years afterward, and the results may also be very variable from person to person. Only a carefully controlled experiment on two samples of subjects chosen randomly from the same population can provide an adequate answer. Theoretical reasoning, and even short-run observation of one or both groups, are almost surely inadequate to provide a valid answer.

When immediate observation is insufficient, and when experts and libraries do not yield the answers you need, you must turn to scientifically disciplined research. And when I say "must," I mean that failure to use scientifically sound methods means fooling yourself into potential difficulty, or fooling others with results that will be fraudulent at best and disastrous at worst. Please note, however, that "scientific" does not mean *experimental*. Astronomy and population censuses are two important examples of scientific enterprises that do not use experimentation. Experiments have great advantages when they are feasible, but when they are not feasible, other methods are usually available.

Journalism Ignores Scientific Methods at Our Peril

The failure to use scientifically sound methods is an ever greater affliction upon the public as newspapers and television become more important influences upon us and as our attention is increasingly upon events outside of our own immediate surroundings where we can check the situation for ourselves. The public is systematically misled about such issues as the extent of welfare abuse by immigrants, the dangers of nuclear plants and nuclear waste, and trends in the availability of natural resources and the cleanliness of our environment, among many others, because journalists apply to these issues the same techniques that their profession has used so successfully in covering warehouse fires and corrupt politicians. But these nonscientific techniques systematically provide unsound answers to the more global questions.

Nowadays newspapers recognize that scientific polling methods are required for useful forecasts about the outcomes of elections; gathering opinion the old way in bars and barber shops is not enough. But in too many other cases, journalists and others barge ahead without the necessary scientific techniques.

Knowing When Science Is Necessary Is Crucial

The most important knowledge about the scientific method is knowing when the special discipline and techniques of science are necessary. The reporter should know that scientific sampling is necessary to get a valid answer about comparative taxi service, though casual observation rather than special techniques is sufficient for covering a fire. Therefore, we proceed to discuss the characteristics of situations that indicate the need for scientific discipline, or instead indicate that casual observation should suffice.

Conditions That Require the Discipline of Science

In general, scientific discipline is necessary when the chunk of the world you wish to understand presents a complex, varied, off-again-on-again picture, rather than a simple, tight, immediate cause-and-effect pattern. Estimating the mortality rate of a nation requires scientific census-taking techniques, whereas finding out who died in a fire does not. Learning the effects of last week's heat wave on ice cream sales needs no special methods, whereas determining whether there has been a rise in the earth's temperature and whether the summer of 1988 was unusual due to the supposed greenhouse effect requires statistical techniques not known even to many climatologists. You can see whether there are cockroaches in your kitchen without any special equipment, but determining how many bacteria there are in the water requires a microscope.

We will see that the presence of the same factors that require scientific techniques leads to the pitfalls in our everyday thinking that will be discussed in chapters 14 and 15.

When There Is Variability in the Phenomenon

When every case you look at yields the same result—when every time you hit the window with a baseball, it shatters—immediate observation tells you what you need to know. But when there is considerable variation from case to case—when some taxi rides are nasty whereas most are fine, or when some people will vote Republican whereas others will vote Democratic—scientific discipline is needed to assess just how much there is of one or the other.

Laypersons tend to underestimate the difficulty of reaching a sound conclusion in the face of variability. Can stock market experts forecast with any accuracy which way the market will go next week? Because many kinds of variability are involved, very subtle statistical techniques are needed to establish that supposed experts cannot forecast better than chance, and laypersons therefore tend to believe that expert forecasting is possible. People tend to underestimate the amount of variability and the likelihood of apparently improbable events, such as a person who has no ability to forecast the market being right ten times in a row—though they would not be so surprised if a coin comes up heads ten times in a row.

A very large proportion of television sportscasters' comments during basketball and football games is sheer nonsense, derived from not understanding the extent and nature of variability. And it is almost impossible to convince people of the operation of this variability. To be able to convince you that there is no such thing as a slump in baseball batting, and no such thing as a hot hand in basketball, is most unlikely indeed, based on my experiences in trying to convince classes and newspaper audiences. Yet it is so. Casual observation breaks down entirely in such matters, and the techniques of science are necessary when there is so much variability from at-bat to at-bat.

Many apparent phenomena really are no more than coincidence—heightened mortality from cancer in particular localities, for example, or from Agent Orange among the American military in the Vietnam War. Yet the coincidences seem so striking to the nonstatistician, and the results are so frightening, that many people do not recognize the need for scientific techniques and will not accept the results even when scientific techniques are used correctly.

The effect of a given amount of variability depends upon the circumstances. Variability in height within the two populations is sufficiently great that scientific methods are necessary to compare the average height of Americans and Yugoslavs. But the difference in the averages among Japanese and Americans is sufficiently great that casual observation is powerful enough to say with accuracy that Japanese (in this generation, at least) tend to be smaller. (And, of course, casual observation, even if not conclusive, can be an invaluable source of ideas to test in more rigorous fashion.)

When There Are Large Volumes of Events and Data

When there are just fifty people in a small town, you may be able to judge whether the current cohort of women are having more children than did the cohort ten years earlier. But it is not usually possible to make a valid judgment about fertility change for a large population such as the United States without careful measurement techniques. It is very difficult to draw a sample of a large and varied population that will be sufficiently representative. You must sample from all the subgroups in proportion to their representation in the population.

Lack of recognition of the difficulty of drawing a representative sample from the large "universe" of taxi rides—perhaps along with lack of recognition of the problem of variability—probably is responsible for the journalistic foolishness of drawing conclusions about the quality of rides in different cities on the basis of casual observation.

Amazing blunders are made by people untrained in a field—even though highly trained in other fields—by not recognizing and overcoming the difficulties of representative sampling of a large set of data. For example, biologists wished to determine how much of the Amazon forest had been cut down. One of the estimates of deforestation most relied upon by biologists who forecast the denuding of tropical forests was based on observations only from the sides of roads through the Amazon and elsewhere. No matter how clever the theoretical assumptions one makes to supplement such observations, one is most unlikely to soundly judge the state of the forests that are *not* near roads with such evidence.

When a Check on Personal Bias Is Necessary

Whenever personal interests are present in a situation—and this is most of the time—the *objectivity* feature of scientific research offers protection. Fundamental to every piece of research deserving the label "scientific" is that the procedures are stated publicly in such fashion that another investigator may repeat the essentials of the research. This enables others to check upon the claims that are made by the investigator. And the objective statement of the procedures itself—if given honestly—enables others to judge whether the research was done in a fair and unbiased manner.

This matter comes up frequently in commercial research that is intended to prove the value of a particular product. For example, a firm that develops a new drug for high blood pressure has a stake in research results that prove the drug's efficacy. If such research is to be meaningful, it must be conducted and written up in a sufficiently objective manner so that other investigators can repeat the work and verify the results.

Multiple Causation, Hidden Causation, and Reverse Causation

Two gentlepeople got drunk on successive nights with brandy and soda, whiskey and soda, and bourbon and soda. Should they have agreed that the soda must have caused their inebriations?

More seriously now: Most countries with high birthrates are poor. Does this mean that high birthrates *cause* countries to be poor? Perhaps there are other lines of causation, perhaps involving one or more other causes, such as the social system of the country.

If the social system and (contrary to fact) high birthrates cause slow economic development, that would be a case of *multiple* causation. It is nearly impossible to separate the effects of such two possibly causal variables from each other without scientifically disciplined experiment or statistical analysis.

Another possibility is that the social system (which had not been one of the factors you originally considered) causes *both* high birthrates *and* low income (and low growth of income). This would be a case of *hidden causation.*

Still another possibility is that low income causes high birthrates, a case of *reverse causation.*

In these cases, too, scientific techniques would be necessary to disentangle the causal relations.

Steps in a Scientific Investigation

The basic principles of scientific research can be thought of as the steps that are applicable when you must create reliable knowledge on your own. As a checklist to keep in mind, and as a sequential order in which you should consider them, these principles can be useful. Violations of these same principles are much the same as the errors we make in drawing everyday conclusions, as will be discussed in chapters 14 and 15. And many of the same principles are the converse of the logical fallacies that have been known to philosophers since the Greeks. This is a nice example of how the same principles of thinking appear in several different contexts.

Here is a checklist of steps for a scientific investigation. The sequence is not rigid. In practice you often skip some of the steps—though sometimes you fall into error because you do so. And in practice you go back and forth among the steps, rather than proceeding smoothly through the sequence.

1. *Make sure the question is worth studying.* The best-chosen methods and the fanciest, most rigorous, and sophisticated techniques are worthless unless the problem is important. I once heard a commercial researcher put it this way: *Study issues that scream, not issues that whisper.* In the back of your mind should be a cost-benefit framework, such as discussed in part I, applied to the evaluation of the research—the benefits not being limited to private benefits, of course.

2. *Ask: "What do I want to find out?"* This is another of the intellectual devices that pops up in many different contexts in this book. When you are unclear as to the direction to take, ask yourself the appropriate variation of the question: What am I trying to do?

Answering this question with reasonable precision is hard work. It is easier to wave your hands around and say something vague like "I'm interested in getting some answers about juvenile delinquency." What answers? To what questions? Do you want to know how many delinquents there are? Or whether parents' incomes affect the rate of juvenile delinquency? Or whether delinquents enjoy their delinquency? Or what?

3. *Establish the purpose of the project.* Why do you want to know the answers to the research question you are asking? How will the information be used and by whom? Is the information about taxi rides intended to affect legislation regulating taxi service, or is it just for the amuse-

ment of newspaper readers? The purpose is likely to determine the methods, including how big a sample you take.

4. *Determine the value of the research.* If you have several projects you are considering, you would like to do the most valuable one. Again, a cost-benefit analysis is appropriate. This is another example of how cost-benefit thinking has application far beyond business. Indeed, we do cost-benefit thinking all the time, but because we do not do it explicitly, we often do it poorly.

5. *Saturate yourself in the problem.* It is amazing what foolish ideas you can hold until you experience a situation first-hand. The sociologist William Caudill committed himself to a mental institution to increase his intuitive understanding of the situation, though I do not recommend such heroic measures in all cases. This is an example of a principle of thinking that appears in several contexts in the book, the necessity for concrete experience. Years ago the advertising agency Cunningham and Walsh sent every writer and account executive to work in a retail store one week in every year to hear what consumers had to say first-hand, and to observe buyer reactions to the products they worked on. Unfortunately, we often are too hurried or too lazy to enforce this sort of discipline upon ourselves.

6. *Choose empirical variables.* This is another stage in the sequence of getting more specific. At this point, you decide what you will actually measure. Will you count the number of complaints to the taxi commission about bad rides, or the verbal comments of riders, or a sample of rides that you take yourself?

7. *Calculate the benefits of accuracy and the costs of error.* This is another stage in the sequence of relating your actions to their values. How much would it be worth to the public if four times as large a survey were taken and the error in the results of the taxi survey were cut in half? It is difficult to render this calculation in the money terms that are necessary to relate to the costs of increasing the sample survey, but the exercise of doing so is very valuable, just as in the case of cost-benefit analyses for nonprofit firms described in chapter 9.

8. *Determine the most important research obstacles.* The patterns of nature and social life are often obscure. The factors discussed earlier that make scientific discipline necessary constitute obstacles to getting knowledge in casual fashion, and require special devices to surmount them. For example, a randomly drawn sample is a device to overcome the obstacle of an unrepresentative collection of taxi rides. There are

also many other obstacles, such as people's unwillingness to tell the truth about delicate matters such as their incomes, and the ethical barrier against human experimentation in some drug investigations. My book on research methods catalogs these methods and discusses devices to overcome the various obstacles.

9. *Choose methods.* After the important obstacles have been identified, you are ready to select the methods that will surmount the obstacles most effectively. It is important to consider the *widest possible range* of methods even if they are not commonly used in your trade. For example, though experimentation is seldom used in mainstream economics, economists should keep this method in mind as a possibility for unusual circumstances.

Often it is best to use two or more quite different methods so that one imperfect method (all methods always are imperfect) can serve as a check upon another. For example, a journalist might use records of complaints to the taxi bureau along with a survey of riders.

10. *Check the ethics of your proposed research* both because it is the right thing to do and because it is the safe thing to do. It is easy to forget the ethical problems when doing studies such as surveys of people's private behavior. Remembering to think through the ethics can avoid a lot of grief.

11. *Prepare a detailed design of the method.* Now it is time to get specific and operational. It is important to identify problems *before* they occur. If an agronomist forgets to vary the amounts of fertilizer as well as test different seeds, there will be no way to make good that oversight and recover the experiment later.

12. *Collect the data.* Carefully. Don't forget that your theory and personal biases can harm your objectivity.

13. *Analyze the data.* Look at the data every which way. Use as many tables as possible. You will find that designing tables and graphs is very demanding work, which is a proof of its importance in clarifying your thinking.

14. *Write up the research work.* Do this as early as possible, even before the data have been collected. Doing so will help you do a good job collecting the data and analyzing it.

Warning

Here the same warning is needed as about formal cost-benefit analysis: Please do not conclude from the neat, clean look of this set of steps that most scientific thinking goes forth on this model. Skilled scientists jump back and forth from one step to the other, and you will constrain yourself in a mental straitjacket if you insist on proceeding strictly by the numbers. Indeed, the philosophy of science threw sand into the gears of science for a while when it insisted on the "hypothetico-deductive" process—that is, first making a formal speculation and then limiting the empirical and statistical work to the test of the original hypothesis. This is a perfect recipe for blinding yourself to new discoveries. On the other hand, working systematically down the series of steps can be extremely useful in helping you find your way out of confusion or saving you from forgetting some important activities.

Summary

The feature that distinguishes scientific from nonscientific knowledge-getting is *not* a special body of techniques, but rather the use of procedures that are disciplined instead of casual. The most important knowledge about the scientific method is knowledge of when the special discipline and techniques of science are necessary. The characteristics of a situation that call for such disciplined procedures are when the situation is complex, varied, and off-again-on-again, rather than simple, tight, and with immediate cause and effect. Other characteristics that call for scientific methods are (1) the existence of possible personal bias, (2) multiple, hidden, or reverse causation, and (3) the presence of large volumes of events and data.

Notes

1. Bob Levey, *Washington Post*, February 16, 1987, p. C17.
2. Geoffrey Norman, "The Hustle and Hypocrisy of Andrew Young's Atlanta," *American Spectator* (June 1988): 24.
3. Julian L. Simon and Paul Burstein, *Basic Research Methods in Social Science*, 3d ed. (New York: Random House, 1985).

Chapter 13

Assessing Consequences
and Likelihoods

Brief Outline

- Range of Procedures That Can Help You Make Estimates
- Some Principles for Estimating Costs and Benefits
- Estimating Probabilities
- Summary
- Exercises

How much would it cost to construct a building like that one over there? How many baseball gloves should your store plan to sell this spring if you price and advertise them as you did last year? What is the probability that a vaccine against AIDS will be discovered in the next five years at the current rate of government support of AIDS research? What are the chances that you will be a good enough violinist to make a living playing professionally?

The Promise: This chapter does not promise to help you get *sure* answers to these questions. But it does promise to give you devices that will reduce the amount of uncertainty about events in the future.

Range of Procedures That Can Help You Make Estimates

Estimating the likelihood of the good and bad consequences that may follow a given course of action, and attaching values to them, are crucial activities in determining the overall "present value" of the option being considered. There usually are many possible ways of making estimates, based on some blend of abstract ideas, the body of theory in a science, information already available, information you will develop from scratch, experience and ideas of other people, and other modes of operation of the human brain.

Sometimes you can do most or even all of the job with systematic scientific procedures of the sort described in the previous chapter. For example, if you wish to know the probabilities for sales of various quantities of baseball gloves in your store in April, a systematic study of the April sales in the past four or five years, combined with the forecasting techniques described in chapter 5, will probably provide a very reliable "probability distribution," as the result is called. But if this is the first year your store is open, you have no history to analyze scientifically, and hence you must use other methods of the sort described in this chapter.

Or, how good a chance is there that a space launch will blow up before getting into orbit? Or that a vaccine against AIDS will be discovered before the year 2005? Or that the Roman Catholic Church will allow women to serve as priests as of the year 2020? These questions are different from the sort that are usually tackled with standard methods of empirical research. This chapter discusses a few selected issues in the practice of guesstimating answers to such questions. The estimation task is closely related to the discussions of experts, libraries, and scientific inquiry in chapters 11 and 12, and to the assessment of your basic values discussed in chapter 1.

Sometimes an estimate is expressed as a single physical quantity, as, for example, the response to "How many people do you think will show up for the concert tonight?" And sometimes the estimate is expressed as the *probability* of a given "simple" event, such as the discovery of an AIDS vaccine. This chapter concentrates on the special problem of phrasing the estimate in the form of the probabilities associated with the event.

The Modes of Thought That Come into Play

The main modes of thought that enter into estimation may be characterized as, on the one hand, *speculative* or *theoretical* or *engineering calculations* and, on the other hand, *historical*, *experiential*, or *empirical*. The estimation may be any possible combination of the two modes. If the process is mainly experiential and if the experience is systematically gathered, the process is that described in chapter 12. The remarks in this chapter refer to the theoretical mode, and its combination with unsystematically gathered experience using various heuristics.

It is common for theory and experience to contend for dominance, either within your own thinking or between two people working on the same estimate. In my experience, people tend to give too much weight to abstract thinking and too little to the available data. When a body of experience is available, I recommend that you lean on it to the greatest extent possible, and almost never push it aside in favor of theorizing. Of course there are situations when it is prudent to ignore the data completely and rely wholly on the theory—for example, if a small set of observations suggests that a higher price of wood produces more sales than does a lower price, or that drinking alcohol improves people's golf scores—but such situations are rare.

Some Principles for Estimating Costs and Benefits

1. *Ensure that all the relevant costs and benefits are included and none are forgotten.* It is amazingly easy to overlook a crucial factor—for example, the raw materials needed, or the cost of taxes—when estimating the cost of a building or the benefit of the learning you will acquire in the course of a job. With respect to costs, the best technique for ensuring that all crucial factors are included is to refer to past experience, because it necessarily embodies all the relevant factors.

Let's consider the issue in the context of estimating costs in a business situation.

More specifically, imagine estimating the expenditures connected with a task with which the firm already has a great deal of experience—say, a construction firm concerned with a bid on a small parking lot of the sort that the firm has done many times before. Another example might be a firm that has manufactured only one product—say, men's shirts—and wishes to estimate the cost of a batch. A third example is estimation of the cost of another hamburger shop to a chain-franchising operation.

A firm with considerable relevant experience may estimate cost directly from its own records. In the case of another hamburger shop, the estimate may simply be the average total cost of shops recently built by the chain, as already computed by them. In the case of the parking lot or excavation, the construction firm may be able to estimate with good accuracy the amounts required of the main components, labor and machine time, and their current prices. The shirt manufacturer may have to do a more detailed analysis to estimate the cost of a batch of shirts if the garments have design specifications. That firm may consult its past purchase records for quantities and prices of yarn, buttons, wrapping, labor, and so on.

Even if your firm has a great deal of experience with a process, however, cost estimation may run into many snags. For example, the firm may want information about costs at output levels different from those it has produced at before, and it may not have sufficient records about the inputs necessary to operate at those output levels. One must also check that there was no stockpiling and no depletion of stockpiles during past observation periods. And, of course, machines with long lives are a big problem. Because of the change of technology over time, records alone may not show what the relevant expenditures on machinery will be during the period for which the decision will be made (which must almost always be a long time period if there are long-lived machines). Perhaps the only case in which all the necessary information on equipment costs could come from records would be where the firm does construction or other jobs on an ad hoc contractual basis—rents all its equipment and hires workers for the one job only.

If the firm does not have direct experience with the process being costed, then it must make (or have made) an analysis of the process, together with estimates of the requirements for each aspect of the job. For example, after it has built a hundred identical McDonald's hamburger franchises, the firm can refer directly to its records to learn the necessary inputs of wood, tile, paint, plumbing labor, carpentry labor, and so on. But before it has built the first such shop, the firm must get, from architects, engineers, and contractors, estimates of how much of each input the planned building would require. These construction experts analyze the various operations required and measure the extent of each operation (such as the number of electrical outlets needed). Then they estimate the material and labor required for each aspect of the work on the basis of their general knowledge and experience with similar projects.

Big construction projects such as dams or spacecraft for moon shots exemplify jobs whose cost estimation draws little from past records and requires careful analysis by engineers and designers. But even in already operating assembly-line operations, one must often use engineering analysis to estimate the relevant expenditures, especially when dealing with new or altered items. For example, an auto manufacturer needs to know the outlays on material and labor and the amount of assembly-line time that will be required for various proposed new models of cars. The aspects of the car that continue the same as in the past years can be costed from past years' records; but the new aspects must be costed by analysis done by designers, engineers, and skilled crafts-men. Analysis is also necessary when a firm considers producing a quan-tity of output at a level of capacity different from the one at which it has been working. For example, if the highest previous level of operation has been 10,000 units per week, and the firm wants to know the expen-ditures relevant to producing 15,000 units a week, the judgment of su-pervisors, plant engineers, maintenance men, and so on must be sought and used.

Movie-making is an industry in which cost estimation is notoriously treacherous. Films that started out with budgets of $30 million have ended up costing $300 million (and then flopped!). Perhaps careful esti-mation can be done for such items as travel, set construction, and so on. But how can one predict in advance that the female star will get furious at the male star and walk off the set halfway through the filming?

In costing new operations, experimentation is particularly useful. Consider the example of an engineer who wants to estimate the cost of digging a foundation for a building in half-frozen ground for the new pipeline, in an area where no building has been done before. He may put a man on a bulldozer to work for a day to see how fast the work goes. Or, if a shoe manufacturer wants to determine the cost of a new style, she often may have the people at the benches try out some of the necessary operations to see how long they take and to find out how much material is required. Experimentation is also used as an adjunct to other estima-tion methods to fill gaps in records or knowledge.

Experiential Versus Theoretical Estimations

The two ways of estimating cost—theoretical engineering calculations and historical experience—are mirrored in the two modes of estimation in many other circumstances. In medicine, for example, a physician may attempt to estimate the likelihood that a patient who has had a stroke will have another stroke on the basis of the patient's "risk factors" of weight, smoking behavior, blood pressure, race, and cholesterol, per-haps adding in the physician's specific knowledge of this patient's physi-cal and mental condition, using the physician's knowledge of the scientific literature but without relying on specific calculations. This is called the *clinical* approach. Or the physician may focus only on the statistics that an average person who has had one stroke will have an-other, an experiential approach. If there are no such statistics, the physician would have to rely on the clinical approach, but in the presence of such data, it would be poor thinking to ignore them. It would also be poor thinking to rely *only* on the *average* data without taking into account the specific characteristics of *this* patient. Raw statistics on the entire population that do not present separately the information by the categories of risk are too broad, and the physician would be wise to adjust such aggregate data in light of the patient's particular risk factors. That is, it would be wise to make engineering-type adjustments to the experiential information in such a situation. An even better prediction for a given patient could be developed using formal methods of statistical analysis, but not even the best physicians have gone this far yet. And too many of them simply ignore the experiential data and proceed on clinical judgment alone—whatever that means—often because they are not comfortable with statistical data.

Another example of the tension between theory and experience is found in estimating the availability of raw materials in the future based on geological and Malthusian theory, versus the history of raw-material scarcity based upon prices throughout human history. The two approaches give diametrically opposed predictions, with the latter being the approach that is validated by history, of course.

The issue is not simply theory versus empirical knowledge in the abstract, but rather how good the particular theory and data are. A good theory will fit the known facts reasonably well, and is soundly constructed; a bad theory does not do so, and is worse than no theory. Yet abstractions have an amazing power to bewitch us, and perhaps the more so if we have more education. An example is the theory of economies of scale in manufacturing, the cornerstone of government monopoly operation under the banner of greater efficiency. But this theory leaves out the stimulating forces of competition and the deadening effect of their absence, which accounts for government monopoly doing worse than private enterprise in almost every case—even the extreme (and amazing) case of competing electric utilities up and down the same streets.

Typically, bad theories leave out a crucial factor—as for example, the importance of energizing competition in the electrical-utility example above—or include a wrong assumption—such as the Marxian theory that people will work just as hard for the community when they do not feel exploited by the capitalist class as they do when they own the enterprise (such as the farm). This assumption has since the 1990s been massively discredited by the happenings in Eastern Europe.

2. *It is important to ensure that all the important impacts, upon all the people and groups that are affected, are brought into the estimation.* The failure to do so is one of the great errors in thinking, discussed at length in chapter 15. Sometimes the effect is merely offensive to one's tastes or values, as when people in (for example) the United States quantify the loss of life in the Vietnam War only with respect to American lives, omitting the loss of Vietnamese and others. Sometimes the effect is socially destructive, as when a chemical plant takes into account only its own direct costs and ignores the costs to the community of the pollutants that it dumps into the river. Other examples of focusing only on the "seen" and neglecting the "unseen" effects may be found in chapter 15.

Sometimes even obvious elements are neglected because the estimation seems difficult. A university is likely to ignore the value of a piece of land in its building plans simply because the accountants find it difficult to assign a value to the land.

Here are some of the factors often neglected when estimating the overall value of a course of conduct: (1) Knowledge gained. A wise person or business will often take on a job that does not seem obviously profitable in order to learn skills that can be valuable later on. This includes information about the environment as well as individual knowhow. (2) Credit and reputation. An activity that enhances those crucial elements leaves you better prepared for the future; a detrimental activity does the opposite. (3) Attention. The number of activities that you can keep your eye on is limited. When you hire someone to paint your house, you must count as a cost the attention you will have to pay to make sure the job is getting done right. You may decide that a more expensive painter, whom you will not need to check on at all, would be a better buy, or you may even decide to forgo having the job done because you cannot afford to divert attention to it.

3. *Subjective benefits and costs are very slippery.* What is the money cost to *you* of sitting and reading this hour? Costs other than money? How do *you* learn *my* costs of sitting here? How do I learn what my costs will be *five years* from now? One of the greatest difficulties in thinking about costs and benefits is that your assessment of them right now may be importantly different than your assessment of them later on, after the event is over. The shock of jumping into cold water seems insignificant after you jump, but beforehand it looms so large that you may shilly-shally about jumping for many minutes. And the value of

making a trip to the deathbed of a dying friend may come to loom larger in your mind years after the friend dies.

It often helps to assess these costs and benefits if you try to imagine that now it is five years later. Ask yourself how you would assess the cost or benefit from that perspective.

These later-on assessments tie into the subject of making binding commitments. A method of integrating this present-standpoint distortion into your decision-making apparatus is described in chapter 5.

4. *The tougher and more important the issue, usually the less information there is to go on.* It is in the nature of important issues that they come along infrequently, and each one is different than others. Hence there is little information to draw on when a very important issue arises. If the situation becomes repetitive, information accumulates. Before the first prototype aircraft is built, there are great "unk-unks"—industry slang for unknown unknowns. Afterward, learning reduces the uncertainty greatly.

Estimating Probabilities

Every estimate is a matter of estimating probabilities. If you estimate that a building is 500 feet high, you may not actually add "give or take 75 feet," but some such assessment of the possible error in your estimate is implicit. And even that sort of statement is a vague substitute for the "probability distribution"—the probability of the building's being between 400 and 425 feet high, the probability of its being between 425 and 450 feet high, and so on. In that fashion, every estimate is implicitly a distribution of probabilities.

Probabilities can be known with considerable reliability if a great deal of data exists. For example, probabilities of death by age and sex for randomly selected individuals may be estimated on the basis of large amounts of experience, as may the probability of outcomes on a roulette wheel. In other cases, one feels as if the probability is being picked out of the air almost without foundation. For example, our family once was in Chaco Canyon when drops of rain began to fall. The road was a dirt track. Would we be unable to leave because of mud if we did not leave immediately? Would we be trapped in mud if we did leave? We had nothing to go on, no knowledge of the likelihood of heavy rain in that desert area, no knowledge of the effect of rain on the road, and so on. Nor did we have any way of obtaining information. Yet we had to make some estimates in order to decide what to do. (I remember that we decided to leave, and we made it successfully, but I do not remember how we reasoned.)

Mortality estimates are considered to be "objective," in contrast to our "subjective" estimates about being trapped in Chaco Canyon mud. There is much philosophical discussion relevant to these matters, but from an operational point of view we treat these probabilities in identical fashion. Some statisticians worry that people inevitably estimate subjective probabilities in a fashion that will fool themselves. Maybe. But there is no alternative to making such probability estimates.

Decision-makers[1] do not enjoy estimating probabilities. Physicians, for example, often say it cannot be done. But there is plenty of evidence that people will and can estimate probabilities with some accuracy.

Sometimes it is necessary to push hard on oneself, or on someone else, to extract the probability estimates—a process neatly called "executive psychoanalysis." The devices sketched out in this section should, however, help you to extract meaningful and useful probability estimates.

The probability-estimation process discussed here is intended for use in all kinds of decision-making—business, politics, war, or other policy or action situations. Estimating probabilities for use in "pure" science is a subcategory of the estimation procedures described here and is subject to special limitations to which probability estimation for decision-making is not subject. More later about probabilities in science.

Probability Estimation by the Decision-Maker

The operational estimate of a probability (or probability distribution) begins with an overall estimate by the decision-maker or deputy. For example, consider the situation in which the firm is making a decision about whether to raise its price. The likelihood of the main competitor's responding with a price raise is a crucial aspect of the price decision. The estimate of that likelihood will then probably begin as a rough horseback judgment by the executive in charge. If she is experienced and wise, the initial estimate may be sound; if not, not. The wise decision-maker uses all knowledge and mental facilities, taking everything into account that she can think of. This sort of estimate is informal and follows no explicit rules. But if the executive forces herself to organize her thinking on paper or for presentation to other people, she may thereby improve her thinking very greatly. This suggestion to use pencil and paper (or computer) may be the most useful one in the chapter.

If the decision is an important one, and if the decision-maker is willing to do some even harder thinking, he may be able to improve his estimate by some mental gimmicks whose purpose is (1) to make sure that his thinking is consistent, and (2) to explore his mind for thoughts that have not yet come to light.

In addition to using the gimmicks below, your estimates of probabilities can benefit from keeping in mind the kinds of pitfalls in thinking discussed in part IV, chapters 14 and 15.

Gimmick 1. Make sure that the mutually exclusive probability estimates add to unity. It is, of course, just a *convention* (an agreed-upon definition) that probabilities add up to 1, but all our probabilistic reasoning is based upon this convention. Therefore you must arrange your estimates—in the simple two-possibility case, the probabilities of "yes" and "no"—to add up to 1.

It is often helpful to estimate *separately* the probabilities of "yes" and "no." This check often reveals inconsistency. For example, the executive might estimate the probability of a competitor's price raise as .40. If his assistant then asks him the chance that the competitor will *not* raise his price, the executive may say, "50–50." This reveals an inconsistency, because .40 and .50 do not add up to 1. Further thinking to resolve the inconsistency and make the probabilities add up to 1 should improve the estimate.

Gimmick 2. If you find it difficult to form a numerical probability estimate, it may help to proceed in stages. For example, first ask yourself whether the chance is more or less likely than 50–50. If less than .50, next ask yourself if you think the probability is closer to 0 or to .50. And so on.

Gimmick 3. Sometimes it is useful to compare your situation to a clearcut gambling machine, such as a thirty-two-slot roulette wheel. You might first ask yourself whether the likelihood in your situation is about the same as the probability of the ball falling into *one* of the thirty-two slots. If you feel that the probability is greater than that, then ask yourself whether the chance is about the same as the ball falling into one of *two* given slots of the wheel, or *three*, and so on. Then convert to probabilities.

Gimmick 4. As a consistency check, try actually making a small wager with a friend on the matter to be estimated. See whether you would be willing to bet $3 to $1, say, that the competitor will raise his price if you raise yours. After you find the worst odds at which you would be willing to take a bet that he *will* raise his price, turn the bet around and figure the worst odds you would take that he *will not* raise his price. Together these two sets of odds give an estimate for your decision. (It is worth noting that many people who say it is impossible to make probability estimates of business events, because there is no "scientific" basis to go on, have no reluctance or difficulty in making a bet on a football game.)

Gimmick 5. Use the "bet-yourself" technique, another consistency check.[2] Imagine that you will receive a big prize—say, a trip around the world—if you are right about whether an event will occur. Then ask which side of a wager you would pick concerning the probability of that event's occurring. For example, assume that you are trying to estimate the distribution of breakdowns that you can expect in the factory next year, and you must begin with an estimate of the median. You first guess that the median number is ten. Now ask yourself if you would bet on more, *or* on less, than ten breakdowns, with the round-the-world trip as a prize if you are correct. You answer that with considerable confidence you would bet on *more* than ten breakdowns. If so, your best guess of the median is more than ten, because you should be *undecided* about which way you would place the bet when the median has been correctly chosen. So now move your estimate of the median to, say, eleven, and ask which way you would then bet to get the prize. If you are then undecided, you can stop. But if you are still pretty sure you would bet on more than eleven, you must next consider a number higher than eleven as the median, and so on, until you reach the point at which you really are undecided about which way you would bet to receive the prize.

Gimmick 6. Sometimes it helps to ask yourself what *proportion* of such events would be "yes" *if the same situation were to be rerun 1,000 times.* This mental trick may produce an acceptable estimate even when it seems very difficult to attach an estimate to a single event in isolation.

Gimmick 7. Sometimes it helps to ask yourself—or the decision-maker you are assisting—for a *range* of probability estimates rather than just a single point estimate. For example, you may find it easier to estimate the probability of the competitor's raising his price, if you raise yours, as somewhere between 30 and 50 percent, rather than a point estimate of 40 percent. If the range is thus fairly narrow, you can safely work with the midpoint in subsequent calculations.[3]

Gimmick 8. As is true of other approximations, it is often wise to break the estimation job into constituent parts if there are several identifiable important aspects to it. For example, you might wish to estimate the probability that a competitor will bring out a plastic contact lens if you do so. And you know that the likelihood of his doing so depends heavily on his being willing to invest money in research and development to develop the necessary new technology. Instead of estimating in one jump the probability of his bringing out the plastic lens, you might separately estimate the probabilities for the two stages. After you estimate these sets of probabilities separately, you can multiply the two probabilities to get an unconditional probability estimate for the overall event.

If there are more than a very few identifiable events that may have an influence on the outcome, you *may* be better off estimating the probability of the outcome in a single jump rather than building a fairly complex tree composed of many probabilities, all of which are uncertain. But, on the average, breaking a complex sequence of events such as a plan into its constituent parts has been shown to lead to more accurate estimation.[4] Estimates made directly about the probability of success for a plan tend to be more biased toward a successful outcome than are estimates that take into account the probabilities of the individual events that must occur if the plan is to succeed. Perhaps this is because when one makes an estimate of the probability of success directly, one tends to focus on the first event that must occur, and then lets that number influence the overall estimate. For example, assume we are estimating the probability that a building will be completed a year from now. The number of hitches that can occur, contingent on one another, is very large. But if we do not take each of them into account very explicitly, we may find that the high probability of the first event—acquiring the land, which has a probability of, say, 70 percent—influences our immediate view of the overall success of the project.

In the previous example, the estimation task was broken into separate sequential stages. Another situation where it may be wise to break up an estimation job is where there may be several *alternative* events to the one you are interested in. Consider, for example, a firm bidding on the contract to produce 2,500 Puritanian flags. Assume there are five other possible competitors. One might simply estimate directly the likelihood of *none* of them bidding lower than some specified bid—say, $20,000. Another procedure is to estimate the likelihoods for each of them individually, and then to combine the probabilities.

Perhaps you estimate their probabilities of not bidding under $20,000 as follows:

Firm	Probability
A	.7
B	.8
C	.7
D	.9
E	.9

If so, the probability of *none* of them bidding under $20,000 is .7 x .8 x .7 x .9 x .9 = .32, and that is your probability of your making a successful bid at $20,000.

It is interesting and useful to know that if you do not break up a *sequential* situation, such as a construction plan, into stages, you tend to *overestimate* the likelihood of a "success" occurring. But if you do not break up a *simultaneous* event, such as a bid, into the various other events, you tend to *underestimate* the probability of a "success."[5]

Gimmick 9. Ask some other qualified people to estimate the probabilities, and find a consensus by comparing the estimates. The best people to choose (and obviously the hardest to find) are those who are well informed but have no emotional involvement in the situation.

The Delphi technique is a systematic technique for developing the consensus of a group of people. First, people are asked for their individual estimates of the probabilities. Then they are presented with the estimates of all the other people and asked how they will change their own estimates, if at all. If a respondent's new estimates are still far away from the group's previous average, the respondent is required to offer an explanation. Then the process is repeated, a total of perhaps three or four times. There is some reason to believe that the last set of probabilities is better than the first set in many cases, if only because people have had to think harder about their estimates as time goes on. Of course, the possibility exists that some of the people who hold "far out" views are right and the majority wrong, in which case the Delphi process could lead to progressively worse estimates. So the process is imperfect—but so is life.

We have been working with the yes-or-no type of probability estimate. In many cases one works instead with the estimation of a probability distribution with a wider variety of possibilities. Demand and cost functions are common examples. But this technique may be left to more technical works (for example, my *Applied Managerial Economics*[6]).

Keep a Record of Your Own Estimates for Calibration

It may be instructive and useful to keep a record of your own probability estimates, and then examine how they compare with actual outcomes. This is especially useful if you are engaged in estimating some series of repeated events, such as the demand for various kinds of musical performers. If you find out that you systematically overestimate or underestimate, you can try to make corrections in advance for your propensity.

Perhaps the most pervasive cause of bias toward over- or underestimates is the estimator's emotional state—his hopes and fears, his optimism and pessimism, the rewards and punishments that he expects contingent upon various possible outcomes. One device suggested earlier to get around this bias is to solicit judgments from people who are not involved actually or emotionally. But often this device is not feasible. Perhaps the best tactic in estimating probabilities when one is involved is to *make explicit* to oneself what one's feelings are. And the best way to do this is by writing them down, as honestly as one can. Once the feelings are out in the open and labeled, one can try to counteract them in the estimates.

Summary

Estimating probabilities is difficult, but it must be done. The better one's information about the situation, the better the estimate is likely to be. Sometimes the probability estimate can be made on the basis of existing information. Sometimes experts should be consulted on scientific research undertaken.

Various devices can help you extract reasonable probability estimates from yourself. You should separately estimate the probabilities of both "success" and "failure" to see that they add up to 1. You may proceed in stages, beginning with the midpoint and then estimating midpoints between other points. You may make wagers with yourself or with others to make the matter more immediate and to check your feelings. And often it is useful to make a range of estimates—or "high," "low," and "medium" estimates—instead of just a single point estimate. And if the planned alternative has several events in sequence, or if there are several possible outcomes alternative to the one you are interested in, it is helpful to estimate the probabilities of the separate events and then to combine them.

gated by the various devices discussed in this chapter. But the greater danger comes from one's emotional situation—one's hopes and fears, expected rewards and punishments, influencing one's judgment. The only antidote is to make one's feelings explicit in as honest a manner as possible.

Exercises

1. Estimate the probabilities that you will find employment at various salaries when you next look for a job, and tell the bases for your estimation.

2. How would you go about estimating the probabilities of various quantities of this book being sold next year? After it is revised the next time?

3. A man and wife teach psychology and physics respectively at Bluewater State University. They want to move to the University of Hawaii. How should they estimate the probabilities of their both finding jobs there? How about if they both teach psychology?

4. If Ford puts a backseat or side-door airbag into next year's cars as a standard item even though the law does not require it, what is the probability that General Motors also will in the following year at the latest? Chrysler? Both? What about other manufacturers? How should Ford go about making its estimate?

Notes

1. This material is more fully covered in Robert O. Schlaifer, *Analysis of Decisions Under Uncertainty* (New York: McGraw-Hill, 1969), especially when read in connection with Howard Raiffa, *Decision Analysis* (Reading, MA: Addison-Wesley, 1969). Many of the ideas in this chapter have been drawn from these two sources.

2. William A. Spurr and Charles P. Bonini, in *Statistical Analysis for Business Decisions*, rev. ed. (Homewood, IL.: Irwin-Dorsey, 1973), discuss this technique at length on pages 117–120.

3. A similar comment has been made about *all* estimations, probabilistic and nonprobabilistic, by Alain Enthoven:

We have found that in cases of uncertainty, it is often useful to carry three sets of factors through the calculations: an "Optimistic" and a "Pessimistic" estimate that bracket the range of uncertainty, and a "Best Estimate" that has the highest likelihood. These terms are not very rigorous. A subjective judgment is required. But it is surprising how often reasonable men studying the same evidence can agree on three numbers where they cannot agree on one. In fact, one of the great benefits of this approach has been to eliminate much senseless quibbling over minor variations in numerical estimates of very uncertain magnitudes. Alain C. Enthoven, "Economic Analysis in the Department of Defense," *American Economic Review* 53 (May 1963): 413–423.

4. Amos Tverksy and Daniel Kahneman discuss this matter in "Judgment under Uncertainty: Heuristics and Biases," paper written for the Fourth Conference on Subjective Probability, Utility, and Decision Making, Rome, 1973.

5. Ibid.

6. Julian L. Simon, *Applied Managerial Economics* (Englewood Cliffs, NJ: Prentice Hall, 1975), chapter 3.

PART IV

WORKING WITH INFORMATION AND KNOWLEDGE

Though the distinction is far from neat, let us distinguish between the *collection* of knowledge and the *analysis* of knowledge. Whereas part III discussed how to increase our stocks of ideas and information, part IV discusses the mental operations that we ought (or ought not) apply to the stocks of knowledge that we possess, in order to draw out the meaning of the information that we have in hand.

Chapters 14 and 15 discuss various pitfalls that may ensnare our thinking, and especially our judgments. There are lots of different ways we can befoul our thinking—logical fallacies, linguistic traps, faulty conclusions due to insufficient information-gathering, and uneven attention to the information that is available, among others. Many of the pitfalls in thinking that are discussed in this chapter are forms of lazy, undisciplined, casual thinking. They are the kinds of thinking that children employ when they are very young. Unbiased and error-free thinking is impossible in principle, and perfect rationality is not even a good standard of comparison. Chapter 15 offers some guides around the pitfalls so as to arrive more closely at mental clarity.

A person can take in only a tiny fraction of the sensations and information that are available and relevant to our activities. And our machinery for processing the information impinging upon us cranks out crude approximations at best. Therefore, the state of our knowledge and judgments is necessarily imperfect, and almost necessarily it is systematically biased in one direction or another.

A variety of factors—notably the traps embedded in the language we employ and the influence of our hopes and fears upon our judgments—often corrupt our judgmental processes so that we do not even come close to the feasible quality of thinking. Chapter 16 contains suggestions about how we can improve our judgments.

Habits and self-discipline are the subject of chapter 17. They may be the most important learning we do, because they control the learning of other subjects. If a child lacks the discipline to do homework or practice shooting baskets left-handed, that child will not become a skilled practitioner of algebra or basketball.

It came as something of a surprise to me that so much of part IV is drawn from my text on research methods. The techniques that are appropriate for collecting and analyzing scientific data are also appropriate for the data that we work with in our everyday lives, both private and public. And the errors in our everyday judgments stem from the pitfalls that are much the same as the obstacles that must be overcome if a scientific study is to be valid.

This similarity between valid scientific and everyday thinking has been emphasized recently by psychologists who study "cognitive thought"—that is, the processes with which we infer conclusions from the data that impinge upon our lives (for example, Nisbett and Ross 1980). This is one of the welcome converging movements among the branches of knowledge. Cognitive psychologists also discern cost-benefit evaluations in our everyday thinking that are similar to the cost-benefit evaluations of obtaining more or better information that are a central feature of managerial economics. The students of mental disorder who group under the label "cognitive therapy" also see cost-benefit processes at work. This is another such movement of convergence.

Finally, chapter 18 discusses interpersonal relationships, including the art of negotiation and skills needed for motivating and supervising peers, subordinates, partners, and other types of colleagues in a wide range of situations.

Chapter 14

Pitfalls That Entrap Our Thinking

Brief Outline

- Two Helpful Tactics
- The Main Types of Pitfalls and Fallacies
- The Classical Logical Pitfalls
- Pitfalls in Dealing With Information
- Fallacies in the Way We Use Language
- Summary

When I was nine years old, we moved to a block with a tree nursery at the end of it. The nursery seemed as huge as a jungle to us kids. (As an adult I am shocked at how small an area it covers—about large enough for two houses back-to-back.) In our game "tribe war," one of our favorite stratagems was to dig an "Ethiopian elephant pitfall trap"—a pit in the path covered with slight sticks and grass for concealment—and then lead the other tribe of two or three boys through the path in hopes that one would fall into the pit (all the way up to one knee). We never worried about spraining joints or breaking bones, of course.

Those elephant traps are my image of the pitfalls that we face in thinking clearly, except that the thinking traps are not created by malicious nature to trap any of us in particular. Rather, they lie in wait for all of us impartially, without design. But if we do not learn to avoid them, we fall again and again, which not only prevents us from getting ahead, but also engenders such fear of falling that we stand immovable in one spot.

This chapter promises to help you spot and recognize the signals of impending pitfalls.

Two Helpful Tactics

Two tactics help avoid pitfalls. First, know the pitfalls so that you can spot their signs, the way a wary elephant somehow senses that something is amiss and steps around the trap, or tests it gingerly with a foot. Second, go slowly, do not be induced into running heedlessly by others running before you, and test every abstract idea against the concrete experience of first-hand knowledge and scientific data. Do not think that the path is safe just because others seem to run safely in it. The saying "Make speed slowly" fits well here.

The Main Types of Pitfalls and Fallacies

Now we proceed to the more technical task of analyzing some of the main pitfalls to help you identify them before they trap you. The more you read about the fallacies, the more sensitive to them you will become.

Fallacies are here classified as failures of *logic, evidence, language, relevance* (perhaps including relevant comparisons), and *overconfidence.* Most fallacies could easily be classified under a heading different from the heading under which I put them, however.

Perhaps the use of the familiar concept of fallacies is itself a fallacy. The types of thinking under discussion here are perfectly normal among children, and we expect such thinking from them. Part of the maturation process consists of forgoing these childish ways of cognition in favor of more disciplined thinking. The maturation process in cognition has some parallel to the process by which a person acquires the discipline to focus the mind in disciplined thought for longer and longer periods. Schools help in the latter process by giving gradually increasing amounts of homework, and requiring longer periods of quiet for pupils. And objective reality gradually forces adults to change more and more from childish ways of thinking to mature ways. But reality is never a perfect teacher of sound cognition, especially for those persons who are endowed with gifts such as wealth, beauty, and mental and verbal agility that enable them to get what they want without having to exert disciplined thought and effort. Hence the "fallacies" discussed here may just as well be thought of as childish modes of thought that have not yet been left behind.

The Classical Logical Pitfalls

The study of logic, and of the logical fallacies, has traditionally been offered as a means of improving your purposeful thinking.[1] But *deductive logic is only one part of reasoning*, and reasoning is only one part of thinking. The *quality of the facts* that one adduces obviously matters greatly. If you assume that energy is getting more scarce when in fact it has been becoming less scarce over the centuries, a logical argument based on a premise of increasing scarcity will necessarily be unsound even though its logic may be airtight. The quality of the theories you use matters, too. If you invoke the simple Malthusian theory that the scarcity of oil *must* eventually increase because there is a limited amount of oil and we use some of it up, yet this theory is inappropriate because we create more oil by growing oil-bearing plants, then your conclusion will be unsound though your deductive logic may be airtight.

Confusion of Assumptions and Facts

Enormous energy is wasted and wrong paths are taken because people make assumptions contrary to the facts and proceed with their deductive theorizing on the basis of those assumed (but wrong) facts.

The most serious drawback of logic is that the propositions it studies are misleading examples of the intellectual material that we must come to grips with. Studies of logic tend to utilize isolated arguments such as "Mammals breathe through lungs. Whales are mammals. Whales therefore breathe through lungs." But most of our thinking concerns propositions that are interlocked with many other propositions, usually in a hierarchical fashion, and therefore cannot be evaluated in isolation. It is the relationship of a proposition to the entire body of our thinking that creates the most subtle problems, but the most important ones. For example, the Malthusian argument about the scarcity of oil is itself a branch of an entire tree of theory and data, and the statement about oil therefore cannot be sensibly evaluated without reference to the entire hierarchy of arguments. This is typical of scientific work. Focusing on single isolated propositions distracts our attention from that larger task.

The classical logical fallacies are variations on a single theme: a faulty or missing link in the argument. The arguer gets away with this if the audience is not paying attention. The obvious protection against logical fallacies is to check every link in the argument.

Circularity, Tautology

One of the neatest ways to err is to logically pull yourself up by your own bootstraps using a tautological argument or adducing a circular process. For example, in 1973 there was a great deal of newspaper coverage of an oil price increase due to international tensions, and the term "energy crisis" was used frequently. Then public polls asked people whether they thought there to be a serious problem concerning energy, and of course large numbers of people agreed because of the press coverage. Then politicians and the newspapers adduced the results of the polls as grounds for arguing that there were grounds for governmental action to deal with the "energy crisis." By this time the high prices had abated, but the results of the polls that had in effect been manufactured by the misleading press coverage and political statements were now being used as the evidence to prove that action was needed.

Begging the question, and *circular reasoning* are two varieties of assuming that something is so just because it is said to be so. You beg the question (really, you beg that an assumption will be accepted) when you say, "Will you grant that statement A is true? If so, then we can deduce that . . . " And you go on from there. Or you just keep repeating A until it seems believable just because it has been heard so often.

The circular fallacy consists of proving A with B, and then proving B with A. "Why should you believe in God? Because the Bible says so. Why should you believe what the Bible says? Because it is the word of God."

Non Sequitur

In Latin "non sequitur" means "it does not follow." That is, there is a break in the logic of the argument. For example, in centuries past, in anti-Jewish riots in Russia (pogroms) this cry was frequently heard: "Save Mother Russia. Beat up the Jews." There is no stated connection between the two ideas. But amidst the passions of riots, the hearer does not pay attention to the break in the argument and simply acts as if one proposition implies the other.

Post Hoc Ergo Propter Hoc

The Latin title of this fallacy means "After it and therefore because of it"—that is, because B came after A, A is assumed to have caused B. But do the birds that fly south cause winter to follow? Precedence alone is a very weak test of causation. It is at the same level of thinking as the superstition that because every time you had cornflakes for breakfast you did well in the tennis match, cornflakes cause you to play well. At best this is a clue to investigate dietary influences, rather than reasonable proof of a causal effect.

Indeed, *no* purely logical argument alone can establish causality. In a complex situation, the decision to describe a relationship as causal is subtle and requires judgment.

False Alternative

"If you are against abortion, you must work for a law against it." This fallacy is rather obvious: You may think that abortion is a bad thing, but also think that a law against it is even worse. Or you may be against abortion but judge that the effort to have it made illegal is even worse.

The rhetorical device known as "false alternative" attempts to box you into a corner from which you cannot escape except by accepting the speaker's desired alternative. It does so by implicitly suggesting that there are only two alternatives, one that you do not accept and the other the speaker's desired alternative. But usually there are many other alternatives. To avoid being dragged into this fallacy, you need only use your imagination to postulate other alternatives, and have the force of personality to deny the speaker's false narrowing of the alternatives.

Long Chains of Reasoning

The longer the chain of argument, the harder it is to check every link in the chain, and therefore the easier it is for an undetected fallacy to occur. A computer program is a nice example of a chain of logical argument. It is obviously easier for an error to slip by when a program contains hundreds or thousands of lines of programming code, all interrelated to other lines of code with a myriad of connections running every which way, than when a program contains just three or four lines of code where the logic is easy to grasp and an error therefore is obvious to your eye. The same is true of a long argument in mathematics or symbolic logic.

The longer and more complex the argument or computer program, therefore, the more important it is to check it, not only by examining its logic but also by examining the output to see if it makes sense and squares with your everyday knowledge. All things being equal, therefore, a policy of a government or an organization that hinges on a shorter line of argument is more attractive than a policy that hinges on a longer line of argument that ostensibly proves that the policy is sound.

Reasoning by Analogy

Analogies are fine to help the listener understand. But they are not a mode of proof.

"Like jumping from the Empire State Building and reporting that it is fine as one passes the 40th floor."

"Giving cheap energy to the United States is like giving a machine gun to an idiot."

Pitfalls in Dealing With Information

Gathering and evaluating information is a skill. If you do it poorly, your thinking suffers. Lack of skill is a bit different than a fallacy, however, because the same actions that are unsound in one situation are sound in another situation. The key questions about evidence are *which* and *how much*—how much evidence to gather, how much attention to give to particular pieces of evidence, which evidence you should consider relevant, and so on.

Let's briefly classify the places where error may occur: *First*, the aspects of gathering and evaluating evidence are: (1) the *elements* (observations), (2) the *dimensions* (variables), (3) the *deductive logic* used, (4) the *devices* used to extend the data, (5) predisposing *abstractions* (theories and world views), (6) *mechanisms* used, and (perhaps surprisingly) (7) the *honesty* of your character. *Second*, for each of these aspects of the information-developing process, there are issues about (1) what to *include*, (2) what to *emphasize and de-emphasize* (the weights given to various elements), and (3) what to *exclude*. Space is lacking to cover this classification systematically, so I'll simply touch on some high points.

Many fallacies result from a lack of scientific discipline. Indeed, fallacy and scientific discipline are the names of the two opposite sides of the same coin. Hence I'll refer frequently to chapter 12, which discussed scientific methods for gathering information.

We tend to gather and process information in ways that are convenient for us.[2] This implies that the information that is closest at hand, easiest to notice, and most familiar to us is more likely to enter into our thinking than information that is harder to come by and less distinct. Sometimes this economy of thought works well. Sometimes, however, we risk falling into error by collecting information hit-or-miss, the easy way.

The fallacy of *post hoc ergo propter hoc* is an example of this kind of erroneous thinking. The event that precedes another event comes to mind as the cause simply because it is the most available explanation of the occurrence.[3] The "availability heuristic" has in recent decades been found by cognitive psychologists (following Tversky and Kahneman) to be a powerful explanation of much of our behavior—a shortcut that often leads nowhere or worse.

We also use convenient similarities as a way of guessing the nature of new instances. For example, Jacques Barzun tells us that many professors pigeonhole a new student on the basis of her or his similarity to students they have taught earlier. This practice certainly saves a lot of time in studying the new student. (Barzun even recommends the practice.) But it is easy to be fooled by surface characteristics and hence to put the student into the wrong pigeonhole in your mind.

Even (or especially) scientists fall into this pitfall. You have probably read and believed, as I have, that air travel is safer than auto travel per mile. But driving 600 miles on a rural interstate highway by a 40-year-old seat-belted, alcohol-free driver in a car 700 pounds or more above average weight is slightly safer than an air trip of 600 miles. Also, driving 300 miles on the interstate is twice as safe as a 300-mile air trip. Surprise. And that's for the driver; a passenger sitting in back is even safer.[4] But then again, though fatalities may be no greater in such a highway trip, the rate of *injuries* is about *seventy* times as great as for an air trip. And for a young, drunk, unseat-belted driver of a small car on a winding country road, the fatality rate is more than a thousand times higher than the safe-situation rate.[5] Now how should we think about the matter? (For some purposes one might wish to compute a measure of "total accident bodily damage" by adding an economic measure of the cost of injuries plus fatalities, using the sort of valuations of injuries and deaths that a court might arrive at—very tricky business. Clearly determining your purpose in advance might be the toughest part of this exercise.)

These are some pitfalls that scientific discipline helps you avoid:

Insufficient Evidence and Neglect of Variability

A single swallow does not make a summer, and a single anecdote does not constitute proof of a general phenomenon. The fact that Simka had a happy time in Salt Lake City does not imply that Salt Lake City is the best place to go to have a happy time. But a single demonstration that an artificial heart keeps a patient alive does indeed prove that an artificial heart can work. This error of neglecting variability is so important that it is discussed at further length in the next chapter.

The point I want to hammer again (and again) is the importance of recognizing variability in a phenomenon, and responding to variability by collecting a sample of evidence large enough and representative enough to give you a reliable picture despite the variability, as in the chapter 12 example of the quality of taxi rides in various cities. (You can't also study in sufficient depth a sample before making a decision—a sample of potential spouses, for example. But you can try to learn from a variety of experiences belonging to others.)

Improper Weighting of the Elements of Evidence

A single vivid illustration can overwhelm a mass of other evidence. A single picture of a brand-new immigrant receiving welfare can overpower careful statistical study that shows that immigrant families receive less in welfare than do average native families. The impression of awesome power projected by a marching army on parade can lead to a decision to go to war, under the illusion that the enemy's power can be defeated. Somewhere I have read Gamal Nasser saying that such an impression influenced him to plan war on Israel in 1967. In the opposite direction, Charles de Gaulle wrote that Nazi parades of war equipment in 1937 convinced French observers in Berlin that Germany was undefeatable, which led to French concessions with respect to Central Europe.[6]

Another illustration: Many people who lived through the depression were so seared by the trauma of money worries that they saved obsessively in later years. The expression "Once burned, twice shy" accurately reflects this facet of our minds.

An important variant of improper weighting of the evidence arises from neglect of the *proportions* of the elements being considered. We often give equal weight to all the elements when they differ greatly in their importance and ought to be weighted very differently. This is like the story of the rabbit-and-horse stew—proportions 50–50, one rabbit, one horse. This error is discussed at greater length in the next chapter.

I fell into this pitfall yesterday. A friend told me that he was worried he had a brain tumor because he noticed that one eye was foggy, and he ran into a man who had had a foggy eye and it turned out to be a brain tumor. I reassured him that the odds probably were twenty to one in his favor because there must be twenty causes of a foggy eye other than a brain tumor. Today he called and told me good news—at worst it is a cataract, not a very serious matter nowadays. (It turned out to be nothing at all.) And I realized afterward that there may be a thousand (I'm guessing) cataract sufferers for each occurrence of brain tumor, let alone other explanations of a foggy eye, and hence the odds I gave him were way off the mark. I had made the elementary error of ignoring the *frequencies* of the explanations, and counting each one equally.

Unsound Biasing Preconceptions and Theories

The fallacy of being biased by unsound prior expectations is as big as the world—literally. Indeed, an unsound conclusion often stems from an unsound world view. For example, if you flip a penny ten times and get ten heads, you may expect a tail on the eleventh flip because you wrongly believe that there is a tendency for such things to "average out." (This is factually wrong, of course; as it is said, the coin has no memory.) Indeed, you may even "see" a tail on the eleventh flip though it really is heads, because you are so sure that it must come out that way, as a result of the unsound theory of "the law of averages."

Or you may have acquired the view that Asians work harder than other groups, and you may therefore "observe" that an Asian in your office works harder than anyone else even though this is not so.

Yet you must make *some* generalizations—about which type of dog is particularly friendly to children and which plants make you sneeze— or you could not get through the day.

Some people conclude from the evidence of the workings of bias that objective science and law are impossible, and they therefore argue that science and law can never be more "truthful" than a collision of political powers. But the fact that science cannot be *perfectly* objective does not imply that scientists cannot aspire to, and achieve, closer and closer approaches to truthful and objective work. They do so by constantly attending to possible biases and purging themselves of these biases to the considerable extent possible. And this is indeed possible for hardworking, conscientious individuals who are sincere in their attempts to get at the truth.

Biasing Hopes

"Hope springs eternal in the human breast." And a good thing it does, from the points of view of our happiness and our ability to deal with life successfully. If we had a correct vision of what will transpire, we might be downcast much of the time. As Will Durant wrote, "A short perspective is the best prescription for happiness."

Furthermore, "Where there's life, there's hope." That, too, is a good thing. But there can be too much of this good thing. Our hopes can be so out of line with the facts of the situation that our judgment is distorted. If survivors continue to believe that persons who are dead will return—as sometimes happens—this can injure their lives.

Hoping that one can pass an examination without studying for it can lead one not to study—with ill consequences. Hoping that one can safely swim across a wide body of water without company or supplies can be disastrous. Hoping that you can succeed in opening a restaurant where a dozen others have failed can cost you your life's savings.

Chapter 16 cites the evidence showing that people are systematically overconfident in the correctness of their judgments in many sorts of situations. Trying to keep in mind the propensity for hope to outrun the facts can help you temper your hope-influenced assessments with sounder judgments.

The Desire to Believe

Too often we fool ourselves because we want to believe in the proposition at hand rather than on the basis of evidence and sound arguments. We say, "I'll do it tomorrow," and allow ourselves to be convinced, though we put off the matter again and again with the same argument. This sort of thinking is a staple for all of us.

Our capacity to fool ourselves comes home to me every time I tiptoe so as not to wake someone up. I can feel myself mentally closing my ear passages to make it less likely that I will hear the sounds that I make. In other words, I have an almost built-in mechanism to convince myself that I am making less noise than I really am.

Fallacies in the Way We Use Language

"A human being is nothing but another species of animal."

Philosophers have known for centuries how easy it is for others—and among philosophers, too, or even *especially* among philosophers—to think unsoundly due to pitfalls that are hidden in language. Indeed, the entire body of philosophical pseudo-knowledge called "metaphysics" is a collection of linguistic fallacies. Some of these pitfalls are specific to certain languages, but the most important of them are the result of speaking *any* language, rather than being specific to particular languages.

Confusion Between Words and Entities

The root of linguistic fallacies is confusion between words and things. People often assume that because there is a word for something, the subject of the word is not just an illusion. This is a flaw in metaphysics. Just because philosophers have been talking about "the Good" for millennia does not imply that there is a meaningful entity corresponding to that term.

Consider the confusion created by the great biologist Konrad Lorenz by the use of such terms as "married love" for some behavior of geese. An unwary reader then asks (as one reviewer of a Lorenz book did): "What is married love?" and after associating a set of characteristics with the term—for example, a "commitment" to each other—goes on to say such things as "Would it not be nice if people could have the same commitment toward each other as geese do, instead of being fickle?" (You laugh? People make such errors all the time.)[7]

It helps if, instead of asking what a *word* "means," you ask what *people* mean when they use a word. It may be that there is no agreement on what they mean; if so, the word is a hopeless mass of confusion, as is often the case in metaphysical discussions.

The Operational Definition as a Tool of Clarification

A way to work toward agreement among people about a word is to forge an "operational definition," sometimes called a "working definition," which contains the *operations* to be used in identifying or measuring the phenomenon under discussion. Einstein's great breakthrough with the special theory of relativity was the substitution of an operational definition of time (Einstein defined time as that which you read on a clock) for a definition in terms of its supposed properties.

Just because a writer's language seems to you to be nothing but a mass of confusion, however, to others it may convey useful meaning—perhaps as poetry does rather than as physics does. This may be the situation with some theology (though some other theology may be simply muddle).

No one can be considered safe from such confusions—even the great Newton. The basis of Einstein's great achievement of special relativity was demonstrating that a definition of time with respect to its supposed properties—an idea that had been at the heart of Newton's thinking—was shot full of confusion. Einstein's next step was to replace the ideas of absolute time and absolute space with definitions based on the operations used to measure time—time is simply what one measured on a clock, and nothing more.

Even earlier, Ernst Mach—from whose writings Einstein learned much in his youth—wrote about this "illusory notion" of absolute time, saying, "It would appear as though Newton . . . still stood under the influence of the medieval philosophy. . . . It is an idle metaphysical conception."[8]

If Newton could fall into such a linguistic trap, think how easy it is for the rest of us to be entrapped by language.

The Confusing Verb "To Be"

Perhaps the most troublesome linguistic fallacies stem from the various forms of the verb for existence, "to be" and the common form "is." Especially in an ambiguous discussion, the term "is" (and its related terms such as "are" and "be") is [sic] one of the greatest sources of confusion in English. This verb has two very different uses—first to indicate equality or identity (as in "a car is an automobile" and "two and two are four"), and second, to serve as a joining word (a copula, as in "Jack is skinny" and "Sereno is a fool," examples of use as a "predicate"). People think that by understanding the "is," they learn about the world. I once met a man in a Costa Rican village who said he wanted to write a book on the subject of "What is a human?" He thought that by answering that question, he could somehow find great truths. He was a pleasant gentleman, but it is unlikely that anything except confusion would come out of that endeavor. (How is that for an example of the fallacy of non sequitur?)

One often hears related usages by biologists such as "At bottom, humans are a species of animal." Propositions of that sort then are the foundation of analyses that liken humans to animals and forecast a similar cycle of boom and bust and eventual extinction.

Other examples include: (1) Debates such as "Is statistics a science?" (2) The psychiatrist Erik Erikson's concept of "Who am I?"—that is, what is my "identity"? (3) People ask, "Is a fetus a person?" That is, they first decide whether a fetus "is" or "is not" a child, and then deduce from that definition a conclusion about what is to be done. If they answer "yes," they then conclude that "Destroying a fetus is murder"; if they answer "no," they conclude that the pregnant woman is not precluded from destroying it. Everything here hinges on the word "is." This is a typical example of why, in my view, this is [*sic*] the worst word in the English language—but indispensable. (Hebrew lacks such a word, but in the vernacular, people use a substitute form anyway.) Perhaps the law requires such categorizations as whether a fetus "is" a person. But apart from the law, I seldom find this usage necessary (though it is [*sic*] often convenient), and usually it is [*sic*] confusing when one is talking of morals.

The Use of "E-Prime"

The word "is" is at the root of the grave paradoxes in logic that required unraveling by the pathbreaking discoveries of Bertrand Russell and Alfred North Whitehead. It is a fascinating and illuminating, though difficult, exercise to try to speak or write without using any version of "is," or related terms such as "exist." The result is a purified English, which its inventor, David Bourland Jr., calls "E-prime."[9]

There are a zillion ways in which language can purposely be used to obscure meaning, all of them employed on occasion by politicians and advertisers (though this is not intended to suggest that most politicians and advertisers are not quite honest in their language; I believe them to be no less honest than people in other professions). Someone joked that advertising is the only profession to have invented an entirely new linguistic device, the "indefinite comparative." I see this device now on the dishwashing liquid bottle. "More Real Lemon Juice" says the label. More than what?

Advertising can also claim to have removed one part of our anatomy, the armpit, and replaced it with another, the underarm. Quite an evolutionary achievement, and just with the simple technique of euphemism.

The power of language to mislead us derives in considerable part from its nature as communicator of abstractions through its easy-to-absorb and often emotive symbols. In just three words, the slogan "Peace, Bread, and Jobs" conveys a great load of meaning to many people, enough to move people's minds and bodies. Effort and precise skill are necessary to elucidate what is meant by such slogans. But without such elucidation any reaction is just unthinking herd action.

Summary

Many of the pitfalls in thinking that are discussed in this chapter are forms of lazy, undisciplined, casual thinking. They are the kinds of thinking that children employ when they are very young. As people grow older, they tend to outgrow these practices in their occupational life, because if they use these practices on their job, they will lose their jobs (if they work for someone else) or their money (if they work for themselves). If you assert that square beer cans are better than round cans, and you run a brewery, you better have solid evidence that you are right before you change over to square cans. These are modes of thinking that simply do not work when put to the objective test.

Much of our life is not tested by objective reality in this fashion, however. In our personal lives, we express to others a wide variety of casual observations that are quite untested by fact. At a football game, you might tell your companion that square beer cans are better than round ones, and that breweries should make the shift, and even if you are wrong you can get away with it.

Danger arises when it is not easy to test your statements, and where it might matter if you are wrong—for example, when you give advice to a friend about the best city to move to for the practice of veterinary medicine, or if the price of farmland will go up or down in the next decade, or whether a proposed advertising campaign will be profitable. Even those whose profession is using sound research methods to check on the validity of their assertions—scientists, for example—often don't bother to apply the same standards of evidence outside of their professional work. Many scientists are remarkably unscientific in the views they express outside of their own specialties. And none of us can even come close to being perfect in this respect; there is not time enough in life to make a satisfactory check on most of the ideas we believe to be true—for example, that heating by electricity is more expensive than heating with gas where you live, or that a vacation in Africa will be cheaper than a vacation in South America. The best we can do is try to do better, or to understand which of the ideas we believe to be true are better supported by facts, and which are less well supported.

Notes

1. The following section closely follows David Kelley, *The Art of Reasoning* (New York: W.W. Norton, 1994), chapter 6, pp. 123–132, including some examples.

2. This section refers to the availability and representativeness heuristics of Tversky and Kahneman, as discussed in Richard Nisbett and Lee Ross, *Human Inference: Strategies and Shortcomings of Social Judgment* (Englewood Cliffs, NJ: Prentice-Hall, 1980), who review in a comprehensive and interesting fashion the evidence on reliability in human inference.

3. Amos Tversky and Daniel Kahneman, "The Framing of Decisions and the Psychology of Choice," *Science*, January 30, 1981, vol. 211, pp. 453–458.

4. Leonard Evans, Michael C. Frick, and Richard C. Schwing, "Is It Safer to Fly or Drive?—A Problem in Risk Communication," photocopy, n.d. William Freudenburg was kind enough to provide me with this information.

5. Discussion of Evans et al. in "Numbers Don't Lie—But They Can Mislead," Malcolm Gladwell, *Washington Post*, August 13, 1990, p. A3.

6. "On May 1, 1937, a complete Panzer division, with hundreds of aircraft flying over it, marched through Berlin. The impression produced on the spectators, and first and foremost on M. Francois-Poncet, the French ambassador, and on our military attaches, was of a force that nothing could stop—except a similar force." Charles de Gaulle, *The Complete War Memoirs* (New York: DaCapo, 1984), p. 26.

7. Stephen Jay Gould, review of *Konrad Lorenz* by Alec Nisbett, *New York Times Book Review*, February 27, 1979.

8. "Newton's Views on Time, Space, and Motion," in *The Science of Mechanics* (Chicago: Open Court, 1902), excerpted in *Philosophy of Science*, Arthur Danto and Sidney Morgenbesser, pp. 337–338 (Cleveland: Meridian, 1960).

9. Albert Ellis and Robert A. Harper changed to E-prime when they revised their excellent self-help book, *A New Guide to Rational Living* (Englewood Cliffs, NJ: Prentice-Hall, 1961; 1975), and they assure us that it clarified their thinking greatly. My knowledge of E-prime comes from the introduction to their book.

Chapter 15

My Favorite
Worst Sources of Errors

Causes of error abound, as the long list of pitfalls in chapter 14 demonstrates. But there are some pitfalls that are so frequent and so serious that they deserve special attention here. This chapter includes my personal selection of "favorite" pitfalls and fallacies. They are my favorites because they are interesting in the ways that they operate.

1. *Assuming that the source of a problem is the nature of the individual or group involved, when it is mainly the circumstances that cause the probability of the problem to be high.*

In the *Wall Street Journal* of June 26, 1989, a front-page story talked about how a 33-year-old woman, Deborah Dean, ran a corrupt operation involving billions of dollars at the U.S. Department of Housing and Urban Development (HUD). The story referred to her and her associates as "young adults" and a "kiddie corps." It asked: "Where were the grown-ups?"

Two pages later in the very same paper, a story about transfer of power after the Tiananmen Square massacre headlined "China's Old Men." The story referred to the Chinese leaders as "old guys in their 80s."

Both stories imply that the officials' ages are important determinants of their activities and decisions. The writers suggest that if people of more "appropriate" ages were put into office, the public would be better served.

These stories illustrate a recurrent fallacy in human thinking. In their book *Human Inference*, Robert Nisbett and Lee Ross[1] review data showing that people are likely to err by explaining events with recourse to the characteristics of the actors instead of the structural conditions of the situation. In both China and HUD, the key element is the existence of a governmental entity that puts money and/or power at the disposal of officials. As long as this condition exists, the likelihood of abuse exists. Sometimes the public gets lucky and the officials are honest and humble. But inevitably some officials will take advantage of the opportunities.

The solution, then, is not to call for better officials—of the right age, say, at which people are free of the urge to turn opportunities for money and power to their own advantage. The solution is to change the system.

It is interesting to wonder what Dean and Deng Xiaoping might have done had government jobs not been available and if they had applied their talents and energies in other fields instead. Deng might have clambered to the top of a huge firm in a swashbuckling industry such as ocean shipping. And Dean might have started a bang-up temporary employment firm and franchised it across the country, both enterprises to the great benefit of the public. Perhaps I give both of them too much credit on the skills side. But there is little doubt that the same people who choose the antisocial route in one set of circumstances will choose socially beneficial activities in another set of circumstances. One of the findings of modern psychology is that people tend not to be consistent about whether they are "honest" or "dishonest."

An experience of mine illustrates the principle. After I got out of the Navy, I took a summer course in organic chemistry to complete my qualifications for entering medical school in the fall; most of the other 200 students also were pre-meds. There were two hours of classes and six hours of laboratory work every day—forty hours a week, with lots of homework. The instructor put tough competitive pressure on the students to obtain high yields on their lab experiments. The tension in the laboratory rose so palpably that it became obvious that students would begin to cheat. I passed on that observation to a lab assistant, but nothing was changed. Two-thirds of the way through the course, the cheating began, and then the system broke down completely. The wholesale cheating was not due mainly to the character of the students, but rather to the structure of the system.

Indeed, sometimes the only difference is whether a society calls an activity legal and ethical or illegal and despicable. In the United States, a supermarket manager wins profit and praise for stocking delicacies and supplying them to customers who desire them and are willing to pay a handsome price. In the Soviet Union the outcome is different, as this incident shows: A few years back the director of Moscow's

Gastronom No. 1—a grocery store that sells gourmet foods to the elite—was put to death for selling delicacies like black caviar and wild boar out the back door. In the United States, he could use the front door and he would get a bonus for his initiative.

One of the great advantages of a market system is that people are enabled to make a wider variety of voluntary exchanges legally than in a system where prices are fixed centrally and where supply does not equal demand at the market price.

Of course individuals' values matter, and people will differ in how they behave in particular circumstances. I suggest only that we realize that underlying dispositions of people are far from the whole story, and if we change the circumstances sufficiently we often can alter behavior considerably.

Perhaps one reason that so many people prefer to find the cause of corruption in the individuals involved is that this allows them to cluck their tongues at how immoral other people are, which by implication makes them feel very moral themselves because they are not involved in those dirty dealings.

Attributing poverty or corruption or other undesired behavior to the "cultures" of particular ethnic groups (while attributing positive characteristics to one's own culture, of course) is a related error. This error, such as the "Protestant Ethic" theory of Max Weber, has long thrived among scholars. These beliefs are again and again discredited by the extraordinary differences in behavior of the same cultural group in different circumstances, as for example: (1) The low Catholic and Jewish fertility in the United States now, compared to the high fertility of these groups in Europe in the nineteenth century, supposedly due to religious doctrine. (2) The lack of the Protestant ethic among Chinese and Indians, which supposedly accounted for their poverty in China and India but is discredited by how these same people flourish economically outside of China and India. (3) Once in the Indian city of Jubalpur I met Sara Israel, a member of the small Jewish community there. When I asked her what the various persons in the community did for a living, she mentioned people working for the government railway, the army, and several other civil servants. I asked if any were in business, and she answered, "It is well known that Jews do not have a talent for business." So much for that cultural stereotype.

Too often the "culture" explanation results from some combination of ahistoricity and mental laziness.

2. *My personal favorite among errors: not recognizing the amount of variability in a system, and therefore jumping to a conclusion about what is going on from just a few observations.*

I first noticed this error when I was in the Navy. When the men aboard ship exchanged observations about the European ports at which we called, after every port there were some men who said it was the greatest place ever, whereas others said it was the worst. Nor was this simply the tendency of some to criticize and of others to praise, because the same man might have a very good experience in one port and then a very bad one in the next or vice versa. The obvious explanation was that a person could have only a very limited amount of experience in a given port, and the luck of the draw might therefore influence whether the overall impression was positive or negative.

The fallacy of "regression to the mean"—"regression fallacy" for short—is an interesting special case. The child of very tall parents is likely to be shorter than her parents, though taller than average, and a child of very short parents is likely to be taller than her parents. This is because height is the result of a chance combination of the genes that a person carries, and even if a person carries a set of genes that would on average produce a person somewhat taller than average, a very tall person is an unusual result even for such a person's genes. (Leave aside the complication of there being two parents; the principle is the same.)

By analogy, if you know that people on average have jars half full of red jelly beans and half full of black ones, while you know that you have a jar containing 60 percent red jelly beans, you predict that the next ten jellybeans you draw are more than 50 percent likely to be black. But it would be unlikely—though possible—for you to draw ten that are only red. If you do *not* know the composition of your jar, but you *do* know that the average for everyone taken together is half and half, and you draw a handful of ten red jellybeans, your best guess would not be 100 percent red for your next handful, but rather something over 50 percent. That models the situation for the height of children of tall parents.

Have you noticed that, when you return to a restaurant where you had a remarkably good meal the first time you ate there, the second meal is seldom as good as the first time? That's because the remarkable first meal is likely to have been so good at least partly by chance, and the chance element is unlikely to be repeated again. Another example: The Rookie of the Year in professional sports often produces disappointing results the second year in the league. (From now on, perhaps you will not be surprised when this happens.)

An interesting twist on the regression fallacy was observed by Daniel Kahneman in the training of pilots. When the student made a good maneuver, the trainer would say "good," and move on to the next part of the training. When the student made a bad maneuver, the trainer would say "bad," and have the student repeat the maneuver. On average, the next trial of that maneuver would be less bad—closer to the average just by chance. The trainers therefore concluded that criticism had a better effect on performance than praise. This unwarranted conclusion led them to rely on criticism rather than praise.

3. *Overestimating your mental powers compared to other people's.*

Most of us believe that we know our own situations so much better than another person can know it that we quickly reject advice and ideas about our situations. Sometimes this is well warranted because the advice-giver really does know too little about the situation at hand to offer good advice. This disregard of dispensed knowledge is one of the main reasons that socialist centralized economic planning fails. But sometimes the advice-giver *does* know enough about the situation to offer useful advice on the basis of general knowledge, yet is rejected without sufficient hearing. "You don't understand my industry" or " . . . my family" is too often an automatic response, and often a costly one. That was the universal reaction when I proposed a volunteer auction plan to the airline industry as a way of dealing with the overbooking problem. And it is the reaction of my close friend T when I suggest to him that he do a bit of market research about what consumers like in the garments he sells. He is sure that his accumulated knowledge is sufficiently great that it is not worth spending even a bit of money and time in systematic investigation, though this seems never to have been done in his industry.

Perhaps such self-assurance is necessary, and the absence of it damaging. I probably would have been a better father if, during my children's adolescent years, I was more sure that I knew what I was doing and that my decisions were good ones. Instead, my lack of confidence led me to indecision and weakness in the face of the kids' determined claim that my wife and I should have the same rules as other parents (except where our rules were more lenient, of course), and that the kids knew best what was good for them. This indecision and weakness were unhelpful to the kids (I now speculate), and unnecessarily painful to me (I am sure).

Even if I really did not know well what I was doing, it probably would have been better if I *thought* that I did, and *acted* so.

More generally, people tend to have an inflated assessment of their own capacities relative to those of other people. For example, surveys in several countries show that about 80 percent of the respondents believe that they are better-than-average drivers.[2]

Charming recent research by cognitive psychologists has documented how people tend to be overconfident in their mental abilities in a wide variety of test circumstances. (When their actual chances of being right are low—below, say, 20 percent—they tend to be underconfident, however.)

Corollary 3a. Thinking that you can figure out and control processes and events that are unknowable and uncontrollable.

Our belief in our capacities to decipher patterns feeds on the assumption that there must be a pattern to be discovered. This belief in our pattern-finding abilities emerged strikingly in an experiment I once conducted. I presented a series of randomly generated numbers to people saying that they were stock prices. (They might just as well have been actual stock prices, which look just about identical to randomly generated numbers.) People tried an extraordinary variety of devices to impose pattern on the numbers—drawing curves, taking averages, making assumptions about which directional movements must follow which (for example, an up must follow a down), and so on—even though they had no sound reason in experience or theory to believe that patterns could be found. Even more striking, after I ended the experiment and told the subjects that the numbers were randomly generated, many wanted badly to continue playing and testing their pattern-deciphering systems against other people's results.

Another piece of relevant evidence is the resistance of almost all sports fans to the idea that there are no patterns in baseball batting or basketball shooting that allow the coach to identify "slumps" or "hot hands."

Perhaps it is good that we are not aware of the frailty of our thinking lest we would walk about in fear and trembling. Overconfidence in our capacities may also have the beneficial effect of making us optimistic about the future and contributing toward our being in a good mood. Studies show that depressives have a less positive view of their capacities in laboratory tests than do "normal" people—but the depressives' assessments are *more accurate* in this regard than are those of normal people. The good feeling may be worth the damage caused by the overconfidence.

Corollary 3b. Believing that there is a connection between morality and education or "intelligence."

Many people assume that the more "intelligent" people are (whatever is meant by "intelligence") and the more education they get, the better will be their character. But to my knowledge, there are no data showing this to be the case. One of the reasons that the horrors of World War II had such a crushing effect on many people's world views and their assessment of human progress was that it was thought by many that Germany was the most "enlightened" country in Europe earlier. Yet Germany behaved in ways that were worse than primitive or barbaric. Moral expectations about Germany based on its intellectual accomplishments were simply founded on an unsound assumption. (This is not to say that, on average, moral behavior does not improve somewhat as civilization evolves cultural patterns.)

One of the most painful errors in human conduct is to assume that the people with whom one shares political ideas are of higher character than the others. This especially afflicted the communists in the 1930s. The disappointing let-downs by supposed friends in that party were devastating to many.

4. Overestimating the power of "clever" individuals—others and ourselves—to create sound new social systems and feasible radical solutions for real-life economic and political problems.

Overestimating one's own capacity, and the capacity of others, to decipher complex patterns of relationships in society and in nature has been the source of many of the costliest blunders of the human race. Individuals' blunders are magnified greatly when the blunders are made by officials on behalf of governments. Since the beginning of history, military leaders have led armies to slaughter with a combination of fancy reasoning and slick rhetoric. In modern times the possibilities for catastrophe have increased as countries have developed the totalitarian organization necessary for regimes to rule by force even into the household. The combination of dazzling Marxist theory and equally dazzling Marxian oratory promised that the "rationality" of communism must surely produce greater efficiency and equity than the "chaotic" and "unplanned" system of capitalism.

The proponents of socialism have often been persons with extraordinary intellectual credentials, persons considered clever and intelligent by all the usual tests—from Marx and Engels and Lenin, to Einstein and Russell and Sakharov. The doctrine sounded good. It still sounds good to those unacquainted with its results in practice. Many other new theories of society also sound good. And many of them deserve to be tried. The tragedy is that people can become so convinced of the correctness of a scheme on the basis of speculation and "logic" that they are willing to make vast changes without conducting small-scale experiments first, or without examining evidence that is available on the working of the scheme. One of the key elements in Marxian theory is that under socialist conditions, officials could be expected to act mainly for the good of the public. Another key element of the theory is that ownership of an enterprise such as a farm is unnecessary to motivate people to work hard. Much could have been learned about the validity of these propositions from the behavior of officials and farmers in a variety of other circumstances.

If citizens had been less ready to trust in political leaders on the basis of their intellect, and if they had—in James Michael Curley's immortal phrase—preferred to be governed by the first thousand people in the Boston telephone directory than by the Harvard faculty—these huge errors in governance would have been less likely to occur. While not much intellect is necessary to drag a country into war, considerable intellect usually is required to persuade people to put their trust in new economic schemes. Aside from the Marxists, the most successful economic doctrine of this century came from John Maynard Keynes, in the eyes of his contemporaries the most brilliant of humans, a characteristic that contributed enormously to his success. Bertrand Russell said of Keynes's intellect that it was "the sharpest and clearest that I have ever known. When I argued with him, I felt that I took my life in my hands, and I seldom emerged without feeling something of a fool."[3] But Keynesian doctrine has now been discredited as a policy remedy in most sets of economic circumstances, and it is more of a burden than a benefit to the human community. If people had been less impressed by Keynes's intellect, economic science and economic life almost surely would now be better off.[4]

Many children are awesomely willing to sally forth on the basis of their own reasonings, and to be so sure of their reasoning that they have only contempt for the advice of adults whose experience contradicts those reasonings.

The fallacy of long chains of logic goes hand-in-glove with the fallacy of cleverness and intellectual dexterity. One of the frequent characteristics of people considered clever is that they master mathematics more quickly than do others, and they often purport to prove conclusions with complex mathematical arguments that less-clever people do not follow. This is wrongly taken as a sign of the likely soundness of the long logical argument.

5. *Not taking into account the indirect and far-off consequences of a change, along with the direct and immediate effects.*

Frederic Bastiat was the great expositor of the "seen-unseen" error that occurs frequently in all kinds of cost-benefit analysis. This error of neglecting indirect and long-run consequences is especially common in analyses of social policy in which public opinion is susceptible to the fallacy of giving undue weight to vivid evidence. Consider, for example, social policy with respect to drugs. Legislators vie with each other to propose ever more draconian sanctions against drug use because people are so frightened of the terrible effects of drug use in their families and communities. Horrifying assessments are made of the effects of drug use, which prohibition of drugs is hoped to prevent. But less notice is given to the ill effects of the sanctions themselves. The deaths due to drugs' being illegal—not only from drug-related killings, but also because of unsafe drug use due to the unavailability of quality-controlled drugs legally—total perhaps 8,000 per year.[5] A sound overall cost-benefit analysis in terms of lives or resources might well show drug legalization—or just legalization of marijuana—in a positive light, as the public seems to have decided it has with respect to alcohol legalization.

Another example is the belief that the number of jobs is fixed, and therefore immigration and labor-saving technology necessarily imply more unemployment. This misconception is a classic case of taking into account only "the seen" and not taking account of the "unseen"—the latter being the process of creation of new jobs. And if economic logic alone were not enough to refute this notion, the history of the human enterprise should demonstrate conclusively that new technology on average creates more jobs than it eliminates.

Oscar Wilde is said to have said that a cynic is someone who knows the price of everything and the value of nothing, and the definition has come to be applied to economists. But a *good* economist—or a good thinker with respect to any cost-benefit matter—is a person who calculates value well. The key hurdle to be overcome in calculating well is including the indirect and far-off costs and benefits into the reckoning.

Bastiat's effects occur not only in human affairs but also in the biological and physical realms. For example, biologists have "recently raised the surprising possibility that very low doses of ionizing radiation may not be harmful after all or may even have net benefits."[6] But this should not be very "surprising." Low-level radiation has always been part of the human's environment, and our relationship with our environment is so complex and intimate that it seems reasonable that just about every facet of the environment has mixed effects upon us. Indeed, the same author tells us, "The stimulatory effect of low doses of a wide variety of chemical agents on the growth of organisms had been noted by Hugo Arndt and Rudolph Schultz . . . in the 19th century. They considered the phenomenon to be universal."[7] The "surprise" comes only if you expect to happen only what you have observed to happen in the range of the observations you have already made, and do not expect there to be an extraordinary number of effects which we have not yet learned about.

Similarly, based on the physics that has developed within the last hundred years, many people worry that the world will eventually run out of energy. But this assumes that within the next 7 billion years humans will not find new suns as sources of energy, or new ways to get energy from nature that we do not comprehend (just as nuclear energy was not even imagined a hundred years ago), or that our needs for energy will diminish rapidly, perhaps faster than a fixed supply of energy (as Freeman Dyson has suggested)—a very strong assumption indeed about the state of our current knowledge, it would seem to me, and one that likely illustrates the error of overestimation of our own knowledge and mental powers.

This general point of view influenced my choice of career. I had planned to go to medical school after I got out of the Navy in 1956. But I had an intuitively based belief that people should not take medical drugs except when the need to do so is clear-cut and strong. I feared that that view would cause me to be badly adjusted to the medical profession, which at that time dispensed drugs quite freely as if drugs have only direct effects on a given disease and no side effects except those already known about—and especially no delayed side effects in the far future. One basis of my view was experiments showing that rats and babies often can choose their diets wisely from a cafeteria of possibilities, and also Walter Cannon's notion of "the wisdom of the body." Additionally, my maternal grandmother's face was faintly blue. I had heard that this was due to a physician's prescribing the drug Argyrol to her on a steady basis many decades earlier; only later had it emerged that Argyrol had delayed effects. So I had somehow come to the belief that tampering with a complex system that we still understand so little was inherently dangerous.

Medical practice nowadays is closer to this view. And ecologists' conception of nature is similar to this conception of the human body, if I understand the ecologists correctly. They believe that we ought not to make changes in the existing natural order unless there is pressing reason, and unless our knowledge of the likely consequences is extensive, because so many undesirable effects may be indirectly caused by a particular alteration.

The same view applied to nutrition suggests that one should eat a diet containing a wide variety of foods, because we may have needs that science has not yet discovered, and a varied diet is more likely to fill those needs than is a narrow diet, no matter how healthy the narrow diet may be deemed on the basis of current knowledge. And the same should hold in reverse: Too much of any food may be dangerous because it may contain something that we have not yet identified as harmful. Furthermore, a diet that corresponds roughly to human diets over the millennia is probably safer than a diet that is a large break with human history, because we have evolved in consonance with that traditional diet. Without further knowledge, there would seem to be a reasonable presumption that a traditional diet is reasonably safe. (On the other hand, a diet that people have come to *think* is traditional but that is of fairly recent origin in human history—such as eating a lot of high-fat red meat—can be a killer. As in many matters, the period of time one considers is crucial.)

Is this an argument against any intervention in human as well as nonhuman matters? This charge has been brought against such writers as Hume, Smith, and Hayek. I do not think that the charge is accurate, however. This view does imply that we should study the existing state of affairs very closely before changing it, to check for complex relationships that have heretofore escaped our notice. But knowledge need not be perfect, and never can be. When we are satisfied that we understand the system as best we can, then we should proceed to make changes. This point of view differs from a more interventionist point of view only in emphasis, not in logic. I do not, however, share a more extreme noninterventionist antigrowth point of view with those ecologists who are so convinced that any alteration might knock our whole system out of whack, which would then induce a series of changes to compensate, which would then have even worse effects, and so on until the whole system comes apart or explodes. This is the viewpoint that underlies the famous book *Silent Spring* by Rachel Carson.[8] Interestingly, many persons who espouse the latter view with respect to natural systems are very ready to intervene in human systems.

6. *Misjudging the role of motives.*

Considering the motives of the source of information can cause error in both directions—(1) ignoring motives when appropriate to do so, and hence not making proper allowance for bias, and (2) discounting valuable information on the basis of an assumed motive on the part of the person providing the information, when it is *not* appropriate to do so, and hence rendering the information less valuable.

The great African boxer Battling Siki fought Mike McTigue for the light-heavyweight championship in Dublin on St. Patrick's Day 1923 and lost by a close decision. One would not have to be paranoid to wonder if there might have been some bias in the judging.

Even very young children learn that they should not accept at face value all the impressions that advertisers seek to leave with television audiences. The children understand that the advertisers have a stake in their believing that the advertised products are better than the competition.

The desire of journalists to come up with a scoop, together with the power of scare stories to sell newspapers and attract television audiences, contribute to the propensity of journalists to seek out supposed social problems for stories. It also contributes to their propensity to put a bad-news twist on what is mainly a good-news situation. For example, a story about an improvement in the worldwide food supply, though at a somewhat slower rate than the year before—it is inevitable that the improvement some years be less than others—may be headlined "Food Supply Lags." Another case—this is for real from the esteemed *Washington Post*—"Good Crops a Bad Sign." It is necessary to understand the journalists' motives in order to make sense of a world that is getting better in most material respects and yet is described in horrifying terms every morning and evening. It helps to keep perspective if you notice the subjects of the stories. When the worst problems the journalists can dig up are local scandals and scares about the shortages of places to dump disposable diapers, you can infer that nothing very bad is happening elsewhere in the world.

Judging information in the light of the supposed motives of the source when it is not appropriate to do so probably leads to more error than neglecting to do so, however. It is said of one of the main human groups that "If you say to a Z that everything you tell a Z, the Z takes personally, the Z will say 'I do not.' " Perhaps this remark should simply be referred to the entire human race rather than to just one group, however.

Journalists habitually ask, "Why is she saying that?" and "What's his angle?" Especially journalists who work in the very political environment of a capital city find it difficult to accept that anyone makes certain statements simply out of love of truth or concern for the public welfare or other enduring value, independent of any personal or institutional benefit. Rather, the journalists assume that there must be some short-run motive. (Politicians tend to share this attitude even though many themselves love truth for its own sake.) This attitude leads to faulty evaluation of information.

The flip side of this fallacy is the attempt to prove that something did not happen because the person had no motive to do it. Consider the statement of Mayor Marion Barry of Washington, D.C., who had been accused of using cocaine:

> Barry said the allegations of convicted crack dealer Charles Lewis were too implausible for anyone to believe. "Anybody who knows anything about America knows any mayor who really wants to get dope can get it without going out on the streets," the mayor said. He also said it would be "idiocy" for any politician to use drugs "around four or five other people," adding: "I've never been accused of being an idiot."[9]

Journalists are not without reason to inquire into motive, however. Politicians routinely deny that their taking fees from a trade association, or owning shares in a corporation, could possibly affect their votes in Congress or their administrative actions. But AT&T long ago understood that owning just a few shares of that corporation's stock could make the owner favorably disposed toward its fortunes, and it therefore set out to sell AT&T shares to as many Americans as possible, with successful results.

It is quite amazing how strongly a person's self-interest can affect the person's interpretation of the facts. A group of South Florida physicians desired to prevent the very large Cleveland Clinic, which has been a pioneer in heart surgery, from entering their market. The physicians arranged that "Carl C. Gill, the chief executive of the Clinic's Florida enterprise, and a surgeon who has done 4,000 [note: an astonishingly large number] open-heart operations, was denied local hospital privileges. The credentials committee of Broward General Medical Center said he lacked enough experience."[10] Who could believe that such a wild charge would stick? But it did.

How could anyone truly believe such a proposition? Every one of us must have come across some religious beliefs (of other groups, of course, not of ours) that seem to us outlandish, passing any possible belief by a sensible person. Yet such beliefs are held by many sensible persons. And there is no obvious difference between those "outlandish" religious views and believing so strongly that a conventional idea is correct that you are impervious to contrary evidence. Even when presented with irrefutable data on the scarcity of raw materials over the centuries, as measured by their prices, many people cannot/will not divest themselves of the belief that raw materials have gotten more scarce, and are likely to become more scarce. The same is true with the cleanliness of urban air and of the drinking water supply in the United States.

Not only may people disbelieve the truth for their own interests, they may even "kill the messenger," as in this case:

> John Kartak . . . was assigned to an Army recruiting station in Minneapolis.
> When he discovered that the office forged high school diplomas and concealed criminal records in order to meet recruiting goals, Kartak called the Army hotline.
> The response from the Army was to order two psychological evaluations on Kartak, with one superior telling hospital officials, "He has lodged numerous complaints recently. . . . I find his behavior highly unstable. I am concerned that he may do something to harm himself or others."

Kartak's superior was indeed afraid that Kartak would do something to harm others—more exactly, harm to the careers of his superiors. And the Army inspector general later found at least fifty-eight in the office guilty of illegal acts.[11]

But again, there are *some* people with the courage and integrity to fight for the truth—John Kartak, in this case.

How can you sort out the courageous truth-lovers from the gutless finks who will bend the truth any which way for their own self-interest? I wish I knew. My only advice is to hold your judgment in abeyance until you see a person tested by events, and try not to let your judgment be swayed by whether the person is pleasant or seems sincere.

It is prudent to attempt to design a fact-finding system so that it is as free as possible of interests that may bias the result. The jury is perhaps the most successful example of such a system. The heart of the jury system is that the individual jurors have no personal stake in the outcome. Their reputations usually are not at stake nor are their personal

economic positions. And because there are twelve jurors, individual prejudices tend to offset one another. Research shows resoundingly that the
jurors generally do behave in a sensible, thoughtful, disinterested
fashion—better than in any other institution that I know of.[12]

Even the jury system can be perverted, however. When I served as
defense counsel aboard a Navy destroyer—a small warship with a
complement of about 300 officers and men, most of whom knew each
other personally—trials were sometimes kangaroo courts, with the ver-
dicts arranged in the officers' wardroom in advance. (The "jurors" were
three officers, unless the enlisted man on trial asked for enlisted person-
nel, and few did.) The defense counsel was "supposed" to be an orches-
trated part of this arranged justice, though I naively did not fully
understand the system until years later: I assumed that a defense counsel was "supposed" to give the accused the best defense possible. In one
case the entire summation of the "trial counsel" (the prosecutor), an-
grily flushed in the face, was: "I know he's guilty. You guys [the three
judges acting as jurors] know he's guilty. Even Simon knows he's guilty
[not quite so]. So find him guilty." He then sat down. And of course the
verdict was "guilty." (On appeal the verdict was reversed—at which
time I found that appealing a verdict off the ship was an even worse
breach of proper behavior than providing a vigorous defense at the trial.)

Perhaps involved here is a belief by many that—to paraphrase Mao
Tse-tung's remark that power comes from the barrel of a gun—truth and
justice are what the majority, or a powerful political bloc, say that they
are. This view of politics asserts that whatever the majority or an effective bloc are able to wrest from the governmental machinery and pock-
etbook is fair game. Indeed, the view of many is that that struggle is the
whole of politics. And in this struggle the only appropriate limitation on
rhetoric is whether it will be sufficiently credible to advance the cause.
(It should be noted that this view is inconsistent with the Constitution of
the United States, which asserts limits upon a majority's power to turn
events in its favor.)

7. *Assuming that effects are either-or when they are actually more-
or-less.*

Ask the person sitting next to you: What would be the effect on the
smoking rate of raising the tax on cigarettes? Your neighbor will probably say, "A raise in the price will never get people to stop," or perhaps,
"Yes, raise it good and high and they will have to stop." In fact, an
increase of 10 percent will lead to *some* people stopping—perhaps 6

percent—and another increase of 10 percent will cause a decrease of another 6 percent, and so on—but many will continue to smoke. The point is that the answer to the question should be phrased in how-much terms and not in yes-no terms.

Converting the discussion from qualitative to quantitative often has a powerful calming effect upon bitter arguments between people with locked-in positions. When people are asked for a how-much estimate, they often find that they are much less opposed to each other than they had thought, and they recognize how imprecise is everyone's knowledge. The parties then find it easier to work toward a reasoned and satisfying conclusion.

The effect of most social policies on people's behavior is best viewed quantitatively—the effects of welfare on the propensity to work, of public transportation upon auto driving, of seatbelt laws upon the use of seatbelts. This is because there is dispersion among people's behavior in response to particular incentives.

8. *Focusing on blame rather than on improvement.*

The human animal has an extraordinary propensity for making himself feel good by charging someone else with being bad. Newspaper journalists spend much of their careers ferreting out who is to blame for public ills, rather than analyzing the underlying causes that may make the bad thing happen again and again, or discussing how to improve the situation. And the rest of us are forever attributing responsibility to others for all the unwelcome events in life. We even curse the chair when it clumsily gets in the way of our shins.

This urge to blame, and to ask people to justify themselves, is sunk deep into our language. Try speaking for a week without using an expression such as "Why didn't you . . . ?" or "Why can't you . . .?" instead of the less blameful "I suggest that next time you . . . ." We even use a related form toward the future, "Why don't you . . . ?" All of these negative terms—don't, can't, didn't—are literally downers, and just put people on the defensive rather than evoking their constructive thoughts.

Maybe the satisfaction that we get out of blaming makes it worth the doing. But there is every other reason for not doing it. Most important, it distracts our attention from looking for solutions to our problems.

***

Following on all this discussion of errors in thinking, you may despair about our ever thinking well enough about any matter to avoid everyday catastrophes. And yet there is irrefutable evidence that civilization advances in material ways, and we live longer and healthier and more comfortably with every decade. How come? There are several partial explanations:

1. Many of the laboratory demonstrations of people's incapacity to think clearly are based on quite subtle situations—for example, people's inability to choose correctly among gambles that are not at all obvious even to trained statisticians. But the decisions that really matter are—by their very definition—those where there is a large difference between the alternatives, and such large differences are easier not to overlook.

The same is true in scientific investigations. If fancy statistical tests and subtle interpretations are necessary, the conclusion usually —though not always—is not earthshaking. Where the results of the study are powerful and important, they can usually be seen in simple tables or graphs.

2. More than one person—sometimes an entire committee—is likely to be involved in important decisions, and the quirky personal aspects of one person's thinking are likely to be neutralized by others' quirks.

3. Many of our decisions are made repeatedly, and we therefore have a chance to learn what is sound and what is erroneous. (Sometimes, however, there is no way to check on the results and therefore learn by experience, and hence we may never improve. This is the problem with choosing a dentist; we have almost no way to determine if she or he is doing good work.)

4. We don't need to be anywhere near perfect in order to do well. This is apparent in our competitions with other persons and organizations. Even the best tennis player in the world, on the best day she or he ever has, makes lots of errors. Think how many more errors a good club player can make and still win. It is much the same in business or politics. And it is true of our struggles with nature, too. Weather forecasting does not need to be perfect to be useful.

5. The worst performers in a situation tend to leave that situation. The weather forecasters with the worst record eventually must find other lines of work. This is not true in politics or religion or even some aspects of science. The persons who prophesied resource scarcities in the late 1960s and early 1970s have been confounded by subsequent events, but continue to offer the same prophecies and continue to be received respectfully. But in most situations that are not so emotionally charged, failure does not persist so successfully.

Summary

1. Misunderstanding the role of variability in human events and not allowing for it. The most frequent form of this error is drawing conclusions based on too few observations.
2. Overestimating one's own mental powers compared to others' powers.
3. Overestimating our powers to figure out other people's thinking.
4. Misjudging the role of human motives in a situation—believing that it is the desires of others rather than the structure of the situation that causes the observed outcomes.
5. Attributing.

Notes

1. Robert Nisbett and Lee Ross. *Human Inference: Strategies and Shortcomings of Social Judgment* (Englewood Cliffs, NJ: Prentice-Hall, 1980).

2. Paul Slovic in *Against All Odds Video Recording: Inside Statistics*, produced by the Consortium for Mathematics and Its Applications (COMAP) and Chedd/Angier, in cooperation with the American Statistical Association and the American Society for Quality Control, 1989 (Washington, DC: Annenberg/CPB Collection, Santa Barbara, California).

3. Robert Jacob Alexander Skidelsky, *John Maynard Keynes* (New York: Viking, 1986), p. 124.

4. It contributed to his "smart" persona in later years that his contemporaries thought him to be very successful in the securities markets. In fact, his performance was quite mixed, and early on he was luckily bailed out and saved from not surviving at all.

5. James Ostraowski, "Thinking About Drug Legalization," *Cato Policy Analysis*, May 25, 1989.

6. Leonard Sagan, "On Radiation, Paradigms, and Hormesis," *Science*, August 11, 1989, pp. 574–575, 621; see also Sheldon Wolff, "Are Radiation-Induced Effects Hormetic?" *Science*, August 11, p. 575.

7. Sagan, "On Radiation," p. 574.

8. Rachel Carson, *Silent Spring* (New York: Houghton Mifflin, 1962; Crest, esp. pp. 16–18, 22).

9. *Washington Post*, September 16, 1989, p. B 1.

10. *Washington Jewish Week*, August 18, 1989, p. 1.

11. *Washington Post*, August 25, 1989, p. A 19.

12. R.J. Simon, *The Jury and the Defense of Insanity* (New Brunswick, NJ: Transaction Books, 1998); and R.J. Simon, *The Jury: Its Role in American Society* (Lexington, MA: Lexington Books, 1980).

Chapter 16

Good Judgment

A key requirement for good judgment is strength of character, says my friend Max Singer. Integrity helps keep your judgment steady when the situation offers inducements to alter your conclusions.

A politician or an executive might change her views about what should be done according to what she thinks is most convenient or profitable either personally or for the political party. A scientist might alter his conclusions according to what he thinks might please the funds-granting agency. Such changeableness might seem as if it is good judgment in the short run. And some people can for a lifetime successfully pull off this trick of trimming their sails to catch the prevailing winds without losing self-respect or career. But for many people the greatest long-run satisfaction comes from doing what you believe ought to be done irrespective of short-run personal inducements.

Character may enable a person to act decisively in a situation where others also see the need to act, but the others continue to drift without facing up to what must be done. This is often the case with the decision to fire an employee. Many people shrink from that action, and fool themselves that perhaps the situation will improve. In contrast, the person with sound character and good judgment recognizes that the sooner the deed is done, the better for all.

Good judgment may be thought of simply as a collection of devices for avoiding the pitfalls that afflict human thinking or, more generally, devices for avoiding the pitfalls of life. But no one can excel at all aspects of thinking. One is unlikely to develop to the fullest the laser-like depth of insight of a great physicist and at the same time have the breadth of knowledge that an outstanding chief executive officer of a major corporation draws upon. In the same way one cannot develop every muscle in the body sufficiently well to qualify for Mr. America and at the same time hone the skills necessary to be a diving champion—partly because of time constraints in training and partly because there may be some mutually exclusive development among some muscles.

Good judgment implies sound balance between depth and breadth. The appropriate balance differs from situation to situation.

Good judgment in each situation usually includes asking questions that are important, and important because they are broad and overarching rather than because they are technically more advanced. For example, at a meeting of engineers about how a bridge should be constructed, one may hear a person with good judgment asking at the end of the meeting—with good reasons, the others agree—whether the discussion suggests that perhaps that bridge should not be built at all. Or a military officer who has good judgment may ask, as the others are deciding on the best strategy for retreat, whether unconditional surrender—which had not previously been discussed—may not be the best tactic.

In the case of the bridge, asking if it should not be built may involve character because a decision against building may imply that the engineering firm would lose an important piece of business. In the case of the retreat, suggesting surrender may require character because others may consider the suggestion traitorous.

Having good judgment implies considering *all the factors* that need to be considered, and doing so *at all times*. In this sense, breadth of knowledge and understanding is the key element in good judgment. Taking into account the forces that come into play in the longer run are an important part of good judgment. Often this requires taking account of adjustment mechanisms that reverse the short-run phenomenon. For example, an expected shortage of a key commodity might allow your firm to raise the price greatly and make a killing. But a person with sound judgment would take into account that the public might react with anger at what it perceives as exploitation. That might lead to customers' leaving you in the future, or even government action to fix the price, which would be very costly for you in the long run.

Taking account of the long-run and indirect effects is particularly important for understanding and forecasting the course of events in the economy and society as a whole.

Good judgment requires steadiness and constancy and an absence of lapses, a quality not required in more technical roles. A person serving in a top job responsible for the activities of an organization and other individuals must function well *every* day, whereas a scientist or artist who functions brilliantly on odd days but gets drunk on even days may be a great asset to the organization and to society.

This also implies that a person with good judgment must avoid being carried away by enthusiasms. It may even be an advantage not to have a copious flow of ideas. An executive can usually obtain satisfactory lists of alternatives from subordinates. One is naturally partial to ideas of one's own. Therefore, not having ideas can help avoid unbalanced judgment. More generally, separating the task at hand from one's own feelings —keeping ego and fears at bay is especially important—is an important element of good judgment.

No one has ever found a way to teach good judgment in any field, to my knowledge, other than exposing the student to a wide range of cases. That is the purpose of an intern's training in a hospital and a law student's training in a legal clinic. Therefore, my best suggestions to improve your judgment are (1) obtain a wide range of experience, and (2) rehearse the habit of asking yourself to check your judgment once more before arriving at a decision—asking yourself whether you have done everything possible to exert good judgment. This is why the greatest advantage of getting older is improved judgment. The more years you live, the more history you have seen, and the more opportunities you have had to see how a complex set of events play out, including the inborn propensities of human nature. This experience can prevent you from falling into pitfalls that younger people might fall into—if you learn from your experience, which is a big "if" indeed.

Understanding the complexities of human nature is one of the main contributions of experience. When you are young, your experience with your parents constitutes a large part of the experience from which you are likely to generalize. But your parents are a very atypical sample of how people at large will behave toward you, partly because they are more likely to have your interests at heart than are other people. As you grow older, your experiences with your parents bulk smaller and therefore affect your judgment less.

An important issue concerns the amount of trust to place in a person's word or competence. Knowing how much faith to place in a consultant or in a prospective partner, for example, is a crucial aspect of an executive's judgment. A child has more reason to believe a parent than a person at large, because a parent is more likely to have the child's welfare at heart than does a stranger. And if a parent promises to protect you from danger, the parent has more at stake than does a stranger, and therefore is more reliable. Hence we expect youth to be more credulous than older persons who have had more time to acquire wider experience. Age does not guarantee acuity, however, and believing that it does would be an error of judgment.

Aside from situations in which a person's good judgment is not wanted by others because it threatens a personal loss to them, sound and seasoned judgment is a highly prized attribute. Indeed, it is the hardest attribute to find when you seek to find a person to fill a job. And when you begin a relationship with a doctor or a lawyer—or a plumber—you should use all your ingenuity to check the person's judgment. Whether you should bring a lawsuit may be an even more important question than how to bring suit, and whether to have surgery more crucial than the quality of the surgery itself.

The greatest affliction with respect to judgment is the belief of most people that they possess it. This is damaging because an important element of good judgment is humility about how little one knows. Perhaps most afflicted by this are shiny new graduates in a field like business or law, sure that they are up on the latest developments in their field, and bursting with energy to wield the tools of their craft that they have been honing for the last several years. The most dangerous are the successful ones who have been getting praise for wielding the tools well. They are unaware that the judgmental aspects of law practice, say, have barely been discussed at law school. If you do not know what you lack, the lack cannot trouble you or affect your practice.

Youths also have not had the traumatic experiences of disaster that one inevitably acquires with time, and therefore youths may lack prudence. An older physician may be less likely than a younger one to advise surgery because she or he has known healthy people to die of anesthesia or complications. But of course this, too, can lead to poor judgment if the older person is so fearful that action is overly inhibited. Certainly it is bad judgment to overemphasize risks: Newspapers and television, which see themselves as watchdogs for the public, often do harm when they emphasize potential dangers—about the environment, for example—to the extent that our judgment about change is warped.

Setting priorities is another test of judgment. What should be done in which order? Which projects must be sacrificed under which conditions? What are the trade-offs? This requires that a person have sound intuition about relative values, as discussed in chapter 1.

A difficult judgment is whether to act now versus purchasing more information with waiting-time and money. It is possible to make some meaningful calculations of this tricky matter, but usually we rely on the decision-maker's intuition.

The test of judgment is how often you are right relative to how often you are wrong. This is unlike the case of a scientist or artist in their actual work. What matters for those practitioners is not how often they are wrong, but rather how many *good* things they do, because the bad things they do are not very costly. Indeed, one scientist said that the job of a scientist is to make mistakes as fast as possible in order to save other scientists from having to make those mistakes. (Einstein put value on the then-unfruitful efforts of his last decades for just this reason.) In contrast, bad decisions are costly for managers; they matter as much as the good decisions. Of course a scientist or artist needs good judgment to choose projects that will turn out well, and in this respect they are functioning as managers rather than as artisans.

Chapter 17

Self-Discipline and Habits of Thought

Brief Outline

- Necessary Values, Norms, and Ethics for Social Functioning

Just *knowing how* to think well is satisfying and enjoyable. But to get the full benefit of the knowledge, you must *do it*. That is, you must get into the *habit* of thinking well. This brings us to the subject of habits, their importance and their acquisition.

These are a few examples of useful *general* habits mentioned elsewhere in the book: (1) Ask "So what?" as a test of an argument's relevance (chapter 15 on fallacies). (2) Ask what the data are, and how big the sample of observations is, when someone asserts the existence of a phenomenon or a change in society or economy. (Examples 1 and 2 both illustrate the more general habit of inquiring about the logical and evidential processes that underlie ideas people present to you, or ideas you come up with yourself.) (3) Check whether there are alternatives that have not been mentioned when offered an unpalatable choice (chapters 4 and 9). (4) Ask "Is there a good reason to compare myself to X?" when you make a painful negative self-comparison to some standard in your mind.

There is also a myriad of very *specific* habits that can help you live more effectively and more enjoyably. Don Aslett, founder of a large commercial cleaning organization and author of amusing and helpful books on how to keep your home clean easily, insists that habits like the following are the key to easy cleanliness: "Anytime, anywhere you pass inches from something that needs to be tucked in, thrown out, adjusted, put back, you can and should do it."[1]

A habit is a psychological device that enables you to repeat an action or thought many times without repeating the effort required to get that action or thought going. For those of you who groove on computers, a habit is like a "do loop," causing the program to repeat an action without your having to rewrite the instructions, or the computer to re-read the instructions, for each repetition.

Habits are devices that economize on our resources (at least, good habits do). As William James, the greatest-ever student of habit, wrote: "Habit diminishes the conscious attention with which our acts are performed." If habit did not "economize the expense of nervous and muscular energy, [humans would] be in a sorry plight." [2] And Alfred North Whitehead puts it this way: "It is a profoundly erroneous truism, repeated by all copy-books and by eminent people when they are making speeches, that we should cultivate the habit of thinking of what we are doing. The precise opposite is the case. Civilization advances by extending the number of important operations which we can perform without thinking about them." [3]

Perhaps some people are born with greater potential for good thinking habits than are others. And it is probable that the home environment you lived in as a child affects your thinking habits, though sometimes children take just the opposite direction than the parents. (The best psychological generalization I've come across was stated by Gordon Allport in my freshman introductory course: The same fire that melts the butter hardens the egg.) But over and beyond the propensities that you start with, you certainly can improve your habits of thought.

Habits and self-discipline may be the most important learning we do, because they control the learning of other subjects. If a child lacks the discipline to do homework, or to practice shooting baskets left-handed, that child will not get to be a skilled practitioner of algebra or basketball.

Jack Barnaby, the successful long-time coach of squash at Harvard, tells this story about Victor Niederhoffer, one of his greatest champions:

> I spent *less* time in the court with Niederhoffer than with my other players. Here's how come. Vic always came to me and said, "Show me about shot X." I'd explain. . . . After we drilled a while, he'd say, "I think I've got the concept" and I'd leave him. He would then drill *himself* for another half hour to an hour, grinding it into himself. He would be using the

shot, correctly and effectively in actual play, a day or so later. . . . Yes, he was talented and all that, but above all, Niederhoffer, before he came to me, had learned how to learn and how to practice.[4]

William James offered suggestions about how to acquire self-discipline: (1) Start the habit with determination. Set up all possible conditions to be consistent with it—make fixed practice times and places, tell everyone that you are doing it, put signs on the wall, and whatever. (2) Do not let yourself make exceptions. None of that "I'll just skip today because I'm feeling tired." James says that "*Continuity* of training is the great means of making the nervous system act infallibly right." (3) Take the habit to the fullest. Do not stop with rehearsing it. "No matter how good one's *sentiments* may be, if one has not taken advantage of every concrete opportunity to *act*, one's character may remain entirely unaffected for the better." [5]

For James, acquiring habits is valuable for more than the effects of the *individual* habits. The *general* habit of exerting effort to attain cherished goals creates will and character—the two being very closely related in James's view of human nature. "It is not simply *particular lines* of discharge, but also *general forms* of discharge, that seem to be grooved out by habit in the brain. . . . *Keep the faculty of effort alive in you by a little gratuitous exercise every day.* That is, be systematically ascetic or heroic in little unnecessary points, do every day or two something for no other reason than that you would rather not do it. . . ." [6] (I go along with James on the latter point, however, only if the ascetic or heroic act is valuable in itself. I don't share his value of suffering for its own sake.)

The statements in this chapter are almost all casual observations of others and mine rather than controlled scientific tests. To reassure you, however, that this is not just hot air to be regarded as no better than some other batch of hot air, here is some systematic evidence—thinner than I would like, but better than nothing—on related matters. Sheldon and Eleanor Glueck began a study of college-entrant boys in the 1940s, and they and George and Caroline Vaillant carried it up through the 1980s, giving them a chance to connect early behavior to later success when the boys were in their late 40s. The extent of industriousness that the boys showed when young, as indicated by doing better in school than their IQ's indicated they would, predicted their later success on the job better than any other variable.[7]

Acquiring the habits of thinking requires effort. You must give up some of the pleasures of self-indulgence in your thinking, and accept the pain of discipline. Ordinarily we can only improve our discipline a bit at a time. That is why schools *gradually* increase the amount of homework that children do, starting with almost none in the lowest grades; very young children are not capable of forcing themselves to do very much of what they perceive as disagreeable.

It is interesting to compare getting rid of an addiction with acquiring a discipline. Addictions must usually be gotten rid of suddenly, and a bit of backsliding is seen as a threat to "staying clean." That is, a single drink usually starts an alcoholic on a slippery slope toward drunkenness (though some recent reports question whether this pattern is invariable). But in contrast to this all-or-nothing pattern with addiction, acquiring a discipline usually cannot be done all at once but rather must be done gradually. The key difference is that the drug gives you a pleasure, and hence experiencing it makes you want more. But the discipline gives you a pain, at first at least, and therefore a bit of it makes you want less rather than more.

I said that discipline gives you a pain *at first*. But, curiously, what starts as a pain often turns into a pleasure. For example, when I was a student and afterward as a beginner, I found that I had to force myself to write. I had to struggle with myself to remain in the chair for fifteen minutes at a time. It was difficult to master the desire to get up and move around and think of other things. But over the years I found that I could write for longer and longer stretches at a time, with less and less need to master the desire to stop. At some point there was no longer any need at all to force myself to write. And there are times when I get so caught up in the writing that I must force myself to stop in order to do other important things. And I have read others describing the same experience.

As with many other matters, there is similarity between the processes of disciplining yourself and disciplining others as a manager. When young men first come to Marine boot camp, much discipline is needed to get them to march at all, let alone march correctly and with style. A few months later those same young Marines, coming back to the barracks after a few beers, will march back under informal joking command of one of them, exaggerating the correct forms, just for laughs. And athletic teams often take pride in how tough their coach is (but only the successful teams?).

This transition from pain to pleasure is not always such a good thing, however. Disciplining yourself not to eat too much is not pleasant for most of us; pigging out is more enjoyable for the moment. But some people get so caught up in disciplining themselves not to eat too much that they eat too little, and they get so much perverse pleasure from not eating that they make themselves sick and even die of anorexia. Perhaps pride in our ability to discipline ourselves is part of the explanation. Certainly there is great satisfaction in overcoming an addiction to, say, smoking or drinking, especially if we do it by ourselves, and especially if we do it cold turkey.

The differences among schools in teaching the capacity to discipline oneself are very great. For example, a study of tenth-grade students found that students did 3.7 hours, 5.6 hours, and 6.0 hours of homework per week in public, Catholic, and private schools respectively.[8] Which studies best teach discipline and good mental habits? My impression is that it matters little whether it be classics, physics, Talmud, being a jockey, or whatever, as long as the course of study is demanding. That is, *what* you study probably is less important than the *quality* of your study. All else being equal, studies that are relevant to your future interests are better, I suppose, as long as there is not too little of broadening material, too much of only "relevant" material, or too little discipline.

Discipline in one aspect of life does not automatically bring about discipline in other areas of life, however. I once had a colleague who had remarkable discipline in running, practicing long hours every day for marathons. But he barely found the discipline to finish a Ph.D. thesis after many years, despite his very great intellectual skills. Ironically, he used marathon practice as an excuse not to work on the thesis.

Believing in the importance of acquiring self-discipline is important. In earlier times, people were fond of pithy verities on the subject, and a few years ago I saw these on the wall of a materially poor school in rural India: "Work is worship." "If you kill time, time will kill you." "Delay breeds corruption." "A path of duty is a way to glory." "Duty is beauty." "Idleness is the nursery of sinful thoughts." "Hard work is key to success." "Learn to obey if you wish to command." Nowadays these sentiments would seem corny in an advanced country. But believing in them fits with acquiring self-discipline.

Not all habit formation is beneficial. Some habits obviously are counterproductive. But even habits of thought that are beneficial on the whole can hinder you by making your thinking more rigid. James talks vividly about increasing rigidity as people grow older and acquire more habits—what Scheffler calls "loss of personal plasticity."[9] James writes:

"Already at the age of twenty-five you see the professional mannerism settling down on the young minister, or the young counselor-at-law. You see . . . the tricks of thought, the prejudices. . . . On the whole, it is best he should not escape. It is well for the world that in most of us, by the age of thirty, the character has set like plaster, and will never soften again."[10]

Here we return to one of the main themes of this book, the value of opposites. Habits are crucial. But also crucial is sufficient freedom from habit to enable you to create new patterns of behavior that are better than the old ones.

Traditions are social habits. Like habits, there is a tension between the virtue of maintaining traditions and the vice of maintaining them so firmly that they inhibit change. There can be no general answer about how important it is for an individual to observe a tradition and for a society to maintain it. Each potential change should be examined individually. Perhaps it is useful to presume that the rule should not be changed unless there is substantial reason to change it. We can learn from Robert Frost: Never pull down a fence unless you know why it was put up. This follows from the truth discovered by David Hume, and presented most forcefully in present times by Friedrich Hayek, that many patterns have great value even though we do not, and cannot, understand why they are what they are. This includes codes of conduct, traditions, and rituals.

Sometimes the logic behind the pattern of behavior is fairly obvious. For example, two games I have played demand that the players observe rules of conduct that are not, and cannot be, fully specified in the written rules of the game, yet are indispensable. In judo, a player throwing the opponent over his shoulder must stop exerting his force at the very last moment—but at a time when it may keep him from an all-out effort— and pull up on the opponent's arm to keep the opponent's shoulder from hitting the mat when he falls; otherwise, the opponent may injure his shoulder. If you don't protect your opponents in friendly matches, you either won't have any partners to play with or someone will purposely do you in by not protecting you, or both. And in the game of squash, which is played within an enclosed court and both players use the same area, you must get out of your opponent's way sufficiently quickly and cleanly so that your opponent can freely go after the ball. Of course, you can gain an advantage by not "clearing" for your opponent quickly enough. But if you repeatedly use that device, you soon won't have anyone to play with or you will find yourself being hit by the ball uncomfortably hard and often.

Many young American men refuse to believe that these games must be played in this fashion. They insist that they should play to win at all costs, as long as you stay within the written rules, the way one can (almost) play tennis or basketball. But if they were to play judo or squash, they would soon learn that in those sports that attitude simply won't work.

Necessary Values, Norms, and Ethics for Social Functioning

Some patterns of voluntary behavior can be understood at the group level though they do not "make sense" for the individual. One of the main propositions of David Hume, Adam Smith, and the founders of the United States—the framers of the Constitution—was that a viable democratic society requires people to behave according to conventions of mutual respect and cooperation far beyond what is required by law. For example, for a society to function well, people must accord legitimacy to the accepted norms of social and business behavior.

Hume and Smith put forth the idea that many of these conventions are the result of the spontaneous growth of traditions in ways that cannot be understood, and for reasons that cannot be understood by rational thinking. These conventions are necessary for cooperative action in the economic as well as other social spheres. If there is a breakdown in the social fabric in such fashion that people refuse to follow these conventions and patterns of behavior willingly, then the society will collapse. This is very far from the vision of a dog-eat-dog competitive society, an idea many who are against a market system impute to such a market system.

Many of these conventions seem to be mere rituals or courtesies, without obvious meaning. That is, many of these activities are connected to underlying values that cannot be explained logically. They may be explicable in terms of some group survival or group good, but this is not the same thing as being explicable in terms of the individual's own welfare. For example, why should a person step aside on the sidewalk for a handicapped older person? Why should a business render assistance to its competitor when the competitor suffers a fire (as very often happens, to the surprise of critics of business)? Why should there be conventions among lawyers or undertakers about what practices for seeking clients are acceptable and which are not? Why should a member of a college class refrain from behavior that is discourteous to the other students or the instructor or is disruptive to the class? It is certainly impossible to demonstrate to any student that it would be good for that student to, for example, refrain from putting feet up on the seat in front of the student. But the attitude expressed by this behavior, and the general atmosphere engendered by it indicating lack of respect for the conventions, is deleterious to the educational process. If one has to make an argument for the observance of each and every one of these conventions, the system will not work. Rather, there must be a propensity and a willingness by the participants to do such things simply because they are done, unsatisfactory as that may seem to the "rational" mind.

These writers whose ideas underlie our democracy and our market economy emphasize again and again that erosion of these values is possible at any time. And such erosion necessarily renders impossible the satisfactory functioning of this sort of society.

John Maynard Keynes and his Bloomsbury set before World War II prided themselves on being free of all social conventions. This is how Keynes assessed the matter later:

> We repudiated all versions of original sin. . . . We were not aware that civilization was a thin and precarious crust . . . only maintained by rules and conventions skillfully put across and guilefully preserved. We had no respect for traditional wisdom and the restraints of custom. We lacked reverence. . . . And as the years wore on towards 1914, the thinness and superficiality as well as the falsity of our view of man's heart became more obvious.[11]

Some social habits—rituals—are particularly hard to understand. Take a wedding ceremony, for example. It is not obvious why it has the pattern it does—the choice of content for the beginning, middle, and end, and the particular acts performed and words spoken in any particular religious tradition. Some couples believe that they can create a better wedding ceremony for themselves starting from scratch. Perhaps some can. But in most cases the ceremony that has evolved from long experience is more satisfying aesthetically and emotionally than a new creation.

Frost's injunction may be too strong, however. Though we can never understand how some patterns evolved, wisdom leads us to sometimes change some of them.

Einstein hated the discipline that German youths were then subjected to, and he believed in the creative powers of freedom. This is too simple,

I think. Some people are more likely to strike off on independent paths if they are given the freedom to do so. But others—perhaps the larger group—get little benefit from the lack of disciplined study and behavior. The best answer probably is that there is no best general answer.

James urges us "to *make our nervous system our ally instead of our enemy*. It is to fund and capitalize our acquisitions, and live at ease upon the interest of the fund. *For this we must make automatic and habitual, as early as possible, as many useful actions as we can.*" [12] This quote is also interesting because its language provides another example of the commonality of some important concepts between psychology and business.

The assumption underlying this chapter is that we can alter important elements of our thought processes if we decide to do so. This relates to a more general philosophy of individual responsibility. Everyone believes that people have *some* capacity to alter their thinking and lives. And everyone also believes that there are *some* constraints upon us, so that we cannot reinvent ourselves entirely at will. The relevant question is the *extent* to which our lives are under our own control. This is one of the great debates throughout history, closely connected to the ongoing debate about how much assistance society should give to persons in need, or if instead it should give people broad latitude to help themselves.

This is an example of the conflict in views:

> A week or so after the woman showed up at the Sarah House for the homeless last year, she was told she no longer could sleep at the shelter. The reason . . . was that the woman refused to be deloused and her lice posed a danger to other residents. . . .
>
> "But even if she had lice," [homeless advocate Mitch] Snyder said, "we wouldn't have put the woman out. You have to start accepting people with dignity. You can't do it with force and coercion."
>
> But [president of the D. C. Coalition for the Homeless Elisabeth] Huguenin explained: "I was not willing to endanger 15 women for one woman. When you love somebody, you can't just let them do anything they want with their lives or to others." [13]

Should the woman be held responsible for getting rid of her lice before being eligible for social services?

A major part of the program of Alcoholics Anonymous is to induce people to take responsibility for their actions. For example, "it treats all attempts to blame third parties as exercises in denial." [14] Our power to control our own minds, and to build habits of joyful and serene thought and feeling, are at the heart of cognitive-behavioral therapy.

Notes

1. *Washington Post*, August 22, 1986, p. D5.

2. William James, *The Principles of Psychology* (New York: Dover, 1890/1950), vol. 1, p. 113. In my discussion of James on habit, I have benefited from reading Israel Scheffler's *Four Pragmatists—A Critical Introduction to Peirce, James, Mead and Dewey* (New York: Routledge and Kegan Paul, 1974), chapter 6.

3. Alfred North Whitehead, *An Introduction to Mathematics* (New York: Oxford University Press, 1958), p. 42.

4. "Squash Tips," *Squash News*, February 1986, p. 16.

5. James, *Principles of Psychology*, pp. 123, 125.

6. Ibid., p. 126.

7. Quoted by Amitai Etzioni in *Self-Discipline, Schools, and the Business Community* (Washington: National Chamber Foundation, 1984), p. 8.

8. Ibid., Table 16.

9. James, *Principles of Psychology*, p. 124.

10. Ibid., p. 121.

11. Quoted by Michael Straight in *After Long Silence* (New York: Norton, 1983), pp. 93–94.

12. James, *Principles of Psychology*, p. 122.

13. *Washington Post*, September 29, 1985, p. C1.

14. A. Lawrence Chickering, "Denial Hardens the Drug Crisis," *Wall Street Journal*, July 25, 1988, p. 16.

Chapter 18

Dealing With People, and Managing Them

Brief Outline

- Infrequent Relationships: Negotiation
- The Art and Science of Negotiation
- Ongoing Relationships

We all want to be admired by colleagues and neighbors, successful in our business relationships, loved by those we care for, and obeyed when we have wishes we would like others to execute. Because we want these responses so much, we often are suckers for those who promise us panaceas for them. And we often fool ourselves for a while that worthless formulas really are working. The moment of disillusion is often painful.

A best-selling book on thinking during the first half of this century (Ernest Dimnet, *The Art of Thinking*) promised that people will be drawn to you, your words will be listened to attentively, and people will regard you as a fount of interesting ideas, if each day you will only follow this simple practice: Read several newspapers, mark and clip items of special interest, group them, and think about them throughout the day.[1] Then "You may meet him again in the evening. A circle of interested but silent listeners surround him. He is an unaffected, lucid and forcible speaker. Every now and then somebody asks him a question, one of those questions which causes everybody else to wish they could answer it. He does so, in a clear way, bringing in facts which you remember catching a glimpse of in the morning paper, but which you thought immaterial, whereas on his lips they actually give you the key to developments of vast importance: " 'This man thinks', you say to yourself."[2]

So there you have a guaranteed all-purpose solution to your needs in relation to other people: Just read several newspapers and clip them. Perhaps things worked so for that author. Or perhaps he just thought they did. Perhaps he just dreamed they would. But will they work that way for you? Fat chance. It ain't that easy.

Once I went to a party where a noted academic savant—an excellent economist—half-danced, half-sashayed around the room, conversing first here and then there. People were fascinated by what he had to say. *Post hoc ergo propter hoc* (see chapters 14 and 15 on fallacies of thought) and hence I figured that the way to fascinate the way he did was to dance-sashay around the room. At the next party I began to do that—for two minutes, until I saw people's eyes widen and their thoughts came very clear: What is that fool doing? End of experiment. Once again, there are no quickly successful gimmicks for success with people.

One more story: Benny Leonard was a boxer famous in the 1920s for being a smart fighter. After an epic fight with Harry Greb, also a famous fighter, Greb was asked: "How were you able to beat Leonard?" Greb replied: "All the time he was out there he was thinkin'. All the time he was thinkin' I was hittin'." So even being "smart" and studying the situation carefully does not guarantee success interpersonally.

Our close personal relationships are among the most complex aspects of human life. The complexity is most marked in our personal relationships. Perhaps because of their back-and-forth multidimensional intimate nature, there are few general principles that work reliably, though there are lots of maxims that sound wise but turn out to be as often inappropriate as appropriate. Hence I will not tackle that subject. Academic studies of social psychology may or may not help you with this set of problems. Novels and biographies may teach you better. But many people, I fear, will only learn about the best way to handle personal relationships by painful and pleasurable experience.

Impersonal relationships may be distinguished into people you will deal with once or at most occasionally, and people whom you will deal with on a continuing basis. The frequency with which you will deal with them affects how they will behave toward you, as Adam Smith noticed about ethical dealings in business.

> [W]hen a person makes perhaps twenty contracts in a day, he cannot gain so much by endeavoring to impose on his neighbours as the very appearance of a cheat would make him lose. When people seldom deal

with one another, we find that they are somewhat disposed to cheat, because they can gain more by a smart trick than they can lose by the injury
which it does their character.[3]

Therefore you must plan to deal differently with the two classes of
relationships. Hence the two types are considered separately below.[4]

Infrequent Relationships: Negotiation

The process of *negotiating* characterizes one-time or infrequent relationships. And the narrowest aspect of negotiating—the bargaining that
goes on if the negotiation has been narrowed down to one or a few clear-
cut issues that are important to both sides—is often thought of as an
arcane art in which perhaps the most important ability is an iron bottom
for outsitting the other side without getting impatient. But research on
labor-management bargaining finds a less exotic characteristic to be most
important in bargaining—doing your homework and knowing as much
as possible about the circumstances.

The Art and Science of Negotiation

There do not seem to be any effective general strategies for bargaining.
All devices seem to have drawbacks. For example, a very high initial
offer, intending to come down later, may boost the level of the final
settlement. But it may also make the other party angry, or even end the
negotiation entirely. And studies find that the famous strategy of Lemuel
Boulware at General Electric—making what he considered to be a "fair"
opening offer and then not budging—does not turn out better (or worse)
than other strategies.[5]

Here is a "theoretical" solution of the problem we are talking about:
Estimate the probabilities of the other side's acceptance of your offer
under various circumstances, then construct a tree-diagram of the paths
leading to such offers, and use the process of backward induction to
choose the best course of conduct (see chapters 7 and 8). But working
out a practical version of this model is bound to be difficult, and no one
has yet shown successful experience with it.

So concentrate on doing your homework carefully on your situation
and that of your opponent, and don't get hung up on the game of head-
to-head bargaining.

Now let us turn to the more general context of negotiation, in which—unlike bargaining where there is just one overriding issue—there are a variety of issues of differing importance to the two sides. The ideas in this section come from *Getting to Yes*, a book summarizing an important body of work than has taken this subject into a more solid and scientific direction than hitherto.[6]

Fisher and Ury begin with the question: What is the best way for people to deal with their differences? Of course you are mainly interested in doing well for your side, so the question comes down to: How can you deal with the differences between you and the other(s) so that the outcome is best for you *in the long run*? But often seeing the whole picture, including how it looks from the other side, helps you get what you want. (That may not *always* be true, however. A salesperson may be more likely to close a sale if he or she avoids learning sound reasons why the customer should not buy. But this raises ethical questions beyond the scope of this chapter.)

Fisher and Ury term their method "principled negotiation," and they use this slogan: Hard on the issues, soft on the people. And they offer a five-part strategy: (1) Separate the people from the problem. (2) Focus on interests, not positions. (3) Generate a variety of possibilities. (4) Broaden the scope of discussion away from the single prominent issue that you both focus on at the start, so as to allow the other party to find benefits in arriving at an agreement with you. (5) Insist that the results be based on some objective standard.

Separate the People from the Problem

Some aspects of separating the people from the problem are these: Do not view the negotiation as a tug of war. Try to see how it looks from the other side's point of view. Do not indulge yourself in the luxury of anger. Avoid getting the opponent's back up. Do not give your opponent a personal stake in making your position worse. (The man who owned the house we bought was anxious that the person he was previously negotiating with not get the house, because he had built up animus against him that benefited us.) Avoid blaming your opponent for the way things are going. Your job is not to demolish the opponent but rather to have your interests served.

Focus on Interests, Not Positions

Don't bargain over positions. Your opposite's ego, and perhaps also her standing in her organization, may be affected by the outcome of the negotiation relative to the position she has taken. Hence it makes sense to detach the discussion from a position that the other side may feel locked into.

One's position tends to take on a life of its own even if it originally was adopted purely for bargaining purposes, simply because it has become yours. It becomes the "anchor" of your thought in subsequent analyses—an illustration of a fallacy discussed in chapter 15.

Related advice: do not *justify* your position. Arguments about whose position is more righteous, based upon the events of the past, inevitably make the negotiation tougher. Yet the temptation to engage in self-justification is almost irresistible—as witness any discussion of Israelis and Arabs about peace in the Middle East, or household discussions about almost any domestic dispute.

The appropriate alternative to struggling about positions is not "soft bargaining." The evidence shows that being a "nice person" in hopes that the other side will reciprocate is unsound strategy, because it does not work.

Figure out what you want, and attempt to understand what they want. Ascertaining your interests and theirs is an important part of doing your homework. If you understand clearly what *you* want, you can often find ways to *help them help you* get what you want, often at little cost to them.

If you understand the other side's interests, you are in position to (1) help them without cost to you, and (2) put pressure on them. Even when the negotiation comes down to head-to-head bargaining over a key issue—such as bargaining over the rent with a prospective landlord—you may be able to find other interests that matter. For example, it is likely that the landlord would like a quiet and helpful tenant, and you may be able to prove from past experience that you fill that bill. If so, you can offer that as an inducement. Try to show the opposite side how you can achieve and advance their interests.

While you're being hard on the interests, be soft on the person. That is, try to be as *personally* respectful and sympathetic as possible, even while insisting that she attend to your interests. This behavior may seem inconsistent, but it is not difficult in practice, and it is very useful. Sometimes you can even get the representative of the other side to sympathize with your position—and then perhaps find yourself sympathizing with his.

Fisher and Ury urge that you explore the two sides' interests *before* discussing any specific proposals.

Generate a Variety of Possibilities

Invent arrangements that will enable both sides to do better than the obvious possibilities. Find benefits you can give the other side with little cost to you. Negotiators have a phrase: "Don't leave money on the table," which means that you should avoid reaching an agreement that does not realize all the benefits possible for both sides. (Sometimes this happens because one side gets interested in hurting the other side as well as helping itself.) Find ways between the horns of apparent dilemmas—that is, innovative ways of satisfying both sides.

A homely illustration by Fisher and Ury: Two people in a library are arguing about whether a window should be open or shut. One wanted cold air while the other wanted no draft. The librarian found a way through the horns of the dilemma, to wit, open a window in the next room. The moral is that the pie is seldom perfectly fixed; a wise negotiator finds ways to expand it. Brainstorm cooperatively with the other side, as if both of you are on the same side of the table, to find ways to make the pie larger. (See chapter 10 on brainstorming.)

Insist That the Results Be Based on Some Objective Standard

When all the above steps have been completed, sometimes there still is head-to-head disagreement on an amount. Fisher and Ury recommend trying to avoid a pushing match. On a head-to-head bargaining issue, seek objective standards of merit rather than settling the issue by a contest of wills. They suggest mediation, or exploring what others in the market would pay for an item, or some other objective test. This enables the other side to not feel pushed around or gypped.

***

The above process has the virtue of simplicity. Keeping it in mind can improve your negotiating attitude, and change you from a warlike state of mind to a diplomatic state of mind. You should focus on giving the other side rational self-interest reasons for doing what you would like them to do, rather than trying to force them to do what you would like. Keeping this process in mind as you negotiate, and not letting your emotions carry you away, is easier said than done, however.

Ongoing Relationships

Motivating and Supervising Others

Now let's consider ongoing impersonal work relationships with subordinates, peers, bosses, partners, suppliers, cooperators of all sorts, in contrast to one-time or occasional negotiations. Inducing associates to cooperate with you in working toward your goals has always been one of the great mysterious talents, almost an art form. In earlier times the art was thought to be the deft manipulation of carrots and sticks. In this century the nature of the human relationship, *aside from* carrots and sticks, has been much discussed by scientists as a determinant of worker motivation and productivity. But the results of this "human relations school" have been mostly inconclusive.

Recently there has been put forth a system for inducing cooperation whose procedure can be written in specific rules, and whose success is supported by a variety of scientific evidence: Tit-for-tat, as developed and described by Robert Axelrod in *The Evolution of Cooperation.*[7] The principle is simple: If the other person does something good for you, you return an equivalent good. You also return an equivalent bad for bad immediately, the very first time and every subsequent time you receive a bad from the other. The word "equivalent" here is important—not half as bad, or twice as bad, but equally as bad, so far as it is possible to act equally. And you start off with a positive action to get the system moving in the right direction. Further research will surely discover situations in which tit for tat is not the best strategy, but it is a starting point for thought.

The live-and-let-live episodes in World War I trench warfare are interesting evidence in favor of the tit-for-tat principle. There were frequent outbreaks of local peace in trench fighting, and when the peace was temporarily broken by some officer or soldier who wished to get fighting going, an equal response from the other side—no less and no more—tended to restore the peace. Price wars in industry also fit the tit-for-tat pattern, as does the reciprocity system among U.S. senators. And computer simulation studies also provide evidence in favor of the principle.

The tit-for-tat system also makes good logical sense. The immediacy and the invariability of the reaction maximizes the likelihood that the effect of a bad or good action will be learned. And the equality of tit for tat means that there is no possibility for the other person to gain by giving you a bad and getting less bad in return, and also no possibility that the bads will escalate in an ascending series of ever-greater bads. Therefore it makes sense that the immediate feedback in the tit-for-tat sequence should change behavior in the desired direction and bring about the cooperation that you seek to achieve. (There always is a problem of measuring goods and bads satisfactorily when it is not money that is involved: What I consider a trivial bump to your shoulder, you may consider a mortal insult. But no system of dealing with other people can ever work automatically without judgments being required.)

Comparing tit for tat to a market exchange is illuminating: You elicit maximum possible cooperation from a grocer by immediately exchanging money for food in the exact amount of the market price, just as the grocer elicits your cooperation by handing over food for money. Tit for tat is also an exchange system that elicits cooperation, but it is not as immediate or as certain as a market exchange. The closer you can approximate a market exchange by making your response certain and immediate, the more cooperation you can expect to elicit. And, just as with market relationships, the more frequent are your dealings with another party, the more reliable is the cooperative behavior, because the parties have more to lose in the breakdown of a system in which they participate regularly than they have at stake in a one-time relationship.

Notes

1. Ernest Dimnet, *The Art of Thinking* (New York: Fawcett, [1928] 1956).

2. Ibid., p. 142.

3. Adam Smith, *Lectures on Policy, Justice, Revenue and Arms* (reported by a student in 1763), edited and with an introduction and notes by Edwin Cannan (Oxford: Clarendon Press, [1762] 1896), p. 318.

4. It is interesting that the distinction that Smith makes in this paragraph turns out to be one of the major "findings" of modern game theory.

5. Howard Raiffa, *The Art and Science of Negotiation* (Cambridge: Harvard University Press, 1982), p. 48.

6. Roger Fisher and William Ury, *Getting to Yes* (New York: Penguin, 1981).

7. Robert Axelrod, *The Evolution of Cooperation*. New York: Basic Books.

Index

About the Author

Julian L. Simon died on February 8, 1998. He was professor of business administration at the University of Maryland from 1983 until his death. Before that, from 1963 to 1983, he taught at the University of Illinois. He was Visiting Professor in the School of Business at Hebrew University in Jerusalem in 1968, 1970–71, and 1974–75. He was the author of some two hundred articles and thirty books, including *The Ultimate Resource, The Economic Consequences of Immigration, The State of Humanity,* and *How to Start and Operate a Mail-Order Business.*